A Report for the John S. and James L. Knight Foundation

NEWS
IN A NEW
AMERICA

BY SALLY LEHRMAN

ABOUT THE AUTHOR

Sally Lehrman, the national diversity chair for the Society of Professional Journalists, is an award-winning independent journalist who covers medicine and science policy.

She has written for a wide range of publications including Scientific American, Health, Salon.com, Nature, Alternative Medicine, The Washington Post and the Los Angeles Times. For 13 years she covered AIDS, biotechnology, health policy and business as a columnist and reporter at The San Francisco Examiner.

Lehrman was part of a team that received a 2002 Peabody Award for a series of public radio documentaries on human genetics. The group also received a Peabody/Robert Wood Johnson Award for excellence in health and medical programming and the 1999 Alfred I. duPont-Columbia Silver Baton. In 1995-96, she was a John S. Knight Fellow at Stanford University.

She is a USC Annenberg Institute for Justice and Journalism Expert Fellow and is active in several organizations that promote diversity in the media. SPJ lauded her work in this area with its highest honor, the Wells Memorial Key.

Significant research support for the appendices was provided by Knight Chair in Journalism Stephen K. Doig of the Walter Cronkite School of Journalism and Mass Communication at Arizona State University, as well as Bill Dedman of The Telegraph in Nashua, N.H., Bob Papper of Ball State University, Amanda Elliott of the Robert C. Maynard Institute for Journalism Education and Kira Wisniewski of the University of Miami. Feedback on the narrative was provided by Teresa Moore of the University of San Francisco, Venise Wagner of San Francisco State University, Karen Reyes of AARP: The Magazine, and author Helen Zia.

Denise Tom and Eric Newton edited the book.

For the John S. and James L. Knight Foundation:

W. Gerald Austen, M.D., chairman, board of trustees
Alberto Ibargüen, president
Michael Maidenberg, vice president and chief program officer
Eric Newton, director of journalism initiatives
Denise Tom, journalism program specialist
Larry Meyer, vice president of communications and secretary
Robertson Adams, communications associate/webmaster
Caroline Wingate, editorial consultant

Design: Jacques Auger Design Associates, Miami Beach, Fla.
Printing: Rex Three, Sunrise, Fla.

More information about Knight Foundation is available at www.knightfdn.org.

Knight Foundation's Journalism Advisory Committee members are: Rich Oppel (chair), editor, Austin American-Statesman; Farai Chideya, host/correspondent, NPR West; John L. Dotson Jr., publisher emeritus, Akron Beacon Journal; Geneva Overholser, Curtis B. Hurley Chair in Public Affairs Reporting, University of Missouri School of Journalism; James V. Risser, retired director, John S. Knight Fellowships for Professional Journalists, Stanford University; Martin Baron, editor, The Boston Globe; Hilary Schneider, senior vice president/operations, Knight Ridder; Eduardo Hauser, founder/CEO, Mydya, a next-generation electronic publishing company.

To request copies of this book or others in our journalism series, contact publications@knightfdn.org. You can download an Acrobat PDF file of this book at www.knightfdn.org/publications.

This book examines news coverage of a changing America. It was commissioned in early 2004 by the John S. and James L. Knight Foundation as a fresh perspective on the issue of news and newsroom diversity. The book also includes a guide to a variety of diversity programs and resources and the results of three surveys showing trends among American journalists and in newspaper and broadcast newsrooms.

ISBN 0-9749702-1-2

CONTENTS

FROM THE FOUNDATION

BY ALBERTO IBARGÜEN

The questions most asked around Knight Foundation's journalism program are: Who, in the future, will give us the information we need to succeed as a democratic society? Who will connect the dots of information so that the towns and cities we live in feel like communities ... or, at least, are comprehensible, not as a series of discrete and independent neighborhoods or interest groups, but as a whole?

In many important ways, this is what Knight newspapers used to do. They gave readers a sense of shared experience by making what happened in one part of town something that happened in *my* part of town because I read about it in *my* newspaper. They gave us shared vocabulary and shared expectations. They defined community.

Who will help us know each other well enough to function as small and large democracies, whether municipal, metropolitan or national? And, as author Sally Lehrman asks in this new publication, will those sources of information provide us the tools we need to understand each other?

In Knight Foundation's home town of Miami, the issues of diversity, of communicating across cultural, ethnic and financial differences influence how we think about the role and value of news and communication. Three-fourths of us who live here were born someplace else. Fifty percent of us were born in another country. Miami is a place worth knowing for what it represents about our globalized future. It offers daily examples about how disparate communities can come together and figure out how to live and work and progress together.

So, in a world where my neighbors are not only possibly, but *likely* to be from another place or culture, it is essential that we find common ground. We need common ground that allows the community to function by letting its residents and visitors see themselves as part of a shared universe.

But to find common ground, we need a medium that paves the way. We need a medium that is the functional successor of newspapers or broadcast television, something that ties us together as newspapers and television used to. Whether it's through a medium or multiple media, we need a method and platform; a way of getting there.

As this book illustrates, U.S. newsrooms still have quite a distance to go before they and the communities they cover are fully served and capably observed. We don't lament here the change in the media landscape. We need to celebrate the evolution of our media and encourage it. Darwin was roughly right: it is not the strongest of the species that survive, nor the most intelligent, but the ones most responsive to change.

News in a New America adds multiple voices and perspectives to this rich and ongoing search for a new understanding. ●

**– Alberto Ibargüen, president
John S. and James L. Knight Foundation**

FOREWORD

BY DORI J. MAYNARD

Good journalists should be able to tackle any assignment, whether it is covering their own community or covering a community with which they have had little or no personal contact.

In short, they should be able to give us news that is as American as America.

That's the ideal.

The truth is, we all have blind spots.

So it helps to make good journalism a group effort, to have colleagues – copy editors, city editors, producers and general managers with diverse backgrounds and different points of view working as a team to help the newsroom as a whole understand the community as a whole.

Some newsrooms operate with a diversity model of "us and them": White men may feel pressured to accept African Americans, Latinos, Native Americans, Pacific Islanders, Asians, gays and women as equal colleagues, while those journalists may feel as if they must work overtime helping white co-workers understand the world outside the mostly white newsroom. Journalists hired for their diverse views, as well as for their skills, become worn down by countless attempts to explain a story to an editor who doesn't appreciate the basic idea that different people can be interested in different things.

This is not the best scenario, nor is it the best approach. A newsroom divided cannot help America understand itself. If we are to fulfill our obligation to accurately, fairly and completely cover all segments of our communities, we as professionals must learn to talk across the fault lines of race, class, gender, generation and geography,

sometimes putting aside our need to agree and striving simply to understand.

My late father, Robert C. Maynard, the former editor and publisher of The Oakland Tribune, used to say that a newspaper should be a tool for community under-standing, a place where you see not only your life, but also the life of your neighbor, accurately and fairly represented. I'm sure that if he were alive today, he would include broadcast, radio and the Internet in that description.

These days that idea may seem a pipe dream, with blue state and red state residents seeming to turn to very different sources of news – talk radio, cable tele-vision, the Internet, the growing ethnic media that increasingly fills the needs of people who don't otherwise see their lives accurately reflected.

Yet it is that media fragmentation that makes it even more urgent to work toward understanding. As changing demographics collide with the ever-growing number of news sources, there is the danger that "mainstream" media may become a niche media in the not-so-distant future if we do not more accurately portray the daily lives of all citizens in all of our coverage.

To understand some of the forces hastening the dismantling of the mass media, one need only look at the slow pace with which we are desegregating the nation's newsrooms.

Back in 1978, the American Society of Newspaper Editors (ASNE) began its annual census. At the time, the goal was for the nation's newsrooms to mirror the nation's society by the year 2000. At the start of the census, journalists of color made up 4 percent of the work force and were growing.

Much of that growth was fueled by the fact that as the civil rights movement morphed into the black consciousness movement, leaders at most news organizations discovered they did not have a staff capable of getting the story.

Then the fires died, both literally and figuratively.

Today, for many newspapers, their most diverse years are in the past, according to a Knight Foundation-funded study (see Appendix I). Among the 200 largest newspapers, 73 percent employ fewer nonwhites, as a share of the newsroom jobs, than they did in some earlier year from 1990 to 2004, Bill Dedman and Steve Doig wrote in the report released in spring 2005.

In 2005 the ASNE annual census found that the share of journalists of color in the nation's newspapers hovered at 13 percent. A similar study done for the Radio and Television News Directors Association found that people of color account for a little more than 21 percent of local news staffs and women about 39 percent. Slightly better, but still far from reflecting a country that is 30 percent people of color and 50 percent women.

Numbers alone, though, are not the entire story. As the report demonstrated, organizations that are truly committed to diversity are the ones making strides, even in papers located far from urban centers. This is counterintuitive to a belief that there is nothing a small town editor or producer can do to increase staff diversity.

More discouraging is the story behind the numbers. As the industry struggles with

retaining its nonwhite work force, journalists of color report that they often leave the business because they find their views of stories and news events often rejected by their colleagues and editors. In other words, one of the skills that led to their hiring – their diverse take on stories – is the very thing that causes them to be rejected once they are hired.

That is why learning how to talk across the fault lines is so essential.

It is not always easy. Though we live in an increasingly diverse world, we also live largely segregated lives.

Researchers at the State University of New York at Albany examined the 2000 U.S. Census and discovered that the average white urban or suburban resident lives in a neighborhood that is 80 percent white. The 2001 study also found that people of color tend to have slightly more integrated lives, as might be expected of a so-called "minority" community living in a majority world.

As a result, many of us do not walk into the workplace with the tools to talk cross-culturally.

There are those who argue that this failure shows in coverage that skews and distorts the daily lives of people of color. In fact, content audits of local news coverage consistently show that people of color are overrepresented in stories about crime, entertainment and sports and are under-represented in stories about everyday life, business, politics and lifestyle.

To start the cross-cultural conversation

that can lead to a more accurate portrayal of all of our communities, news organizations can encourage conversations across the fault lines with the goal of understanding each other's viewpoints. At the same time, we must recognize that our fault lines shape the way we think about ourselves, each other and events around us.

Consequently, two people with different fault-line perspectives can look at the same event and see two very different stories. In today's newsrooms, oftentimes one person's perception wins out, leaving scores of readers and viewers out of the picture.

It is only through honest dialogue through-out the process of reporting and editing that we will learn how to include all pers-pectives and, by extension, many more viewers and readers.

By adopting this approach and having these conversations, we are making it clear that diversity means everyone.

White men no longer have the luxury of sitting it out with the excuse that diversity does not apply to them. Journalists of color no longer have the luxury of walking away because "they (white men) just don't get it." It's time for all of us to do the hard work and to work together.

A successful future for the news industry means true diversity in newsrooms – not "us and them," but journalists from all walks of life disagreeing and agreeing together. It means newsrooms where everyone is respected, appreciated and acknowledged – where everyone is needed and where everyone can cover every story. It means newsrooms that produce American news. ●

Dori J. Maynard is president and CEO of the Robert C. Maynard Institute for Journalism Education, the nation's leading trainer of journalists of color. She is the co-author of Letters to My Children, a compilation of nationally syndicated columns by her late father, Bob Maynard, the first African American to own a major metropolitan newspaper. Dori Maynard was a reporter at The Bakersfield Californian, The Patriot Ledger in Quincy, Mass., and the Detroit Free Press. In 1993, she and her father became the first father-daughter duo to be appointed Nieman Fellows at Harvard University.

AUTHOR'S NOTE

In my research for this book, one theme kept returning: change in news and in newsrooms requires more than good intentions.

A transformation is sweeping the country. The United States is fast becoming a nation of many cultures, with increasing differences between young and old, rich and poor, city and rural. If we are to serve our ideals as journalists, we must work harder to give Americans the tools they need to understand each other.

Diverse sourcing or clever recruitment and retention strategies are not enough. We must go deeper. We need to begin to address the powerful human processes that create misunderstanding, the things that shape interactions both inside and outside the newsroom.

Fortunately, each of us has the power to make the news better. A wealth of research from social scientists, combined with experience from real-world newsgathering, can now speed our effort. Soon, I hope, America's news providers will find a way to include all of America in our words, sounds and imagery.

A word about language: In this book, we aim to respect the terms people use to describe themselves. Since this can vary by region and community, we use both black and African American, Hispanic and Latino, and Native American and American Indian, usually according to usage by the original source. We also recognize that all these terms, as well as Asian Americans, lump a very diverse population together as one. It is not our intention to portray all people within these groups as the same. ●

– Sally Lehrman
Montara, Calif.
December 2005

CHAPTER ONE

NEWS IN A NEW AMERICA

As volunteers in Fremont, Calif., prepared for their 2004 Fourth of July parade, Vice Mayor Steve Cho had an idea. If the local Boy Scout troop carried flags from around the world, he thought, everyone who lived there would feel included and excited about America's birthday. But what at first sounded simple, quickly became complicated. Some residents got angry that Old Glory wouldn't be the only centerpiece. Others questioned the selection of nations to be included. The argument, wrote Jim Herron Zamora, a San Francisco Chronicle reporter, "caused hurt feelings all around and raised the timeliest of questions: What does it mean to be an American?"

Steve Cho

In the end, 50 volunteers carried flags from 25 countries – a sampling of the 120 or so nations representing the heritage of the city's 210,000 residents.

In various ways, Fremont's Fourth of July is happening all over the United States. Today's journalists are covering a key moment in U.S. history, a story of social upheaval as dramatic as the industrialization and immigration that shaped the nation a century ago. In those days, the best journalists uncovered exploitive child labor, dangerous factories and corrupt politicians. Their work helped define the news media's emerging mission of exposing injustice and giving the powerless a chance to be heard. Today, once again, the country is struggling amid technological and demographic change. And again, journalists are called upon to provide – fairly, honestly and fully – the news citizens need to shape their government and their lives.

Despite their inbred skepticism, many reporters and editors believe passionately in these ideals. The Society of Professional Journalists, founded in 1909 to improve and protect journalism, lays out the duties of good journalists in its ethics policy. Reporters, producers, photographers and editors should further justice and democracy by providing a fair and comprehensive account of events and issues. In short: "Seek truth and report it."

THE NEW MATH: OUR NATION IN 2050

But whose "truth" do general-circulation journalists report, ask more and more people in America today. Already, one in three residents in the United States is not of white European descent, according to the U.S. Census Bureau. Following the year 2050, people of color will begin to out-number whites. Then, exactly what will the word *minority* mean in this country? The term, when used as a way to describe those who aren't white, already makes little sense in places such as Hartford, Conn., where a nearly equal mix of African Americans, Asian Americans and whites live; Gary, Ind., and Atlanta, which are majority black; and Daly City and Monterey Park, Calif., both majority Asian American.

"You have a quiet demographic revolution in the making," says Peter Morrison, a demographer for RAND Corp. in Santa Monica, Calif. At the moment, the U.S. Census Bureau describes the population of the nation as 75 percent white, 12 percent African American, 13 percent Hispanic (of any race), 4 percent Asian American, 1 percent American Indian and 3 percent mixed race. Morrison does not doubt that America's racial diversity is accelerating. A few decades from now, will we wonder why we made so much of the skin-color gradations we use to define race? Or will we put even more emphasis on them, creating new forms of segregation and disparities in education, medical care and access to technology?

Age will define the new majority population as Baby Boomers live on, swelling the over-50 crowd. Older people will drive many trends in work, family life and politics, says Morrison. Too energetic and healthy to retire in the conventional sense, they may popularize second or third careers.

At the same time, immigrants will continue to arrive from other nations – primarily Latin America. The Hispanic and African American middle classes will grow stronger. Though racial diversity will continue to spread through the middle of the country, most of the immigrant population will live on the coasts.

Should trends in the news media continue, however, general-circulation newspapers and magazines and broadcast networks will still reflect the culture, economy and politics of a white America. Coverage of the rest of the country will largely be left to ethnic media and the latest incarnations of vehicles such as blogs and videoblogs. Today, even though media executives have pledged their commitment to diversity for more than two decades, at least 86 percent of newspaper editorial employees, about 79 percent of broadcasters and 92 percent of network news sources are white.

News organizations have struggled to move beyond a history where white men dominated media, business and government. Despite their intentions, however, they are diversifying at a snail's pace. The only independent study that covers all media over many years, "The American Journalist in the 21st

Century," by Professor David Weaver and his colleagues at Indiana University, strongly suggests this. In 1992, Weaver says, 8.2 percent of America's journalists were journalists of color; in 2002, only 9.5 percent. (See Appendix III.)

The implication is, to say the least, interesting. If these rates were to hold, by 2050 only 16 percent of America's journalists would be people of color in a nation more than half nonwhite. Weaver predicts that change will accelerate as white men retire and a more diverse work force takes their place. But none of the data collected over the past two-plus decades by Weaver, the American Society of Newspaper Editors or the Radio and Television News Directors Association offer reason for optimism. "Virtually every year, TV falls farther behind the population. Newspapers are even worse," says Bob Papper, a telecommunications professor at Ball State University who studies work-force trends in broadcasting.

If a white minority ends up controlling news flow in a richly pluralistic society, how will a fair and open democracy survive?

"I'm saddened that we are now stagnated in the industry," says Ernest Sotomayor, director of career services at the Columbia University Graduate School of Journalism and former president of UNITY: Journalists of Color. "Our people are getting left behind more and more, and at the same time we are seeing a backlash unlike any in years against immigrant populations."

"I don't see that mainstream media gets it," agrees Patty Talahongva (Hopi), former president of the Native American Journalists Association and managing editor for two syndicated public radio programs about Native American issues.

Part of not getting it is seeing diversity only as a question of staff counts on race or gender. The skew in news today reflects not just who sits in the newsroom, but whom we consult and whom we cover. Though women make up half of the population under 40 and an even bigger proportion of older age groups, for instance, the U.S. network news shows cited women as sources only 15 percent of the time in 2000. Women didn't fare any better as news subjects on television and radio, with broadcast stories featuring just 14 percent of them in 2002 and 2003. Comparable data on the sexual orientation, socioeconomic level or age of news sources and subjects doesn't even exist.

"Journalists default to male and white as authority figures, as experts," says Ina Howard, former U.S. research director for Media Tenor International, a media analysis firm based in Germany. "I think they tend to be thought of as more valuable sources as well. They're thought of as more neutral."

Is this the truth of U.S. society today? After much discussion, the SPJ ethics committee carefully eliminated the article *the* when describing *truth* in order to acknowledge that people with different backgrounds can witness the same events and see different truths. Journalists can only report as thoroughly as possible, test the accuracy of information and seek a variety of interpretations and views as they invite society to understand itself.

REFLECTING THE WORLD AROUND US

Hold on, some will argue. The narrow demographic band of news choices and sourcing simply reflects today's power structure. Journalists are just telling it the way it is.

Yes and no. Granted, most corporate executive officers and high government officials are white men. But their ranks are changing faster than our source lists. And sure, reporters cannot chronicle every nuance of the breadth and depth of the U.S. population in every news story. At the same time, however, journalism involves telling stories that the audience finds relevant. We ignore great numbers of news consumers at our own peril. If we want to stay in business, we must seek news that is important or interesting to our readers, listeners and viewers.

In their own fashion, large corporations such as IBM, Ford, Aetna and Merck get this. They have made work-force diversity and multicultural marketing a priority. At postage-equipment company Pitney Bowes, for example, people of color made up a little over half the entire work force and one-fifth of managers in 2003. The leadership at multinational banker Citigroup is 47 percent female. PepsiCo ties executive compensation to diversity performance.

Diversity isn't a "program" or "goal" at Ford, according to Ray Jensen, former director of supplier diversity development. "It's the way we do business," he says, and a proven means to expand market share. Ford and its corporate brethren are preparing for the $2 trillion in buying power that today's consumers of color will enjoy by the middle of the century.

This commitment to diversity might come as a surprise in many newsrooms. Even business reporters write relatively little about industry's race to catch up with U.S. population demographics. Though companies run by people of color (including the ethnic media) are growing at four times the national average, they remain unusual

REFLECTIONS ON THE FUTURE

Not so long from now, the meaning of the terms *ethnic minority* and *racial minority* will change in the United States of America.

By the year 2050, European Americans will be a so-called "minority" group in this nation.

This has already happened in many American cities, where people of color make up a majority of the population. Even so, America's news system has not caught up to those population changes. This raises the question: Will it ever?

Here are the reflections of seven journalists, who as leaders in UNITY, the four ethnic journalist groups, the National Lesbian and Gay Journalists Association and an organization for women journalists, have volunteered untold hours helping news organizations become more diverse.

Mae Cheng, president of UNITY: Journalists of Color; assistant city editor, Newsday; former president, Asian American Journalists Association:

"We're not making much headway. A lot of newspapers and television stations are treading water right now. We still think we're covering these communities by covering their festivals and holidays. At some point, our readers and viewers are going to call our bluff. Information is so accessible now they don't have to rely on their local media.

"When the people in the suits start feeling it in their pockets, this will be the impetus for change. But I hope we don't have to wait that long. Hopefully, by 2050 we'll be smarter. Between now and then we'll have to provide all our journalists, all the way up the ranks, training on how to cover our communities. We'll have to bring in more people from different backgrounds even when they're not covering those beats – they bring a wealth of resources and knowledge. The number of ethnic media will grow. There will be more collaboration in content, marketing, advertising, and community projects."

Patty Talahongva, managing editor of two syndicated public radio programs, *National Native News* and *Native America Calling*; host of *Native America Calling*; former president, Native American Journalists Association:

Mae Cheng

"I don't see that mainstream media gets it. They're not embracing diversity now, and certainly, native people have been around forever. Everybody talks about diversity, but if you look at the states with the largest populations of Indians – Arizona, New Mexico, Oklahoma, California – none have a Native American anchor on their prime-time broadcasts. Native news doesn't affect just our people; it affects the communities around us. It affects the states and the nation. The biggest business story out there, the class-action lawsuit against the federal government for mismanagement of the more than 500,000 Individual Indian Money accounts (money from lands held "in trust" by the Bureau of Indian Affairs), is bigger than Martha Stewart, it's bigger than Enron. Where is the coverage? On the other hand, the reporting on issues such as mascots and gaming is just a farce. It's never in context, and there is another part of the story that's not being told at all.

"Canada has a good idea, the Aboriginal People's Television Network. I would like to see an American version of that. It's up to us to train our own people and get them out there. As more native people become affluent or even middle class, they're going to want some options. I would hope that our people would stay true to the native media, and along with that, embrace the free press, and encourage their tribal press to flourish unrestricted. If that happens, native people will turn to our own networks."

Herbert Lowe, courts reporter, Newsday; former president, National Association of Black Journalists:

"Will the news media reflect the diversity of the population by 2050? The answer will be set today, tomorrow and through the next decade by the people who are doing the hiring. People with aspirations have to be trained into people with ability; people with ability have to be given responsible positions. For the industry to be diverse, you have to have some diversity in groups such as ASNE, RTNDA and NAA. Otherwise, over 50 years, you have a white publisher replaced by a white publisher replaced by a white publisher. He

Patty Talahongva

Herbert Lowe

Juan Gonzalez

Ernest Sotomayor

hires a white editor who hires a white managing editor who hires a white assistant managing editor. It's hard to aspire higher than where you see others like you. Fundamentally, it's about who gets to hire whom.

"On the optimistic side, we are continuing to see more and more black journalists getting into levels of authority – really, levels of influence. People will always want to know what's going on in their world, what's going on in their communities. In order to pull more black people into the pipeline, journalism has to be portrayed as an important and honorable trade, as a defender of democracy. When pastors rail against journalism, those parents with influence aren't going to want their kids to go into it. Integration and diversity must continue in schools. All kids must learn that no matter what color they are, there cannot be any other choice but diversity. Managers must spot unhappy journalists and pull them back in. Retention is about being able to advance, being satisfied in your job, and being able to enjoy what you're doing."

Juan Gonzalez, columnist, New York Daily News; co-host of the national daily radio and television news show, *Democracy Now!;* former president, National Association of Hispanic Journalists:
"There has to be some sort of incremental change because the companies are going to increasingly depend on people of color as consumers. But newsrooms obviously aren't going to be anywhere near parity unless new, nationwide strategies are developed by some of these news companies. In another 10 to 15 years, you are going to have a strategic opening when the Baby Boomers begin to retire. There will be a lot of openings, particularly in senior management jobs. Are companies going to take advantage of that to downsize, or begin hiring more? What kind of efforts does the industry make to get ready for the strategic opening? That's what we're trying to do with the Parity Project, to

get enough people into the pipeline for when that time comes.

"There's another, even more pernicious trend than the slow diversification of staffing. We've been putting so much attention to getting people in the door, we haven't paid attention to ownership. So while you may have a slow integration of lower level staffing, the attitudes and perspectives of the owners and publishers – the people who set the tone – are astoundingly white. Consider the Pew study on press credibility. The news media are becoming less respected, less credible across the population. That should be a signal that something is not resonating in the population."

Ernest Sotomayor, director of career services, Columbia University Graduate School of Journalism; former president, UNITY: Journalists of Color:

"By 2050, we will see a much more fragmented media society. I use that term because that's what it will be – not an industry. More groups already have vehicles to distribute their information through the Internet and even through low-power radio stations. If general circulation publications are going to survive, they will have to change.

"Broadcast and print have always tried to be generalists in their coverage, to be something for all. I think we have conditioned ourselves over the decades to not count on these companies to reflect the interests and needs of Latinos, African Americans, Asian Americans and Native Americans. They've long been ignoring issues that are primarily of importance to people of color. And for companies to think they can solve the problem by starting a feature here and there on Sunday is folly. It's got to be a long-term process. One way or another, they'll have to cover these issues – and they'll

(Continued on next page)

Amy Bernstein   Eric Hegedus

(Continued from previous page)

have to cover them from a broader range of perspectives. Subjects like immigration and schools affect everybody. I'm optimistic that we will see increasing change in the biggest and most diverse communities because news media will understand the demographics eventually. Otherwise they will have gigantic chunks of their communities simply disappear as readers and audiences.

"This all comes down to power sharing. They didn't erase Jim Crow laws willingly; the laws had to be dismantled by force, by marches, by law. We've had to advocate and lobby and try to make media companies understand the importance of this, to see that they can't survive unless they change. This is something we will continue to struggle with in 2050, and after that."

Amy Bernstein, deputy editor, strategy+business magazine; former president, Journalism and Women Symposium (JAWS):

"At some point the majority of this country will not be WASP. As a result, the forces that keep our newsrooms white will give way. I think we're seeing more people in power in newsrooms who want their staffs to look more like America. It's the thin edge of the wedge, thank heaven. Every woman I know in a position of power in a newsroom looks out for talented women and minorities. It's a conscious act and they think of it as vital to the future of the business. Our judgment of what is important will change, what's accepted and familiar will change.

"You're already seeing it in magazines. For them, it's about markets. When it becomes clear there is an underserved market, people will create magazines to serve it: an Advocate, an Essence, a Latina, or People en Español."

Eric Hegedus, president, National Lesbian and Gay Journalists Association, page designer, New York Post:

"When you consider how diverse the population is getting, the news industry really has to get into pace with that. We need to see more women, African Americans, Asian Americans, just across the board. I don't think it's a stretch to say the industry is made up of largely white, male leaders. We've made strides, but is everything where it should be? No.

"Diversity matters, period. I can't think of anyone coming up with a clear reason why it doesn't. It absolutely matters who is in the newsroom, because we each have a different perspective. I have a certain understanding of what LGBT (Lesbian, Gay, Bisexual and Transgender) issues are, for instance, and how they should be covered fairly and accurately. The UNITY groups have a right to be unhappy. And I should hope that by 2050, things will be a whole heck of a lot better than they are.

"As far as gay coverage goes, as LGBT people become more of the mainstream, as the younger generation becomes more accepting/tolerant, LGBT people will be more common in the news. And maybe as acceptance grows, LGBT issues will become less important because they will have been resolved. You can see it reflected in entertainment first and foremost. But as time goes on, as you see an increase in civil rights for LGBT people and others, you'll see changes in how things are covered in the news and what is covered regularly." ●

– Sally Lehrman

in the news. Nonwhite and female executives now commonly decide policy and set direction at many corporations, yet they rarely appear as experts on business matters.

The same editorial myopia can be found in other areas of society undergoing a change in leadership. One of three medical school graduates in 2004 was Asian American, Pacific Islander, African American, Native American or Latino, yet journalists seldom ask for their views on hot issues such as prescription-drug benefits or health insurance costs. The voices of women and ethnic minorities who serve in positions of authority in the military, schools and government often go unheard.

Mainstream journalists who push for newsrooms and news coverage that reflect the nation's changing demographics have been accused of dictating a "diversity orthodoxy." Critics of news diversity say journalists are skewing sourcing and preventing balanced discussion of troubling issues such as crime, welfare, drug use, even race itself. They worry that a commitment to hiring journalists of color will translate into biased coverage. In fact, the opposite is true. Good journalism, as the SPJ code recommends, should "tell the story of the diversity and magnitude of the human experience boldly."

The real news of today, not the imaginary news of the future, tends to oversimplify, to stereotype, to come loaded with the bias (conscious or not) of its creators. At the extreme: Latinos are swarming in from Mexico to grab all the U.S. jobs. Asian Americans are stealing coveted academic opportunities. Native Americans are building casinos and exploiting local civic resources. Women are always tempted by the "mommy track." People with disabilities are heroes or objects of pity. Deeply religious folks are crazy conservatives. Gays and lesbians? They all want to get married and upset the nuclear family.

In their 2001 book, *The Black Image in the White Mind*, Robert Entman and Andrew Rojecki detail the distorted pattern of broadcast news coverage of black people. Local and network news producers nearly always place African Americans in narrowly defined roles, they report: at the center of crime and sports, as social victims or as supplicants on the public dole. Newspapers follow suit. It was race news in 2003 when the esteemed civil rights scholar Christopher Edley arrived at the University of California, Berkeley. The San Francisco Chronicle headline: "Black to lead UC Law School."

ARE JOURNALISTS HUMAN?

Journalists don't build social bias into stories deliberately. Our own human filters – race, gender, generation, geography, class and ideology – help create it. (Later chapters will talk in detail about that phenomenon.) It's also true that shortcuts in writing and editing help produce much of this imagery, as do news values that rely on conflict, immediacy and symbolic characters to carry the narrative. Still, a newsroom's composition plays a huge role. Even as recently as 2005, at least 346 U.S. newspaper newsrooms, or about one of four, were 100 percent white. That number balloons to 621, or 44 percent of all general-circulation newspapers, if you take into account the newsrooms that didn't report their numbers in the 2005 American Society of Newspaper Editors' annual survey. Only a little over a third of daily newspapers (36 percent) are even halfway to parity with the nonwhite population in their communities, according to an

WHAT WORKS: TEN TIPS ON RECRUITING FOR DIVERSITY

(Editor's note: This list was developed for those recruiting for midcareer journalism programs).

1. Join forces. Team up with other midcareer journalism fellowship programs to present panel workshops and receptions at ethnic journalism conventions, attracting more prospective candidates who are interested in fellowships in general. Split the costs and make a bigger splash.

2. Seek more and better visibility for your program. Do a number of things each year to make yourselves known (and always look for new ways): advertise in journalism magazines; send flyers to hundreds of newsrooms and news executives; send paper flyers and e-mail notices to mailing lists of ethnic and other journalism organizations; attend journalism conventions and distribute materials, meet candidates and more.

3. Use your web site as a recruiting tool. In addition to providing background information on your program and application forms that can be downloaded from the web, post testimonials with photos of your alumni (many of them people of color) talking about their fellowship experiences and what it meant to their careers.

4. Invite your alumni to help recruit for your program. With more than half of our U.S. applicants telling us they heard about our program from former fellows, we know alumni are a powerful recruiting tool. Send a letter to your alumni each year with a copy of your updated brochure, asking them to think about who might make a great fellow. This also encourages alumni to think more about recruiting, and to offer names of potential candidates. Consider hosting occasional alumni dinners in different U.S. cities and alumni receptions at the UNITY convention and other such events where alumni are invited to bring a fellowship candidate.

5. Seek out new places and new populations. The ethnic media is a growing area of journalism, and there has been an increase in fellowship applications from U.S. journalists working at publications and broadcast outlets in Spanish, Chinese and other languages. Attend the New America Media convention, where some of these journalists

(Continued on next page)

analysis of ASNE data by Pulitzer Prize-winning investigative reporters Bill Dedman, managing editor of The Telegraph of Nashua, N.H., and Stephen K. Doig, Knight Chair in Journalism at Arizona State University. (See Appendix I.)

Broadcast also is behind the demographic times. In 2005, people of color made up just 21 percent of the television news work force and only 8 percent of radio news workers – even counting the Latinos working in the Spanish-language media, according to a study by the Radio and Television News Directors Association and Ball State. For the past 15 years, the proportion of workers of color in television news has held at about 20 percent, while the proportion in radio has declined. (See Appendix II.)

The effects of these trends are more than skin-deep. In an environment where any single group dominates, reporters must work harder to gather the increasingly varied perspectives and experiences of today's multicultural society. Add to that the aging of newsroom staffs and the heavy influence of the East Coast media on each day's news mix, and the search for truth can be even more difficult.

When Robert McGruder, then-executive editor of the Detroit Free Press, accepted the Helen Thomas Diversity Award in 2000, he explained the importance of going beyond staff percentages. Though his paper's newsroom was one of the few across the nation reaching racial parity with the surrounding community, McGruder believed his paper was not doing all it should. "The issue is not just employment, it is content," he said. "It is what's going into the newspaper. ... Despite some major successes, we know we are not listening to all the voices, showing all the faces and telling all the stories." As an editor, McGruder emphasized that the real bottom line is fairness and equality.

Most reporters and editors would agree that stereotyping and misrepresentation is bad journalism. Unfortunately, many just don't think hard or long about it. We don't pay enough attention to the influence of stories that leave out context when covering issues such as crime, employment and rural poverty.

We may be tempted to dismiss the power of words and images because of the temporary nature of the news. Broadcast news lasts only as long as someone is listening. Newspapers become outdated before they even land on the doorstep. Even so, they really are the first rough draft of history. People still rely on television, magazines and newspapers as a primary source of information about each other. They use the news to decide on the importance of issues, learn specifics about social concerns and gauge the climate of opinion. People will choose to speak out or hold back their own views on affirmative action, for instance, depending on the flavor of coverage. Their opinions become votes.

To understand the power of their work, modern journalists might do well to read the 1968 Kerner Commission report. In analyzing why riots had seethed in U.S. city streets for four summers in a row, the commissioners pinpointed the isolation and neglect of black Americans by white society. They chastised the news media for its part – both before and during the uprisings. "By and large, news organizations have failed to communicate to both their black and white audiences a sense of the problems America faces and the sources of potential solutions," the commission concluded

(Continued from previous page)

meet annually, and send flyers to their members. JAWS – the Journalism and Women Symposium – is a smart and irreverent women's journalism group that has been around for years, but is growing and is now taking advertising in its annual conference, or "Fall Camp," program. Attend JAWS conferences and participate in panel discussions.

6. Be there for candidates. Offer to talk with applicants who were not selected as fellows after the process is over, making suggestions on how they might improve their application if they decide to apply again. Find ways to reach out to journalists in other settings, such as making yourself available for regional journalism conferences and workshops, helping judge journalism contests and inviting journalists to your public events as a way to get the word out about your program that may pay off with more applicants in the future.

7. Show commitment to diversity through your choices. By selecting a diverse group of fellows each year, journalists of color and those from media other than traditional daily newspapers (broadcast, online, etc.) see that you are interested in them and that they should consider applying.

8. Tailor promotion materials. Translate promotional flyers into languages other than English for international candidates; and when you do so, be ready to receive and answer queries in those languages.

9. Solicit top editors and news directors. Journalists in leadership positions in newsrooms and broadcast stations who once were fellows themselves – or understand the power of fellowships – are terrific advocates for programs. Seek them out to find good candidates. In addition, their newsrooms are the ones that often make the best use of fellows when they return, recharged and ready for bigger challenges, after their fellowship.

10. Recruit with the long view in mind. Many of these efforts often take years to pay off from first contact until someone actually applies. Be patient.

– **Dawn Garcia, deputy director John S. Knight Fellowships for Professional Journalists, Stanford University**

bluntly. "The media report and write from the standpoint of a white man's world."

WHAT NEXT?

This work focuses mainly on race because the case here has been documented beyond all reasonable argument. As the United States rapidly becomes more diverse, the conventional news media risk repeating past mistakes – to be again branded as "white," and thus irrelevant for a large portion of the population.

Not long ago, Midwest editors could wave off the nation's increasing blend of race, sexual orientation, religion and national origin as an artifact of coastal cities such as New York, Miami, Los Angeles and San Francisco. But consider the transformation in areas such as Minnesota's Twin Cities, St. Paul and Minneapolis, famed for their light-skinned, Scandinavian immigrant history. St. Paul (population 287,000) is home to more than 30,000 people of Hmong descent – most of whom are second- or third-generation citizens whose parents fled Laos after the Vietnam War. Of the seven million Muslims across the United States, some 75,000 live in this historically Lutheran region. The Hispanic population in Minneapolis more than tripled from 1990 to 2000, and, across the state, the black population has doubled.

In 2000, the St. Paul Pioneer Press profiled five immigrant groups that were transforming the city and conducted a survey in five languages in order to let the new arrivals speak for themselves. With "The New Face of Minnesota," the paper hoped to reconnect longtime residents to their own families' immigrant experiences and generate discussion about how best to allocate resources to the changing population. Just as impor-

tant for the newspaper, the initiative generated background knowledge and a source list that still helps reporters cover the city more inclusively and accurately. The paper has continued to write in depth about immigration, in 2005 publishing a series about the exodus of the Hmong from Laos 30 years ago.

Alas, too few general-circulation media outlets are adapting to the demographic change across America as actively as the Pioneer Press. To be fair, industry statistics note real progress at both Gannett and Knight Ridder, which lead newspaper companies in newsroom diversity. But the American people set the pace here: Newsrooms simply are not changing as fast as the nation. Without major new efforts, most mainstream print and broadcast news organizations risk losing market share and societal influence to niche media.

A probable scenario for 2050: A few far-sighted media companies rise above the rest, and other, more relevant media use ever-cheaper technology to step into the gap. America's journalists will either work at news organizations that reflect their communities, or ones that don't. In a nation where democracy is organized by geography, the news organizations that reflect their communities will stay in business. The others probably won't. What about the individual journalists who chose not to consider the rapidly changing country? They will be giving away the role their predecessors fought for over the centuries: to be right in the middle of the most important debates, to be the town square of a democratic nation. Their readers, listeners and viewers may find themselves, for a time at least, living in a society where vital concerns fester unexpressed and unaddressed.

TO INNOVATE, OPEN UP YOUR NEWS ORGANIZATION

Does your news organization have a diversity committee, but no diversity? Readership or viewership task forces, but no new readers or viewers? Retention programs, but no retention? Web sites but no web revenue?

Innovation means more than a new hire, a new beat or a new edition. It means creating new ways of doing things: ways that help us change with the times while honoring the journalism values of fairness, accuracy, context and truth.

To diversify, to open up coverage, to grow, to innovate and to move fast, news organizations are realizing they need to make big changes. I once described these broad moves toward new people, practices and products in a book about the creation of The Open Newspaper. These days, though, you might want to call it The Open News Organization.

At an open news organization, we agree that each of us sees only a piece of the whole picture. We build the skills of group decision-making. We take time to learn about things that separate people – such as gender, age and race – as well as things that bring people together.

An open news organization builds an institutional open mind – it has a Learning Newsroom, one designed to routinely add knowledge about the community it serves and the people it employs. Such a news organization seeks to grow by attracting new readers and viewers from its core community, instead of only by taking new territory.

The big problems faced by news people today – even such advertising department problems as failure to match online audiences with online revenue – are created or made worse by institutional closed-mindedness.

It doesn't have to be that way. There are, in fact, as many ways to open news organizations as there are journalists, who are, after all, the soul of news and the people whose souls are fed when openness makes things happen.

But here are 10 basic steps:

1. Make diverse hires. Take hiring as seriously as budgeting. Post all openings. Advertise in community and trade publications. Recruit at conferences and colleges. Keep a database of diverse candidates. Hire young and promote in-house. Base managerial bonuses on hiring performance.

2. Connect with your community. Form community advisory boards. Write and distribute media access guidebooks. Offer your cyberspace to schools, neighborhoods, civic groups. Set up guest columns in all sections of the paper. Sponsor community events. Stand up proudly as the citizens responsible for asking good questions.

3. Train. Set up a comprehensive program of in-house training. Arrange for your experienced journalists to coach newcomers. Start writing groups. Fill in gaps with traveling trainers. Make your newspaper a local training hub, working with high schools and colleges. Let the staff know what the research says about your newspaper, readers and community. Spend 2 percent of payroll on training. Send people to the Media Management Center, Poynter, the American Press Institute.

4. Adjust your attitude. Having a growing audience online is a good thing. Having Readership Institute research on who reads what is a good thing. Having interesting stories to tell about a changing America is a good thing. As former Knight Foundation president and CEO, Hodding Carter III puts it: "This is an explosively creative time to be going into journalism – if you are not in search of the past."

5. Open up your reporting. Ask reporters for their own story ideas. Help get them out of the office. Subsidize their reading lists. Build diverse source lists in databases. Use content-audit software to check what you're doing. Gain access to every government database in your region. Use TracFed (*http://tracfed.syr.edu*). Raise writing standards. Issues hide behind every news event: find as many as you can. Answer the question: So what?

6. Open up your editing. Require reporters and editors to talk as a story is edited. Open news meetings on a rotating basis to staff and community members. Have regular planning meetings

(Continued on next page)

(Continued from previous page)

away from the office. Align your training plans with your editorial plans. Don't forget your line editors or producers; they make it happen, make sure there are enough of them. Know your colleagues; use each other as cultural specialists. Set up style rules that respect all your readers. Don't dictate, coach.

7. Expand your mix. You now mix hard with soft, local with wire. Try mixing in stories important to the different people of your community. Look at the paper through the prism of Robert C. Maynard's fault lines: gender, generation, race, class, geography. Try making Page One or newscast decisions by consensus. Let anyone at the meeting nominate any story to be your lead. Don't be afraid to promote your web site.

8. Review and revise. Look at what you are doing daily, weekly, monthly, yearly. Survey readers and the community. Seek out critics. Make your phone numbers available. Speak and meet in the community. Keep rewriting your rules. Have a five-year editorial plan and one-year plans. Organize the newsrooms to reflect the way readers live today. Rules make results: If a newspaper routinely makes 70,000 beat calls to the cops every year, unnecessary police stories will be reported.

9. Brand your standing features. If you work at a newspaper, comics, columns, stock pages and the like take up most of a newspaper's editorial space, yet get the least attention. Order research with sample sizes large enough so no group is "statistically insignificant." Look for alternatives to syndicates that have no demographic readership breakdowns. Make sure you know who reads, listens to or watches what and why. If you have good locally produced columns or commentary or standing features, promote them. Grow your own standing features, columns and special sections by reaching out to the staff and community. Let readers write a special section or send in video.

10. Experiment. Establish a "new products" unit. Find ways to collect the news once and distribute it through five different pipelines. Sell newspapers, books, magazines, parts of the web site, radio, television. Train journalists to do media they don't usually do. Use other media to promote your core product. Become more than a single source. Turn

your news organization into what Bob Maynard called "a geographically discrete dynamic database."

If this sounds like a tall order, perhaps now would be a good time to start.

Change is here. A generation ago, television passed newspapers as America's No. 1 news source. Ten years ago, cable television developed greater reach than newspapers. Today, the web has greater reach. Yet the nation's newspapers – weekly and daily, free and paid – still possess America's greatest news-gathering system, and are best positioned to move quality local news into cyberspace.

To survive and thrive, all news organizations must be ready to change. To propel this great newsgathering system onward into the 21st century, we need to help each other drop the defensive stance and focus on achievement. Seeking the truth is an honorable calling. Let's be open to doing the new things that will help Americans – all Americans – get the news they need to run their nation and their lives. ●

**– Eric Newton, director of Journalism Initiatives
  John S. and James L. Knight Foundation**

The civil conflict and unrest of the 1960s arose in just this sort of disconnected environment, as the Kerner Commission detailed. Does American journalism really need more riots before it starts writing again about social and political issues that concern more than white, middle-class men? Do we need our route to work blocked by fires before we think about polling in more than one language? Given the companies that are trying new formats and approaches to reach young readers, second-generation Asian Americans and Spanish-language consumers, among others, we hope the answer is no. Yet America's demographic clock is ticking. By failing to seek truth and report it, we are robbing people of the news they need to govern themselves. ●

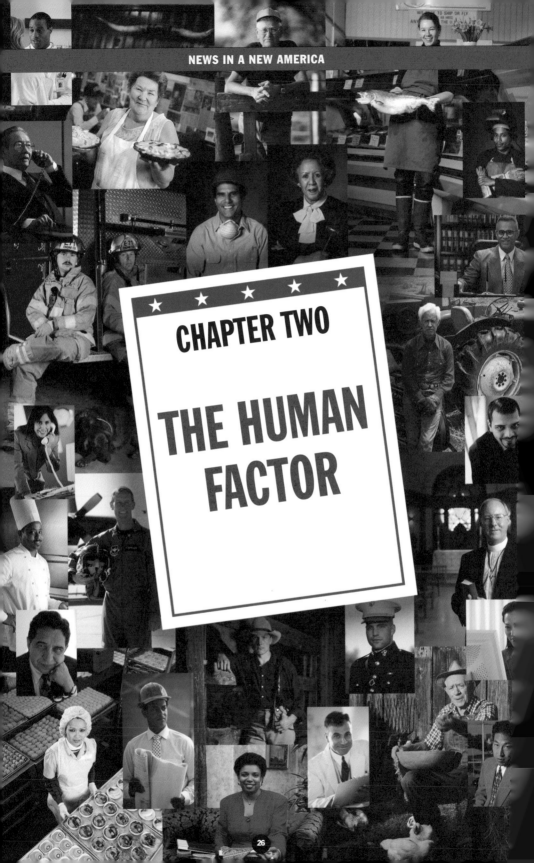

CHAPTER TWO

THE HUMAN FACTOR

B y now, many journalists know to avoid obvious blunders such as dressing disrespectfully in a mosque or describing a person as "wheelchair-bound." We tend to notice wrongheaded word choices, as when The Seattle Times wrote that Californian Michelle Kwan was competing against "Americans" in the 2002 Olympic figure-skating competition. We cringe at a Chicago Sun-Times story that referred to a 2,250-member tribe in Oklahoma as "ghosts of the past" who were troubling the descendants of German settlers in the area.

But the most dangerous of mistakes usually go unnoticed. They are sins of omission and emphasis, errors that can have life-or-death consequences. Look at the missing pieces in most medical reporting. If articles about breast cancer rarely mention Asian Americans, will Japanese American women check for lumps or get mammograms? When they do, they discover malignancies nearly as often as white women. If heart-disease stories don't mention African Americans, how will people in that group know the extremely high mortality rate they share? How often have you seen a report on diabetes featuring American Indians? And yet they are more likely to have the disease than anyone else.

Gaps in coverage and off-base ways of framing a story and its importance, of course, aren't limited to topics that could make a difference in the health of people of color. They show up in news about schools, crime, politics and all the topics of the day. Usually they result from journalists' shortage of background knowledge and a surplus of assumptions. Why would one in five news stories about Native Americans, for instance, focus on reservation life when most native people live in cities?

These problems – while solvable – go deeper than the choices we make in research and reporting. They begin with the very way we perceive the world.

SEEING THINGS OUR WAY

Do journalists routinely consider the way our own situations in life – from education to employment to home ownership – color our "objective" reality? Do we think about how these might affect the way we go about our work? The honest answer is No, not really.

If we have never faced discrimination, for instance, we are less likely to notice the problem. We may have never needed to look for its signs. On our beats, we may be less likely to check for discrimination in school funding, corporate hiring or real estate lending. If we have been raised on images of violent urban youth, we may be oblivious to the problems of youth anger and alienation until suburban young people, such as the boys at Columbine High School in 1999, turn on their classmates with gunfire. We may see medicine only through the experiences of our own family and friends, not even guessing that others may get different standards of care.

Our personal histories can also help us see things that others don't. If we live with a condition that limits our physical abilities, we might pay more attention to access technologies or prescription drug pricing. If we grew up in a religious family, we might find it easier to interview people with fundamentalist beliefs and portray them fairly. If we are the first generation in our family to live in the United States, we may have a finely tuned radar for immigrant achievements and concerns.

As many journalists point out, what we're really after is better news coverage. And that requires an expansion in thought, inclusiveness in *ideas*. Recently The New York Times formally adopted this concept by broadening its definition of diversity. "We will make an extra effort to focus on diversity of religious upbringing and military experience, of region and class," wrote Executive Editor Bill Keller. Hiring a mixed work force is just one aspect, he added. "It calls for a concerted effort by all of us to stretch beyond our predominantly urban, culturally liberal orientation."

True newsroom diversity can lead to a completely different take on the news. Reporting on three studies released in August 2005, the San Francisco Chronicle wrote this headline: "Health care treatment for blacks improving." The San Jose Mercury News, which has a more diverse newsroom and nearly the same market, looked at it differently: "Studies: Health care disparities persist."

How often do we overlook interesting stories about people unlike ourselves? Recent figures collected by Media Tenor International, the media-analysis group based in Germany, offer a clue. Researchers studied race and ethnicity references in Time, Newsweek, The Wall Street Journal, and the NBC, ABC and CBS nightly news shows over 32 months ending in August 2004 (see chart, Page 29). Of 170,212 news reports, African Americans appeared as main characters only 138 times – unless they were well-known entertainers, athletes or government figures. Latinos appeared half that often; Arab Americans a little less often; and Native Americans, about a third as often as African Americans. Asian Americans, the subject of just 13 stories, were nearly invisible.

Our experiences each day as journalists reflect the whole package of our lives to that moment: broadly, our race or ethnicity, class, gender, generation, ideology and the places where we live and grew up. Together these elements influence our news judgment, how we perceive and evaluate issues and events.

Each of us, of course, is a unique mix. But patterns can develop when people who work in a newsroom are a lot alike. According to the latest data, most mainstream American journalists are well-educated, male and white. The news they notice and the sources they consult have led to a statistically provable national media tilt toward the white world. Shaped by newsroom traditions and shared personal backgrounds, a powerful, unconscious belief system has come into play. Because it is woven into the very structure of the organization, it is hard to identify and tough to crack. It determines what journalists collectively see as newsworthy. The less we notice it, the more that system influences choices about whose stories are deemed important and whose are overlooked.

People create routines, but then the routines take on a life of their own. Newsroom cultures are famously defensive. Journalists deal with the ever-changing news stream by avoiding change or even, at times, awareness in how or why they process that stream. You may hear a person of color talk about the "white media." But it would be quite unusual to hear a white broadcast producer or newspaper editor use the phrase. Tom Jacobs, an African American documentary producer who worked in television for three decades, says he hopes one day for "real color TV." In a column for Electronic Media, Jacobs wrote: "White male news executives, producers and writers report on

Who's in the News?

A majority-white news department runs the risk of producing majority-white news. Bolstering that supposition is a study of 32 months of print and television news reports in which people of color were seldom the main characters. The chart below shows the number of news reports in which people of color were the focus.

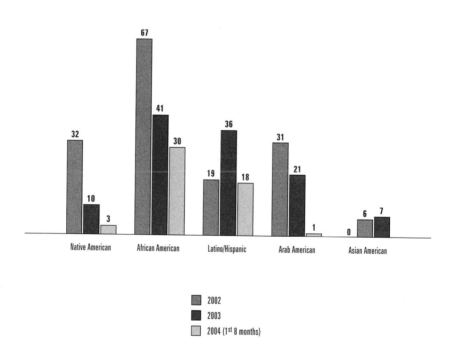

Source: Media Tenor International, 2004, 2005. Based on 170,212 reports in Time, Newsweek, The Wall Street Journal, NBC Nightly News, ABC World News Tonight, CBS Evening News. Jan. 1, 2002, to Aug. 31, 2004.

the world from their point of view. The world, for most of these people, is a white world."

As cognitive psychologists and media analysts explain it, the bias toward the white majority is rarely deliberate or – at least within the newsroom – even noticed. It emerges in news reporting through a lack of cultural awareness, unconscious stereotyping and selective sourcing. It is maintained by news traditions that had grown out of a U.S. social structure where white, upper-income men historically held leadership positions. It especially flourishes in fast-moving, closed, assembly-line style news systems. "Most reporters are embedded in this racial ideology – it's somewhat equivalent to 'common sense,'" says Hemant Shah, journalism and mass

Hemant Shah

communication professor at the University of Wisconsin-Madison. "This comes out in whose culture, whose ideas, whose values are assumed to be proper."

Shah studies how journalists shape, source and write stories. "We look at who are the heroes, the villains, who is to blame," he says. People of color are "portrayed as having concerns that are less important than the majority ... presented in a way that highlights their anger or other emotion instead of the argument they're trying to make."

It would be a mistake to assume this system is solely a problem of the white-majority newsroom. Mistaken assumptions don't come only from notebooks held by people from a certain race, class, gender, generation or region. Fortunately, the reverse is also true. Each of us has the power to change the situation.

PRIMING STEREOTYPES

News helps people learn about the world around them, and to make up not just their minds but also their policies. Most journalists avoid obvious stereotypes. But we may not know that the stories we choose about people or the way we characterize them can activate unconscious stereotypes. They can strengthen assumptions that our audiences already hold.

A 1999 study showed this directly. When immigration reporting focused on jobs and other resources, readers began to think about race – and race-based stereotypes – even if the word was never mentioned. In response to questions after they read news articles with an economics angle, people

David Domke

who thought of Hispanics as "nurturing" said immigration helped the United States. Those who saw Hispanics as violent, of course, said immigration was harmful. When reporting emphasized human rights or ethics instead of economics, though, readers did not associate their views on immigration with any perceptions about Hispanics themselves. Social psychologists call this "priming," a process by which certain subject matter activates unconscious ideas. David Domke, the University of Washington professor who led the research, concluded that journalists may be building a powerful bias into stories just by the angles we choose.

Of all the possible ways to frame it, mainstream journalists by and large reported California's Proposition 187 as a dollars-and-cents issue. The 1995 law – most of which was later ruled unconstitutional – would have blocked undocumented immigrants from education, health care and government services. "It is a matter of limited resources, not race," wrote Evelyn Iritani of the Seattle Post-Intelligencer, paraphrasing a political consultant. But by sticking to an economics angle, journalists may have unintentionally given the proposition an advantage.

Even if government were mainly a financial transaction, there still would be more to the story. When the stories on Proposition 187 covered only one part of the equation – taxes brought in and services going out – without covering any other aspects – culture, history, human rights, moral values or personal responsibility – was that either accurate or fair?

In an analysis of 166 stories about immigration in 2005, University of Missouri-Columbia graduate student Brendan Watson found that reporters across a range of newspapers mostly wrote about conflict. This approach, other researchers have found, often provokes negative reactions by the audience. Watson also found differences in immigration coverage depending on who was doing it. Latino reporters more often wrote from a human-interest perspective. They also used more immigrants and other regular people as sources, instead of officials or academics.

When it comes to economics in general, mainstream news appears to take on a negative tone in covering Latinos. Media Tenor studied news from top national outlets in the 20 months from January 2002 to August 2004. Most stories with a Latino as the main character had a positive tilt – except those about the labor market and, as might be expected, HIV/AIDS (see chart Page 33). Could journalists be influenced by the same triggers linked to race-based stereotypes that we help to cause? Why wouldn't we?

Our unconscious attitudes don't affect just the way we report about race. In a two-year Media Tenor analysis of coverage ending in 2003, most television reports that featured women involved social issues or human interest topics. Even with then National Security Adviser Condoleezza Rice in the news regularly, women featured less often in international policy stories. Once again, who works in the newsroom matters. Women television reporters were more likely then men to use and give time to women sources, according to an analysis of local coverage of the 2002 governor's race in Michigan.

Journalists often pick news angles, words and imagery to make stories more understandable and meaningful. But the choices we make may unintentionally promote a point of view. Domke, a former journalist, studied the use of terms such as "inner city" or "disadvantaged teenagers" in written crime coverage. Not surprisingly, the phrases spurred readers to draw on racial stereotypes when they weighed anti-crime strategies such as a stronger police presence or job programs for youth. Political scientists Franklin D. Gilliam Jr. and Shanto Iyengar found in a 1999 study that people's attitudes shifted significantly when local crime news on television included clear racial elements. Stories with race references triggered white television viewers' support for a punitive criminal justice policy. "Journalists have to recognize that they are fundamentally part of the processes by which people construct their racial reality," Domke says.

Researchers at Stanford University and the University of California, Los Angeles recently tested this phenomenon in a juvenile justice system setting. They found that when police and probation officers had been primed with words such as *dreadlocks* or *homeboy*, they favored tougher punishment.

We have the most influence, studies have found, when our audiences live in places or work in jobs that are not very diverse. That's when they most rely on the news media for information about other groups. When certain types of people don't show up in the news, "long-standing cultural stereotypes and misunderstandings ... readily fill in the blanks," wrote Robert Entman, co-author of *The Black Image in the White Mind: Media and Race in America*, summarizing a 2001 Shorenstein Center Conference on Race and the Press.

The sheer volume of black Americans featured in crime news stories – but not included elsewhere as contributing members of society – helps shape racial prejudices, conclude political scientists Jon Hurwitz and Mark Peffley. They've shown that these biases, in turn, influence social and political choices: whether to build more prisons, or teach inmates technical skills. And when both black and white people have followed news about race relations and affirmative action, they are less likely to blame African Americans themselves for race-based social and economic inequalities.

CATEGORICAL THINKING

Knowing this, why don't journalists just announce that, starting Monday, there will no longer be any bias in the way we tell stories? Because we're people. Humans can't help but think categorically. We naturally sort our environment into comfort zones, using past experiences and visual cues as our guides. "The human mind must think with the aid of categories. ... Orderly

living depends upon it," wrote psychologist Gordon Allport in his influential *The Nature of Prejudice* in 1954.

Categories are everywhere. Letters are letters. Numbers are numbers. But categories can also betray us. Students in a 1995 study described differences in color between a letter and a number – when the symbols were actually the same shade of red.

Socially, people align fast and easily with what psychologists call our "in group," which can be our race, class or gender, our generation or our occupation, our neighborhood or our nation – or even the side of the room we sit on. Quite quickly, we decide on one another's perceived warmth and competence, then react accordingly, says Susan Fiske, a social psychologist at Princeton University. "These associations are in your head, even if you don't have prejudiced values," she says.

While we may not notice our resulting preferences and distinctions, we act on them all the time. In 1998, social scientists now at Harvard University, the University of Washington and the University of Virginia designed the Implicit Association Test to learn more about unconscious bias and categorization. Their quizzes, available on the Internet to anyone, measures automatic responses to images and words. Over six years, visitors to the web site (*http://implicit.harvard.edu*) have taken more than three million tests.

Most people show a more positive attitude toward whites than blacks and a stronger liking for young over old. Regardless of their conscious beliefs, they more often link women with liberal arts and family, while they pair men with technical subjects and careers. We can even hold an unconscious

How the Media Covers Latinos

Mainstream news outlets are generally evenhanded when reporting on the most common topics involving Latinos – except when it comes to jobs and health. As this chart illustrates, print and broadcast media took a negative view of the Latino community in the areas of the labor market and HIV/AIDS during 32 months of reporting.

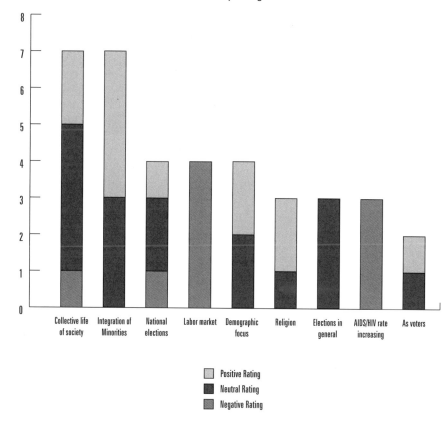

Source: Media Tenor International, 2004, 2005. Based on 73 reports on Hispanics out of 170,212 stories in Time, Newsweek, The Wall Street Journal, NBC Nightly News, ABC World News Tonight, CBS Evening News. Jan. 1, 2002, to Aug. 31, 2004.

bias against people like ourselves. About 40 percent of African Americans in the study so far show a pro-white bias, 40 percent show a pro-black one, and the rest have been neutral.

The response is very deep. Harvard University psychologist Mahzarin Banaji, a collaborator on the test, explains that these reactions reflect social conditioning and an ancient fear of people who seem different from us, whether physically or due to different beliefs or cultures. If we have little contact with people of another race, followed by one bad experience with someone, we are likely to reflexively fear everyone in that group. Banaji said she was encouraged that the effect can be overcome – first of all just by spending time with people unfamiliar to us and learning about them. "Above all it seems to be contact with other groups that's positive," Banaji says.

As journalists, we may unconsciously act on these reflexive attitudes. They may influence whom we rush to interview, and whom we avoid. They may cause us to think of some people as representative, and others, not. Banaji and Thierry Devos at San Diego State University tested the idea of "American" in six studies. They found that both white and black people viewed Asian Americans as less "American" than themselves. And both white people and Asian Americans thought whites were more American than anyone. For all groups, "to be American is to be white," the researchers concluded. Do we think of this phenomenon when we rush out to get reactions on a breaking news story? Not usually. Could it be one reason white sources dominate in every area of news? Could it help explain why so many reporters called the people leaving New Orleans "refugees" during the week

following Hurricane Katrina? The term usually describes people fleeing from one country to another. Before September 2005, it had been mainly associated with Sudan and Afghanistan, according to the Global Language Monitor, a media tracking company. Some residents of New Orleans, including those sheltered in the Houston Astrodome, felt the word turned them into outsiders. "The fact is they are our own people," Donna Jo Napoli, a Swarthmore College linguistics professor, told the Associated Press. Some news outlets dropped the word. But others insisted on it. "Refugee," said Associated Press Executive Editor Kathleen Carroll, captured the "sweep and scope of this historic natural disaster on a vast number of our citizens."

News coverage of the hurricane brought more African American faces to television screens and newspapers than had been seen in decades. Some wondered why reporters were so quick to repeat unsubstantiated rumors of armed carjacking and rape. Why the emphasis on people who were pulling food, clothes or tools out of ruined stores? Were there really "wild gangs" and an "urban menace," as Fox's Bill O'Reilly warned, blocking rescues? In a column that ran in black community newspapers, Freedom Forum Diversity Institute training editor Dwight Cunningham predicted that reporters will be much less eager to cover Katrina's ongoing impact on African American families across the nation. Now is the time for journalists to monitor the fairness of the rebuilding effort, to report on government responsibility to the poor and to African Americans, he urged. Journalists, he wrote, should "embrace their basic ideals. For all the people."

Can we undo our natural inclinations? Yes, social psychologists say. Some very simple strategies work, they have found. First, we can pay attention to these tendencies and notice what triggers them. Over time, they are likely to have less influence. And we can do what we already know how to do. We can spend time with the people who make us feel uncomfortable. We can visit community gatherings, cultural events; we can observe and ask questions. We can learn how others do things, and why they do things the way they do.

THE IN CROWD

Many journalists are trying to reach diverse audiences and to portray all of society fairly. They know that they must respond more deeply than counting up staff members or thinking more carefully about topics and sources. They are looking for ways to recognize our built-in bias, to better see how this may infiltrate the news. Compared to the scientists, though, we have a long way to go.

Jack Dovidio

Jack Dovidio, a University of Connecticut psychologist who studies stereotyping and prejudice, points to a phenomenon called "linguistic intergroup bias." This builds on the theory that people unconsciously favor their own kind.

Dovidio finds that even simple sentences can come out of our heads with bias built in. Describing positive behavior in our own group, we tend to convey a general sense of a person's inner goodness: "She is helpful." But if the person isn't in our group, it's just the facts: "she helped someone," as though tomorrow, maybe she won't.

When a group member behaves poorly, they get the concrete, one-time language:

"She hit the man." But if the person is outside the group, it tends to be a sweeping indictment: "She's hostile."

Does this sound familiar? It might. Similar patterns show up in coverage choices. Every day, journalists decide what will be "spot news" – a one-time story that just happened – and what will be more: a big feature, a running story worth many days, an investigative series, a major trend.

Here's an example: In 2001, there seemed to be plenty of news coverage of Coca-Cola's agreement to pay $192.5 million to remedy racial inequities in the workplace. But a bigger story, unearthed by Rutgers law professors Alfred and Ruth Blumrosen the following year, 2002, got little attention. These two former EEOC officials studied Equal Opportunity Commission data from 1999, the most recent year available. They found that workplace discrimination went far beyond Coca-Cola. A whopping 37 percent of mid- to large-sized U.S. companies intentionally avoided hiring nonwhites in nine job categories that year and 29 percent discriminated against women. (See chart Page 37 for a look at the risk of discrimination by occupation.)

What's a bigger story? One company, or nearly four in 10?

When we cover social disparity on a sporadic basis and shy away from documenting discrimination, social scientists say, we influence the way people think about it. Instead of getting concerned about a social issue, they say, our audiences think in terms of victimization and personal responsibility. "Media coverage and debates about affirmative action may help to amplify a form of racial resentment that runs through the opinions of many whites today," wrote Oscar Gandy, a professor at the University of Pennsylvania Annenberg School for Communication, in a study on the ways news influences attitudes about inequality.

TREATING PEOPLE DIFFERENTLY

The unconscious human tendency to categorize others and treat them accordingly also helps explain why change is so difficult – in any enterprise, but especially in pressure-cooker workplaces. When several journalism organizations complained about a news story that described a man who had been murdered as "Oriental," KMPH FOX 26 in Fresno, Calif., apologized and tried to explain. "Our staff was in a rush to report the story 'live' on the air," wrote General Manager Charles Pfaff in a letter to the groups. Without a thought, the reporter had repeated the term a police officer had used.

At KRON-TV 4 in San Francisco, the staff has worked hard to avoid such errors. They now have guidelines on when and where it is appropriate to use race in a story or to use descriptions that might point to race. But sometimes, the result is still "information that stereotypes rather than informs," says producer Kevin McCormack. Crime news especially – because of frightening content and tight deadlines – attracts quick-reflex mistakes. "Unconscious framing happens a lot," he says. Often these stories are set in predominantly African American or Latino neighborhoods. Reporters "will get whatever pictures they can of the scene, and grab whatever interviews they can," McCormack explains. "There is little time to think, let alone to look for other sources, other perspectives. So the end result is a one-dimensional view of the story."

Organizational analysts compare the newsroom culture to hospital emergency rooms. Both are places where people must think and act quickly. They know time pressure and stress like the back of their hands. Medical schools even train doctors to quickly evaluate someone's health by making guesses based on that person's appearance, age and social circumstances. So how do doctors handle the intensity? Are they able to sweep aside stereotypes and unconscious assumptions that might steer them wrong?

In many cases, probably not.

Though health care overall is improving, white men enjoy the benefits more than others. Black Americans still die disproportionately from heart disease and cancer. Latinos in the Northeast have twice the death rate from asthma as white people. In some parts of the country, Native American men generally live only into their mid-50s.

Why? Biology? Lifestyle? Physicians have blamed these things.

But more than 100 medical studies document the biggest reason: unequal care.

In 2003, a panel of experts convened by the Institute of Medicine analyzed all the data on health disparities. Their final report, "Unequal Treatment: Confronting Racial and Ethnic Disparities in Health Care," concluded "there was no disease area where the studies did not show differences in the quality of care."

Black people and Latinos are less likely than white patients to receive the proper cardiac medicine. They're less likely to get analgesia when they break their bones.

Discrimination by Job Category

This chart, based on a study of EEOC data from 1999, shows the likelihood that an applicant will face intentional discrimination because of race, sex or national origin each time a job is sought in a given occupation. The figures indicate the percent of establishments that discriminate in each occupation.

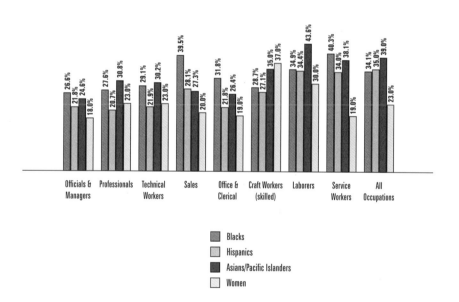

Source: Blumrosen, Alfred W., and Ruth G. Blumrosen. "The Reality of Intentional Job Discrimination in Metropolitan America – 1999." Rutgers University Law School, 2002.

THINGS JOURNALISTS CAN DO

To learn more about bias and stereotyping, you can read some of the references at the end of this book. In addition, you may wish to:

➤ Try the implicit association test to better identify and understand your unconscious biases. You can find the test at *http://implicit.harvard.edu*.

➤ Study other cultures. Your writing will become richer in detail and context if you come to each story with a better understanding of the people and cultures you cover, as well as their history in your area. One way to do this is to visit cultural centers and museums for a look into community histories. Another way is to read *A Different Mirror: A History of Multicultural America* by Ronald Takaki and *Africana: Civil Rights, An A-Z Reference of the Movement that Changed America*, edited by Kwame Anthony Appiah and Henry Louis Gates Jr.

➤ Build new relationships. Spend more time with sources and subjects so you can write about them with detail and nuance. Visit community hangouts and get to know people. When you can include revealing details, your news reports become stronger.

➤ Widen your sourcing. People of color; elderly people; gay and lesbian people, and people with disabilities all have more to talk about than "their issues." Include the total community in all your coverage.

➤ Audit your "big" and follow-up stories. What do you consider trends worth writing about? What do you treat as just one-day stories? Is your work as a whole oriented too much toward institutions and not enough toward a diverse group of people?

➤ Audit overall coverage and sourcing regularly. The Maynard Institute for Journalism Education offers "Reality Checks," a web-based diagnostic tool to analyze coverage and track progress.

➤ Look at the language. Do you see cases where abstract descriptions have been used to favor an "in group" or to negatively label an outsider? Are quotes from women and people of color used differently than those from white

(Continued on next page)

Doctors amputate the limbs of people of color more often than those of white patients. They give their patients of color anti-psychotic medications more often than they do people who are white.

Along with structural and institutional reasons, the institute's panel concluded that the unconscious biases and stereotypes held by doctors themselves are an important factor. Studies on physician-patient interactions have found that class, race, gender and age all play a role. In one study that ruled out other possible reasons for their judgments, cardiologists rated the African Americans they treated as less educated, less intelligent and less likely to comply with medical advice than their white patients. "These processes are fairly universal; we all need to be on guard and know that stereotypes may affect judgment," says Brian Smedley, who directed the national project.

The diversity among physicians nearly matches that in newsrooms: about 14 percent are people of color. Asian Americans make up 8.4 percent of doctors; Hispanics, 3.3 percent; African Americans, 2.4 percent; and American Native/Alaska Natives, a little under 1 percent, according to the American Medical Association. Men outnumber women as doctors by two to one.

With such similarities in the work environment, perhaps the strategies that medical institutions are using against unconscious stereotyping and bias may work in journalism, too. The Institute of Medicine's recommendations may even sound familiar:

➢ Hire a more diverse staff.

➢ Provide interpreters.

➢ Monitor progress.

But that's only a start. To change the culture that builds in unequal treatment, Smedley and his colleagues would like to see doctors learn about disparities and about cultures different from their own. They recommend more research on the unconscious processes that can undermine good care. They suggest new procedures that help remove subjectivity from decision-making.

Both the IOM and the American Medical Association emphasize cross-cultural education and encourage doctors to build stronger personal relationships across differences, whatever they may be. The Department of Health and Human Services Health Resources and Services Administration offers a downloadable course (www.hrsa.gov/financeMC/ftp/cultural-competence.pdf) for physicians. The training describes successful practices such as listening to the needs of historically underserved groups, involving them in problem-solving and taking the time to learn about knowledge, beliefs and attitudes shared by the community.

TRAINING AND EXPOSURE

The effort reaches back to medical school. The American Association of Medical Colleges offers programs to broaden interest in high school, support diversity among medical students, encourage faculty of color and raise awareness. Many schools have begun courses on racism and racial profiling. They teach students cultural traditions and customs, and do exercises intended to improve doctor-patient interactions.

(Continued from previous page)

men – for example, to add emotion to the story, but not analysis?

➢ Encourage the newsroom to apply checklists that will help keep fairness in the forefront. KRON-TV 4 in San Francisco has guidelines to help producers decide when race is appropriate to include in stories (http:www.ciij.org/newswatch?id=145). The Columbia Workshop on Race and Ethnicity suggests a list that reporters can use to review their work at http://www.jrn.columbia.edu/events/race/APME/growingyourcontent_diversity.asp.

➢ Find out about the sociology, psychology, politics and history of relations between groups in the United States. Check for resources on better reporting and media analysis at the Manship School of Communication Forum on Media Diversity: http://www.masscommunicating.lsu.edu/bibliography.

➢ Try the Writing for Change section of the Southern Poverty Law Center's teachingtolerance.org. The center's 10-minute writing exercises focus on unconscious bias in word choice, phrasing and perspective. Written for college students, they are also useful for newsrooms. http://www.tolerance.org/teach/expand/wfc/wfc_sctn1_4.html.

➢ Create friendly, open forums within the newsroom where stories can be discussed and ideas suggested. Keep the focus on improving future work.

➢ Go out to neighborhoods and invite people from the community into the newsroom to talk about coverage and offer their suggestions. Some newsrooms do spot checks on accuracy by sending letters to sources from randomly selected stories. Others use diverse editorial boards.

➢ Learn who lives in the community you cover. Consult the "American FactFinder" on the U.S. Census web site http://www.census.gov. You can get fact sheets on communities down to the size of a census tract, with details on the languages people speak, whether they own or rent their houses, where they work and how they get there each day. ●

– Sally Lehrman

It's a complicated challenge. People trying to address cultural diversity and health-care disparities in medicine can run up against the very problems they are trying to address, says Letha Mosley, an occupational therapist and faculty member at the University of Central Arkansas. "They often have to deal with issues of racism and sexism even as they are trying to incorporate such programming into their institution," she says.

Mosley studied diversity efforts at four accredited medical schools; two in historically black colleges, two in historically white ones. The strategies that worked might easily transfer into newsrooms. Program planners measured progress. They made sure people throughout the school knew about the diversity effort and its success. And they integrated cultural sensitivity of all types – not just about race – into the most important courses of the school. When interviewing patients for the first time, students at some schools met people of different races and genders with a range of physical abilities, linguistic skills and socioeconomic backgrounds. They learned about culture, context and history. The most successful medical schools cultivated the assumption that diversity and responding to disparities was a central mission. "It was a given, rather than a goal," Mosley says.

Stanford Medical School aims to incorporate cross-cultural awareness in every aspect of its curriculum. "You've got to look at the whole system," says Ronald Garcia, a psychologist who directs the Center of Excellence in Diversity. To begin, the school is offering one course that introduces students to the role of race in society, epidemiological differences between racial and ethnic groups and culture-based understandings about

disease. Stanford also brings in prestigious speakers for a quarterly lecture series on multicultural health. "I try to tweak their interest to know that culture is part of every encounter," Garcia says. "You have to be immersed in it, use it and value it."

Garcia sends his charges out into the community for everyday experiences, such as grocery shopping or visiting the library. He asks them to study a culture different from their own and to research each ethnic group's history in the area. He urges them to find "guides" into a community and to build relationships with "cultural brokers," people who serve as informal bridges between groups of people. His father, a business agent for the Longshoremen's Union in Southern California, was one. Cultural, educational and political paths crossed inside their house in Ventura, Calif., as visitors of all races, classes and backgrounds stopped by. "It's about trust, it's about honesty, it's about time and being available," Garcia says. "That may be too intimate for journalists. But you can't have a relationship without nurturing it. You will always be on the outside."

Every good journalist knows to cultivate the informed and connected people on his or her beat. Think of it that way, no matter who you are meeting, suggests Patty Talahongva, managing editor for the syndicated radio shows *National Native News* and *Native America Calling* and an on-air host for the latter. "You have to win trust with every story you do," she says. "Why is it so hard to talk to an Indian? Yes, you have to approach it with a certain amount of caution, respect and sensitivity – but you do that every day. Just pick up the phone, call the Indian and meet them." •

'INTELLECTUALS LOST TRACK ... OF RACISM'

Many Americans would agree that open racial bigotry is mostly a thing of the past.

But stark race-based disparities in daily life persist. Academic researchers, the U.S. Census Bureau and the Institute of Medicine continue to document examples like these:

➤ African Americans with a college diploma find themselves jobless almost twice as often as white people with the same education.

➤ Hispanics must get by on about half the individual income that Asian Americans and European Americans are able to divvy up among the bills.

And what happens when blacks and Latinos go to the hospital with a heart problem? They are less likely than whites to receive catheterization, be sent home with certain heart-protecting medicines or even be advised to take aspirin to protect their health.

Sociologists who study the reasons behind these disparities have begun to develop a new framework to understand racism and come up with solutions. "It's not just Archie Bunker anymore," says Troy Duster, a sociology professor at the University of California, Berkeley, and New York University.

Troy Duster

In recent books, Duster and other researchers say overt prejudice and direct discrimination happen less often in today's world. But bias, they contend, remains sewn into the fabric of work, school and the medical system. They document policies and practices throughout U.S. institutions that favor white people. And even the most well-intentioned white man or woman, they report, benefits from unseen preference built up over generations.

These researchers give historical and social context to proposals for "color-blind" government policies that might create a more equitable society. They offer a way of thinking about ongoing racial injustice that they hope will help U.S. society overcome a history of favoritism and bias.

When legislators outlawed discrimination by employers based on race, sex, religion or national origin, people assumed the practice would simply end. "Intellectuals lost track of the ability to discuss what racism is," says UC Berkeley sociologist Andrew Barlow. As social theories about race develop, he adds, "We are really at the beginning of a new era."

This emerging school of sociologists is also reacting to other intellectuals who contend that discrimination – and even the idea of race itself – is old news. Stephen and Abigail Thernstrom, who wrote *America in Black and White: One Nation Indivisible* in 1997, and Shelby Steele, author of *A Dream Deferred* in 1999, argue in their books that the nation ought to forget about race. It's time to appreciate progress made over the past several decades, they say. Race-conscious policies make white people resentful, they argue, and at the same time, do little for people of color. Instead, they say, such rules promote low ambition by holding some groups to a lower standard.

Those who want do away with race-based programs point to the Human Genome Project. When researchers had completed a rough draft of all human genes in 2000, they announced that race has no basis in biology. In a 1998 statement, the American Anthropological Association explained how modern ideas of "race" started. The concept arose in the 18th century as a way to justify status differences between European settlers and the people they conquered and enslaved. The Nazis later built on the idea to support the extermination of Jews, gypsies and others.

Since race is not biologically "real," the association proposed, the U.S. Census should plan to stop asking people about it by 2010. Instead, the term "ethnic group" would provide a "more nonracist and accurate" means to show U.S. diversity.

Soon, some proposed to abolish the idea of "race" in other arenas, such as education and medicine. A proposition on the California ballot in 2004 would have stopped most state agencies from collecting race-based data. As the initiative headed toward the ballot, the American Sociological Association attacked the suggestion as wrongheaded. The professional society urged scientists to continue using race categories in order to study how these groupings affect people's daily lives, access to resources and overall well-being. "A vast body of

(Continued on next page)

(Continued from previous page)

sociological research … shows that racial hierarchies are embedded in the routine practices of social groups and institutions," the society wrote in a 2003 statement.

The statement sparked some debate. California State University, Los Angeles, professor Yehudi Webster complained that sociologists who use race terminology promote racial awareness and separatism. These in turn lead to exclusion and discrimination. Journalists, government officials and educators should stop talking about race, too, he said. The human history of intermarriage, migration and genetic change make such boundaries meaningless, Webster wrote in the society newsletter.

While race may not hold up as a biological concept, others responded, its influence cannot be ignored. "Not everything 'real' is genetic," says Pilar Ossorio, a microbiologist and assistant professor of law and medical ethics at the University of Wisconsin. "We use racial categories to interact with each other in ways that have significant consequences."

The association urged its members to study race-related data to understand disparities in a deeper way and to develop policy ideas for greater social justice. Discrimination on an individual level does not explain much anymore, an increasing number of sociologists now say. They hope to unravel the ways racial privilege may be hidden inside the day-to-day workings of institutions from education to public transportation to criminal justice.

White-Washing Race: The Myth of a Color-Blind Society, written by seven scholars including Duster, begins the story in the 1930s with Franklin Roosevelt's New Deal, which was aimed to protect the working class. Congress then revised the law to protect racial segregation, too. The Social Security Act excluded domestic and agricultural workers from old-age pension and unemployment payments. Three-quarters of the black population, from domestic workers to sharecroppers, fell through the net. Similarly, the Wagner Act, which gave power to unions, also allowed labor to shut out black workers from closed shops. Loans under the Federal Housing Act differentially provided whites the wherewithal to move into new suburbs. Federal

Andrew L. Barlow

subsidies built public housing, which would contain black migrants from the South in urban areas.

The GI Bill, enacted in 1944, deepened the race bias built into the economic provisions of the time. Millions of returning veterans and war industry workers could get low-interest mortgages and free access to higher education. But white Americans benefited most, the book's authors write. First, federal lending rules favored segregated suburbs. And white people more often had the educational credentials to go to college. The policies of the time created an economic advantage for many white families that continued to grow as each generation built upon the wealth of its parents.

Like interest on a bank deposit, children collect economic potential for themselves from the property and social standing of their parents, Duster explains. Privileges in housing, jobs, education and other arenas, in turn, build upon one another. Disadvantages such as barriers to well-paying jobs, safe housing and fair-priced loans pass from parent to child, too. As a result, the racial hierarchy developed over the middle of the 20th century has pretty much held fast, he says.

Some think that the disparities built into American society may even be growing worse. *In Between Fear and Hope*, a book on globalization and race, Barlow writes about this change. In the 1960s and '70s, he says, business regulation, low-income housing, job training, public-health measures and other social programs began to undo the advantages long held by white people. But in the 1980s, the economy started to change. Service jobs replaced industry, businesses became internationally mobile, and deregulation and tax cuts became common. Wages dropped, health benefits declined and many jobs headed overseas. In 2004, household incomes had not improved during five consecutive years. The U.S. Census Bureau said they had stayed stable only because people were working more hours.

With more worries about jobs and pay, according to Barlow, many white people began to feel threatened. "Growing inequality makes more and more of the middle class experience a sense of crisis, so they try to buffer themselves," he says. He points to attacks on affirmative action and tough-on-crime laws that have put more African Americans and Latinos in jail. "We need to think about racism in a new way," Barlow contends.

Scholars now are studying the effects of race in society in more detail. Julie Sze, an assistant professor at University of California, Davis, looks at links between health and policy decisions such as where city planners place garbage dumps. Some research explores segregation in housing and how it limits people's job options. Others are looking at hidden racial animosities and the ways teachers treat students of different races.

Barlow, Duster and colleagues emphasize that whites may have no awareness of their privilege. They may not even know when they are trying to protect it. Say parents decide to fight to save funding for suburban high schools. Their work helps create more advanced-placement classes and leadership opportunities. Graduates can then more easily win a spot in the best colleges. But in urban areas, schools rarely have parents pushing for more money. They can't offer the same academic advantages. And the parents and graduates of top-tier schools? They understandably consider their achievements solely the result of the young peoples' own hard work.

While they may agree that race-based disparities exist, Barlow says, white people often know little about the history that tilts opportunities toward them. Instead they often suspect a lack of ambition or effort on the part of people of color. "You don't need to be a racist to promote policies that are race-conscious," says David Wellman, a professor of community studies at University of California, Santa Cruz and one of the *White-Washing Race* authors. Most whites don't see white as a race, he says. "Like a fish in water, they don't think about whiteness because it's so beneficial to them." ●

– Sally Lehrman

This article was adapted from a three-part series on race for the Institute for Justice and Journalism at the University of Southern California's Annenberg School of Communication.

★ ★ ★ ★ ★

CHAPTER THREE

PRESSURES IN THE NEWSROOM

Tim Kalich, editor and publisher of The Greenwood Commonwealth, had just hired his only black reporter. This boosted the nine-member newsroom to 11 percent African American. "You hope coverage changes," he says. "Common sense tells you that if you're in a community that's majority black, you'll be more able to tap into that."

Tim Kalich

African Americans dominate city government and school board leadership in Greenwood, Miss., population 18,425. White people own most of the businesses. Kalich says his white reporters try to cover everyone, sometimes by relying on the paper's black circulation director for tips. Indeed, the paper has won awards for the best paper of its size in Mississippi for the past four years. But coverage could be better, Kalich acknowledges. "The stories you don't get," he says, "are the ones passed on at the grocery story or at church, through daily interactions with people."

Charles Brown

Kalich's new hire was Charles Brown, 25 years old at the time and raised in a town an hour away. Yes, some community members were more willing to talk to him. And he noticed different stories. When a press release came in about June-teenth, for example, Brown learned that some of his colleagues didn't know that communities across the country celebrate June 19 as the day U.S. slavery finally ended. They didn't know that news of the Emancipation Proclamation, which took effect on Jan. 1, 1863, did not reach Texas slaves until two years later – June 19, 1865 – when a Union regiment arrived in Galveston, Texas, to order the last remaining slaves in the country freed.

The Greenwood Commonwealth was among the 346 papers that reported an all-white staff to the American Society of Newspaper Editors in 2005. Though such publications are small, together they reach at least 3.3 million readers across the country. The Commonwealth, with its circulation peaking at nearly 7,800 on Sundays, serves one of the most diverse areas on ASNE's all-white newsroom list. Of the 50,000 who live in or near Greenwood, 66 percent are black, Hispanic, Asian American or Native American. At the paper, the number of journalists of color has ping-ponged between zero and one during the past 20 years. Though Kalich can offer a starting salary of $22,000 to $25,000, he says nonwhite reporters and editors are hard to attract and keep. "They're in such high demand," explains Kalich, 47, editor and publisher for 10 of his 23 years at the paper. "When you take that small crop of candidates attracted to journalism, we're kind of on the bottom rung."

'WASTING OUR TIME'

Many newsroom managers do make an effort to hire, promote and encourage people of all backgrounds to succeed. Yet America's newsrooms have remained mostly white and male. Why? Sociologists and psychologists have discovered hidden barriers that help explain the glacial pace of change within many an industry, even when the best intentions really exist. Without realizing it, they say, people favor those most like themselves. These natural human processes play into newsroom cultures and systems that tend to give white and male journalists an advantage.

Minority Employment in Daily Newspapers
The American Society of Newspaper Editors has surveyed minority representation in U.S. newsrooms since 1978. The results of this annual census are shown here. The figures are based on newspapers' responses to the survey, and are rounded off.

	Total Work Force	Minorities in Work Force	Minority Percentage in Work Force
1978	43,000	1,700	3.95
1979	45,000	1,900	4.22
1980	47,000	2,300	4.89
1981	45,500	2,400	5.25
1982	49,000	2,700	5.51
1983	50,000	2,800	5.60
1984	50,400	2,900	5.75
1985	53,800	3,100	5.76
1986	54,000	3,400	6.30
1987	54,700	3,600	6.56
1988	55,300	3,900	7.02
1989	56,200	4,200	7.54
1990	56,900	4,500	7.86
1991	55,700	4,900	8.72
1992	54,500	5,100	9.39
1993	53,600	5,500	10.25
1994	53,700	5,600	10.49
1995	53,800	5,900	10.91
1996	55,000	6,100	11.02
1997	54,000	6,100	11.35
1998	54,700	6,300	11.46
1999	55,100	6,400	11.55
2000	56,200	6,700	11.85
2001	56,400	6,600	11.64
2002	54,400	6,600	12.07
2003	54,700	6,900	12.53
2004	54,200	7,000	12.95
2005	54,100	7,300	13.42

Source: American Society of Newspaper Editors Survey of Employment in U.S. Newsrooms, 2005

Kalich may think the Commonwealth is unusual. In aggregate, however, staffing at the 926 daily newspapers that sent in their numbers isn't terribly different from his own paper's. ASNE's leaders committed a quarter century ago to change their newsrooms to reflect the U.S. population. Today, at newspapers across the country, the share of journalists of color has reached just 13.4 percent. (See chart Page 46, which tracks minority representation in U.S. newsrooms since 1978.)

The U.S. public is now one-third Latino, Asian American, African American and Native American. The country will, the U.S. Census says, be half "minority" by 2050. Yet 40 percent of the daily papers that reported on hiring and retention employ no journalists of color at all.

Plus, not all editors provide data every year. Of the papers that didn't answer the 2005 survey, 275 had earlier reported all-white newsrooms. So the actual number of journalists of color at U.S. daily newspapers could be at least a point lower than ASNE believes. In 2002, when ASNE had for several years been reporting close to 12 percent journalists of color in U.S. news-papers, Indiana University's American Journalist Survey made this estimate: just 9.5 percent.

Broadcast data is equally discouraging – almost all of the numbers for journalists of color slipped last year, especially in radio. Television newsrooms are nearly 80 percent white, according to the Radio and Television News Directors Association, while radio newsrooms are 92 percent white.

Women now hold about 37 percent of print and 39 percent of television editorial jobs.

Yet they make up 51 percent of the population and more than two-thirds of the journalism and mass communications graduates. The proportion of women with executive jobs is even smaller – about one out of five people who head up newspaper or local television news departments. Perhaps worse, an American Press Institute/Pew survey found that one out of two female editors plans to leave her job soon – and maybe leave the business entirely. Salaries for women languish at $10,000 per year less than those of their male counterparts.

"What we're doing now is wasting our time," says Herbert Lowe, a Newsday reporter who is immediate past president of the National Association of Black Journalists. Newspapers must integrate up and down the ladder if they intend to change, he and other minority journalist association leaders insist. "Fundamentally," Lowe says, "it's all about who gets to hire whom."

'BEGIN TO TAKE A TOLL'

As it turned out, Charles Brown left The Greenwood Commonwealth. While the experience was great, he says, the hours were brutal: 6:30 a.m. to 11 p.m. many a day. His new job involves covering the campus and developing press materials for the historically black Mississippi Valley State University. Brown earns more money and enjoys a more reasonable schedule. And there's something else. "I feel more comfortable here," he says. He can relate to his colleagues easily, and they can relate to him. They can talk about personal things. "It wasn't a really big problem," Brown goes on, hesitating as he tries to explain. "It's like your finger hurts, it doesn't really bother you, but it will begin to take a toll."

INSIDE THE NEWSROOM: CONSENSUS MATTERS

The Poynter Institute's News and Race Project surveyed 970 journalists about their attitudes on diversity. They found:

➤ Journalists of color were more supportive of diversity goals than white journalists.

➤ Journalists of color were more critical of their company's current diversity efforts.

➤ The smaller the differences of opinion between journalists of color and white journalists, the greater the chance a newsroom is actually diversifying its staff and coverage.

In the chart below, the "climate" score is calculated as a mathematical ratio of how far apart journalists of color and white journalists are on diversity goals and efforts. A "newsroom diversity climate" score of 0 would mean there was no disagreement over diversity goals and efforts. Higher scores indicate greater disagreement. The full 2001 research report by Edward Pease, Erna Smith and Federico Subervi may be downloaded at *https://www.poynter.org/content/content_view.asp?id=5045&sid=5*.

News organization	Newsroom diversity climate
The Dallas Morning News	145
St. Louis Post-Dispatch	234
San Jose Mercury News	35
The Seattle Times	141
South Florida Sun-Sentinel	109
KRON, San Francisco	238
KTVA, Anchorage	126
KVIA, El Paso	108
WFLA, Tampa	290
WNBC, New York	70
WXYZ, Detroit	247

In 2001, ASNE leaders reported that America's daily newspapers had a retention problem. An ongoing exodus of journalists of color was undermining efforts to build racially diverse newsrooms. For every six journalists of color that editors had hired that year, seven had departed. The disillusioned émigrés complained about limits to their professional challenge and growth, according to a study by Lawrence McGill, a sociologist now at Princeton University. "Journalists of color are not convinced that they have equal opportunities for advancement," McGill wrote at the time, "or that they are being judged by the same evaluative criteria as white journalists."

Which journalists get to serve on newsroom committees, chase the best stories or write for the front page? In survey after survey, journalists of color say they feel they are the last to be chosen. "People who leave the field tend to do so accompanied by the feeling that what they had to offer was not given a chance to bloom," McGill wrote.

From assignments to daily news lineups, many newsrooms operate on the gut instincts of managers. Journalists trust in quick reflexes and timeliness. Many see things like job descriptions and written assignments as a waste of time. A Maynard Institute for Journalism Education workbook calls this approach "the closed newspaper." There's little give-and-take between editors and reporters. Editors assign, and reporters write what their editors expect. The bosses dictate news priorities.

In this kind of environment, both the way we work and our hidden biases can create a culture that shuts people out. Even today, many editors will tell you they know exactly what they want in an "ideal journalist"–

in job postings on journalismjobs.com, they seek reporters who are "goal-driven" and "aggressive," prepared to compete with the "big boys." Important qualities, certainly, but is male stereotype really all there is to it? What about being persistent, verbally talented, or good at developing trust with sources? These skills, stereotypically female, are just as important.

Because they operate at an unconscious level, stereotypes have their most power when people make subjective choices or must rely on incomplete information. Absent professional personnel practices, that's the way newsrooms tend to assign and promote. And so most women who do rise to executive jobs find themselves running departments such as marketing or community affairs. Here they can exercise those excellent communications skills – but are unlikely to be groomed for higher positions.

David Lawrence Jr., former publisher of The Miami Herald and before that the Detroit Free Press, put it this way when he accepted the 2004 Robert McGruder Diversity Award:

"Surely we cannot keep good people if we do not encourage them ... if we do not give them good role models ... if we do not give them good assignments ... if we do not give them real evidence of our commitment to their personal and professional growth ... if good people do not have a sense of being needed, wanted, fulfilled."

Some organizations say they are "colorblind" – meaning fair – when what they really are is blind to the issue of bias. When playwright and actress Anna Deveare Smith explored attitudes about diversity at Stanford University Medical School for its strategic-planning retreat, she did not run across instances of overt racism or sexism.

Instead, Smith found that people in the minority because of their gender, race or economic status felt isolated and undervalued. "It doesn't feel like there's any value to having a diverse population," one Latino medical student said. "You're allowed to succeed, but I bet most people feel that no one would cry very hard if they left."

UNCONSCIOUS STEREOTYPES AT WORK

When diversity remains unspoken and invisible except when it's time for staff counts, the ambiguity creates lots of room for guesses and misunderstandings. Scientists who study human interactions say this is when unconscious expectations and imagery – the stories and assumptions that everyone grows up with – can take over. Implicit stereotypes begin to limit people's opportunities, but may go unnoticed and unquestioned. And those in the minority – because of their sexual orientation, disability, or any other reason – may turn to stereotypes as well as they try to interpret and anticipate their colleagues' expectations.

When a stereotype is in play, the people affected by it tend to act unconsciously in alignment with it. Their actual strengths and abilities don't matter. Told that females usually perform poorly on a particular math test, women are likely to do just that. Otherwise they score just as well as white men. The same thing happens when black people are asked to mark their race at the beginning of a difficult verbal test or are told that it measures intellectual ability. Or when a teacher starts talking about "white males," those students often begin to feel threatened and uncomfortable. Social psychologists Claude Steele and Joshua Aronson studied this phenomenon at Stanford University. In their research,

MENTORS MAKE A DIFFERENCE

Ray Marcano had dreamed of becoming an R&B star. He studied voice, percussion and piano while growing up in the Bronx. He even won a place at the esteemed High School for Music and Art in New York City. But then he heard his fellow students play, and began to doubt his own talents. That's when an English teacher suggested journalism. Marcano heeded that advice. He is now in his third decade of journalism and one of only 14 black deputy managing editors in the country. "If you want it bad enough and if you're willing to do the things that help you grow," he says, "you'll do OK."

Marcano doesn't credit his achievements to any special skills or connections. But he says the welcoming environment he felt at Cox Newspapers has made all the difference in the world. "Cox, unlike a lot of other newsrooms, *gets* diversity," Marcano says, explaining why he has remained at the Dayton (Ohio) Daily News for more than two decades. "I don't think I could find anywhere I'd feel as comfortable."

Ray Marcano

Brad Tillson Jr.

Marcano applied for his first newspaper job before he even finished his journalism degree at Lehman College of City University in New York. He spotted the Vinita (Okla.) Daily Journal's ad in Editor & Publisher and wrote in right away. Then he called to check on his application every week for a month.

The publisher agreed to give Marcano a try. Vinita, Okla., home to the annual Will Rogers Memorial Rodeo and the World's Largest Calf Fry Festival and Cook-off, was originally the northern capital of the displaced Cherokee nation. When Marcano got there in 1981, the town of 6,700 was about 12 percent Native American and 6 percent African American – and, he recalls, segregated.

He arrived to join the six-person news and advertising staff sporting a Mod Squad-style Afro. It was culture shock both ways. To Marcano, the town felt "98 percent white." Susan Ryals, who runs the Vinita Public Library, remembers that people did notice him. "Because he wasn't from here, he was a little more Yankee," she says. Marcano didn't know about local specialties like the "coney" – a chili-covered hot dog – yet

"people were very, very warm," he recalls. Just one bad incident sticks in his mind – when he tried to get a haircut and the barber refused.

During his second year in Vinita, Marcano completed his journalism studies. He would get off work, drive about an hour and half to Northeastern State University in Tahlequah, return at about midnight, sleep a few hours, then hit the desk at 7 a.m. He was sports editor, lifestyle editor, then news editor.

Marcano wanted to make it back to New York. He decided to go to a bigger paper and set his sights on Tulsa. At the Tulsa World, Marcano covered night cops. He liked the demanding beat. Then, one night, as he joined the news crew covering a gathering tornado, a police officer stopped him. He ordered Marcano to turn around and leave. When the reporter protested, the cop slapped handcuffs on him.

Even though he was released shortly afterwards, the incident disheartened Marcano. He isn't sure whether race had anything to do with what happened. After a couple of close friends left the paper, though, he decided to go, too. "I said, I'm outta here," he remembers. He promptly sent out resumes to newspapers of about the same size in Ohio and Pennsylvania.

Soon Marcano landed a minority affairs job in Dayton. And, after a week of training at The Poynter Institute in St. Petersburg, Fla., he says, the quality of his work began to climb. So did his level of responsibility. He began to fill in as an editor on Sunday, next taking over the night assistant city editor slot. "I wanted to be in a position where I could shape a newsroom, where I could be a leader," Marcano says. Every chance he could, he told his bosses about his goals to move up.

They listened. Marcano rose through several department-level positions and finally became metro editor. But then he hit a rough spot. That old self-doubt began to set in. "It was a very, very demanding job and I seriously wondered whether I really had the stuff to run a newspaper," Marcano says. He would agonize over the decisions he had made. He wondered what his boss would have done, what his boss' boss would have done. "That'll just eat you up," he says.

A call from a recruiter changed everything. Before Marcano knew it, he had an offer. While he decided not to go, his self-image was transformed. Like other managers of color, he had held himself to an incredibly high standard. "If a paper of that quality thinks I could be managing editor, I thought, I must have something going for me," Marcano says. "We all feel the same way, we can't make a mistake: You've got to be perfect."

Even though he's not very good at doing so himself, Marcano advises other journalists of color to try to let go of that feeling. "That's simply a byproduct of my mother's upbringing," he says. "I'm only four generations removed from the slave plantations. We've got another generation or so before black people can walk into any job situation and not feel like they have to be better and have to work harder."

With a renewed sense of his own potential, Marcano applied to open several new bureaus as a regional editor. Soon he rose to assistant managing editor for production. In 2000, he won the presidency of the Society of Professional Journalists. Then, much to Marcano's surprise, Brad Tillson Jr., at the time the publisher of the Dayton Daily News and chief executive over eight Cox papers, called him into his office and asked to be his mentor. "I was floored," Marcano says. "I'm thinking, how can I not screw this up?"

The relationship began as part of a formal mentoring program that Cox was testing. (Cox, a national leader in newsroom training, ranks No. 5 on the Dedman-Doig newsroom diversity index of newspaper companies.) Tillson recalls that Marcano had always made it clear he was looking for opportunities. "There are people who never put their hands up; and there are people who sometimes put their hands up," Tillson explains. "And then there are people like Ray, who always have their hands up."

Yet Tillson feared that the relationship might be awkward because of the men's relative positions within the organization. He certainly couldn't share everything he knew about the company as a top executive. He worried about perceptions of favoritism and the like. Plus there was the time commitment. All these concerns fell away as the two began to meet.

"I really looked forward to the time with him and felt it was an important part of the job," Tillson

says now. They got together regularly, mainly over lunch. Marcano set the agenda with his questions and concerns. "We developed a very open relationship," Tillson says. "If I thought he was going about something the wrong way, I wouldn't hesitate to tell him that."

The conversations ranged from distribution to finance to how Marcano interacted with others. Marcano decided to go back to school for an MBA and graduated in March 2003. The exchanges with Tillson continued informally even into the publisher's retirement. When someone across the table really cares about your development, Marcano says, "It makes a real difference." ●

– Sally Lehrman

ADVICE FOR WOULD-BE MANAGERS

Over 15 years, the percentage of journalists of color on the staff at the Dayton Daily News increased from about 12 percent to nearly 14 percent in 2005, in a circulation area that is 16 percent nonwhite. Gender diversity has improved, too.

"Coverage has changed," says deputy managing editor Ray Marcano. "People bring different ideas to the table. You notice things you didn't before." His advice for women and people of color who want to be managers:

"You've got to take care of yourself, you've got to take care of your family. It's not going to do anybody any good if you work your 14th hour on the seventh day of the week and you have a heart attack coming home.

"You've got to hang on to your confidence. Stick to a right decision. Just because somebody disagrees with you doesn't mean you're wrong. Talk it through and find out why they differ, but you can't get down on yourself and start judging yourself.

"Try to let go of the feeling that you've got to be perfect; that you've got to work harder than everyone else. You can't be anybody but who you are."

THINGS NEWS MANAGERS CAN DO

1. Set priorities for diversity and explain them clearly. Evaluate assignments, promotions, pay and other rewards to make sure they are fairly distributed among the staff.

2. Use compensation and comparable rewards to hold managers accountable. The news media companies with the best diversity track records reward managers with bonuses for creating a diverse staff.

3. Set goals and monitor progress by collecting data on hiring and promotion, and by doing regular content analyses.

4. Make sure procedures and criteria for hiring are designed to include, not exclude. Review job qualifications to get rid of stereotype-laden ideals and replace these with specific, equally relevant skills that are less tied to race or gender. Begin by selecting from a diverse pool of qualified candidates.

5. Encourage every staff member to create goals and objectives that include learning new skills, developing leadership and stretching into more creative or challenging assignments. Develop systems to make sure managers know about staff members' ambitions.

6. Encourage mentoring. Make sure management performance appraisals include demonstrable support for the advancement of people of color, women, gays and lesbians, and people with disabilities. Consider building in systems to mentor up, as well as mentor down.

7. Make sure that the criteria for coveted assignments and promotions are explicit and defined by the actual skills needed, not by a manager's subjective judgment.

8. Take the Implicit Association test to understand how unconscious stereotyping and reactions occur. Encourage others to take it, too.

You can find the test at:

https://implicit.harvard.edu/implicit/demo/index.jsp or *http://www.tolerance.org/hidden_bias/02.html*

(Continued on next page)

Claude Steele

students' scores reflected racial and sexual stereotypes when the test situation "primed" them in some way. Otherwise, they fared the same as everyone else.

For journalists of color, Steele says, "stereotype threat" is often exhausting. Every grammatical mistake or misidentified source feels magnified, suggesting some deeper incompetence. "Every interaction is shrouded with this possibility of being seen stereotypically and devalued," he says. This "burden of suspicion" can cause a wearing self-consciousness that in turn interferes with performance.

Our confidence can rise and fall along with the limits and expectations that we believe society places on us. Our race, gender, sexual orientation or physical characteristics, of course, help set the bar. The infamous Jayson Blair, in the wake of his departure from The New York Times, has given a boost to stereotype threat for many young journalists, especially those of color. While Stephen Glass of The New Republic and Jack Kelley from USA Today also made up stories and faked sources, their misdeeds didn't prompt the same kind of reaction. People in newsrooms didn't start saying, "Well, we better be more careful about hiring those white guys." Nor did you hear anyone saying, "As a white man, I feel more pressure at work because of what Glass and Kelley did."

Some white people do worry about being stereotyped another way, though: as racist. Blair clearly was felled by his drug abuse, compulsive fabrication and plagiarism. His bosses just as clearly failed to practice good management. They didn't monitor the expense reimbursements that would have given him away. But Steele also gets the sense that both Blair and his bosses were frantically combating felt stereotypes. At least some of his editors may have avoided confronting him because they were afraid of being seen as unfair to African American reporters. Macarena Hernández, a former colleague whose work Blair copied, took this view a step further in an op-ed piece for the Los Angeles Times: "If The New York Times was sincerely committed to diversity, Blair's editors would have chopped off his fingers at the first sign of trouble instead of helping him polish his claws."

Stereotype threat can stand in the way of mentoring, an important means for less-experienced journalists to develop their skills and climb the ladder. White men might avoid relationships with people of another gender, race, physical ability or sexual orientation for fear of making a misstep or being judged. Yet they are the ones most often in a position to offer support and advice. In experiments at Stanford, when white men thought they'd be discussing racial profiling with black men instead of love and relationships, they moved their chairs further away. "What's interesting is that it's not related to how prejudiced they are," Steele says.

A FAILURE TO COMMUNICATE

Journalists of color, women, people with disabilities, and gays and lesbians enter a double bind the moment they enter a newsroom.

Suppose, for example, you become the only Latino journalist in a newsroom in a town with a large Latino population. You aspire to be a political reporter. You know you'll have to work up to it. The first job you get is general assignment, and the

(Continued from previous page)

9. Include diversity in every aspect of professional-development training. Teach reporters, editors and managers about the ways that unconscious stereo-typing and majority privilege influence every workplace.

10. Provide a forum for systematic and safe discussion of race, gender, sexual orientation, disability and class issues, both as news subjects and as they apply to news operations and life in general. Support intercultural dialogue with specific exchanges, and prepare to bring in a mediator for these.

11. Get feedback from employees and take it seriously. Create safe places for staff members to voice their worries about unfairness or insensitivity. Provide opportunities outside of the day-to-day work environment for people to raise specific complaints such as "You shouldn't use this phrasing," or "You never call on me in meetings or conference calls." Teach others how to respond to such concerns thoughtfully and well.

12. Avoid labeling people who speak up about race, generation, gender and other issues as troublemakers. Know that successful discussion about diversity often involves conflict.

13. Create intercultural experiences within news teams as they work together on stories. Build in periodic exercises to support positive collaboration and exchange. Put diversity issues on the agenda of every meeting: from story conferences to news budget meetings to sessions about the organization's overall mission.

14. Support new hires and transfers. Help people who may feel they stand out as unusual in their communities by providing information about churches, restaurants, cultural events and other resources relevant to their interests. Develop cross-media or cross-company networks they can turn to for support and advice. ●

– Sally Lehrman

assigning editor is glad to see you. There have been complaints about the news organization ignoring the Latino community. All your assignments are community stories, mostly about Latinos. You may be new to this town, but you now have the "Hispanic beat," are expected to know what "the Latino community is thinking" and are further asked to help guard against bias or insensitivity throughout the broadcast or news pages.

You now have three jobs: reporter, assigning editor and unofficial ombudsman. And, if no one else is hired, it looks like you'll have them forever. How do you feel? How do your colleagues feel about you? Not only do you become acutely aware of your minority status, but you are put in a position that naturally makes your colleagues defensive.

Newsrooms are no more immune to categorical thinking than other parts of society. We align with our in group, however our minds unconsciously define it, and look for distinctions with others. While the resulting preferences lie outside our awareness, we act on them all the time. Despite their best intentions, people in the dominant group tend to resist letting go. Editors and producers may have a hard time digesting unfamiliar approaches and ideas: they just may not seem relevant or appropriate. And because of the feedback loop they've developed, they might swear, and possibly be right, that their currently declining audience would agree. But how does this way of working allow room for the ideas that expand loyalty and keep news fresh? Whenever they pitched stories about people of color or poor communities, African American news producers Gregory Branch and Claudia Pryor found they ran into resistance. The pattern finally drove them out of the networks to start their own production company.

Race bias in newsrooms? Many news managers, who are mostly white and male, say there isn't. But most journalists of color say there is.

Nonwhite broadcast producers, for example, say racial biases influence news decisions on an on-going basis. Their managers consistently deny such considerations. How can this be? After conducting more than 120 interviews of television journalists in 1999, Freedom Forum Fellow Av Westin found no blatant bigotry. But, he wrote in Nieman Reports: "The interviews reveal a clear sense among the rank and file that news management's attitudes about race play a role in story selection and content, editorial point of view, and the skin color of the person who will provide the 'expert' sound bite."

Such practices may go unspoken, but not unnoticed. The dissonance can add a level of stress. "As a society, we want to live the ideal of a color-blind society – don't talk about it, don't recognize it – and that tends to suffocate dialogue and discourse," says former magazine writer Meta Carstarphen-Delgado, who now studies race and gender in the media context at the University of Oklahoma. She interviewed 60 journalists after they attended a Poynter workshop on covering race and was struck by their descriptions of newsroom silence. White journalists don't want to ask questions that make them look stupid. Reporters of color want to let go of their role as the caretakers of race issues. The result? Frustration. "Nearly all of these journalists believed that discussion about race on the job benefited them, even though only 33 percent said that it was regularly discussed," she reported.

Good diversity training can work, but not the quick and easy kind. "Racism is more complicated than calculus, but we often think we can learn about it in one session," says Jack Dovidio, an expert on prejudice and stereotyping at the University of Connecticut. "Most of us are well-intentioned and want to learn. People will want to come and will listen." But programs that seem geared toward remediation – whether for women, people of color, or white men – can backfire, Steele's work shows. A focus instead on challenge, achievement and the affirmation of each staff member's contributions will yield better results.

TAKING ON THE CHALLENGE

One way newsroom managers beat the retention problem is by nurturing an open, creative environment. Then all journalists can do their best work, says San Francisco State University journalism professor Erna Smith. The most successful news organization becomes an exciting place for everyone, concluded Smith and her colleagues, Edward Pease and Federico Subervi, in the Poynter Institute's News & Race Project. They studied newsroom climate, ethnic diversity and news content. "It's the openness of a place, the willingness to take on new things, the ability to keep people engaged through professional development," Smith says. A newspaper where she has consulted, the South Florida Sun-Sentinel in Fort Lauderdale, allows reporters to rotate through special projects or switch to different desks. "There's always some opportunity around," says Smith. The newspaper employs 28 percent journalists of color in a 36 percent nonwhite community. Its diversity is increasing.

A creative, effective newsroom doesn't just arise on its own, adds Newsday's Lowe, and there's no magic numerical formula. "You can hire a black journalist who simply doesn't get it and that doesn't do us any good," Lowe points out. Diversity, he argues, needs to be built into newsroom practices. "I'd like to see a top editor and publisher agree on a set of principles and post it throughout the newsroom," Lowe says. "I'd like to see them set benchmarks and measure progress. Managers' success should be tied to their work in this area, and they should be fired if they don't do it."

The San Jose Mercury News, for instance, where journalists of color make up nearly a third of the staff, announces its commitment to diversity in a news mission statement every day on Page 2. The paper first focused attention on the area's changing demographics in 1992 when it created the "change pod," a team charged with covering Asian and Latino immigrants. The race and demographics team continues today – plus every other beat aims to bring the pluralism of Silicon Valley into its coverage as well. The parent company of the Mercury News, Knight Ridder, financially rewards executives for recruiting journalists of color and ranks No. 2 after Gannett Co. in its newspapers' average newsroom diversity.

Yet even the Merc faces challenges. As diverse as it is, the newsroom staff has not kept up with its community. For their analysis of ASNE data, Stephen Doig and Bill Dedman came up with a measure called the "newsroom diversity index," which compares staff counts to the population that a newspaper serves. A score of 100 means the publication reflects at least in overall terms the ratio of people of color in its community. More than half of those who live in the San Jose area are people of color, so the Mercury News came in with a diversity index of 61 in 2004-2005.

Another Knight Ridder paper, the Akron Beacon Journal, has a diversity index of 177. At 20 percent journalists of color, its staff is nearly twice as diverse as the population it serves, which is about 12 percent nonwhite. The publisher, Jim Crutchfield, (a Knight Foundation trustee), and executive editor, Debra Adams Simmons, are both African Americans. Simmons says Knight Ridder's commitment to diversity helped her leap headlong into a wild first year as an executive there, and succeed. And yet, she writes in the March 2005 issue of The American Editor, that like others in her situation, she believes she must work twice as hard as other executives. She feels every step she takes – for better or worse – will influence opportunities available for other African American editors.

Whatever their newsroom climate, lots of small papers lose excellent reporters to bigger papers on an ongoing basis. Kathy Spurlock, executive editor of The News-Star in Monroe, La., must constantly recruit. The Gannett Co. paper serves a community that is nearly 40 percent people of color; 37 percent of the population is black. The News-Star works with regional universities and provides year-round internships for students of color. The paper has won grants to develop contacts at historically black colleges and universities that could feed into the staff. "Our staff is heavily committed to a newsroom that looks more like our community, yet we find ourselves filling the same positions over and over because we are not able to offer the financial rewards offered by the major dailies," Spurlock says. Even so, The News-Star keeps working to meet the challenge. The proportion of journalists of color there has fluctuated from 10 to 20 percent over the past decade. In the 2005 report, staff diversity bumped back up to almost 16

percent from just 10 percent in 2004.

'THE WAY WE DO BUSINESS'

Even as news corporations continue to struggle to achieve staff diversity, the organizations we cover seem to have progressed remarkably well. Many nonmedia companies have built diversity into their management framework, leading to accomplishments that leave news media trailing behind. Executives there view broad-based inclusion as a business imperative, and they make this clear up and down the management ladder. They value diversity as a means to support creative exchange, stimulate ideas and enhance competitiveness. They see it as so critical, in fact, that 65 businesses joined friend-of-the-court briefs in both *Grutter v. Bollinger* and *Gratz v. Bollinger*. These parallel cases in 2003 involved law school and undergraduate admissions at the University of Michigan. Eighteen television, print and cable companies that are minority owned or target substantial minority communities joined in one amicus. They cited diversity as necessary for their success and essential to the public interest. The U.S. Supreme Court agreed. The justices decided that programs must be "narrowly tailored," but they upheld the right of universities to consider race.

Many top companies, Ford Motor Co., for instance, try to make inclusiveness a straightforward business priority. The automaker wants to make sure that people from a variety of backgrounds buy its cars. Ford houses its powerful, $4.5 billion supplier diversity effort in the purchasing department, not in human resources. "It really isn't a program, it's the way we do business," says Ray Jensen, former director of minority supplier development. "If you

Ray Jensen

aren't in a position where you can influence who buys from whom, you can't do much." Ford purchases directly from certified minority-owned businesses. The company also demands that its 525 biggest parts and service suppliers do the same – the staff, for instance, even tracks whether its outside law firms bill at least 6 percent of hours to attorneys of color. Ford also has a formal mentoring program that seems to align with psychologist Steele's theories. It's not just top-down, but bottom-up and cross-organizational, with one branch dedicated to helping senior male managers learn about issues important to women.

Each year, the magazine Diversity Inc. ranks the top 50 U.S. companies for best practices in diversity based on advocacy and management measures. Editors there have pinpointed common themes. Whether they sell consumer products, technology, or financial services, the successful businesses evaluated progress by using metrics. Nine of the top 10 in 2004 tied managers' salaries or bonuses to the result. They also created pipeline initiatives to bring in diverse hires, and to develop people for leadership posts. In newsrooms, the same practices work. Instead of calling their friends when openings appear, those who profile the real qualities of the job and recruit widely have more success in creating a welcoming environment for everyone.

Besides bringing diversity values to the fore, all these practices help remove the subjective decision-making that supports unconscious bias.

CLARITY WORKS

Even with all this emphasis, pluralism doesn't necessarily come easy. Ford still struggles with sexual harassment on the assembly floor and settled a race discrimination lawsuit for $9 million in 2005. In that case, plaintiffs argued that a required test had blocked African Americans from its plant apprenticeship programs. In many businesses, the problem comes down to residual policies that encourage unconscious stereotyping – not to outright prejudice or even ill will, says Teresa Demchak, managing partner for Goldstein, Demchak, Baller, Borgen and Dardarian in Oakland. Her firm has litigated civil rights cases involving Denny's, Home Depot and Metropolitan Life Insurance, among others. At Denny's restaurants in California, a general demand went out from headquarters to boost profits and cut losses. Down at the restaurant level, the goals turned into a policy that black youth prepay for their meals, she says. Without information about the cause of losses or suggested solutions, discrimination took hold. California managers, acting on stereotype, assumed that African American youths were most likely to leave without paying. Servers began asking them for cash in advance. As part of a $34.8 million court settlement in 1994, Denny's trained employees not to discriminate and taught them how to serve a multicultural customer base. The company set up a monitoring system to ensure fair treatment.

At Home Depot, managers had passed over women for promotions. The company created job criteria and a formal means for employees to register their interests as part of an $87.5 million settlement in 1997. Hiring and promotion decisions were no longer so subjective – and thus susceptible to guesses about women's interests and capabilities.

Metropolitan Life, which had ignored complaints from women about their slim chances to win top jobs, discovered that a stereotype was at play. Managers had assumed that women were less willing to work long hours or take on tough assignments because of family responsibilities. In fact, they *were* having trouble balancing home and work. So along with offering better management training in a 2003 settlement, the company took steps to accommodate working parents – male and female alike.

"In media, decision-making may well have to be subjective," says Demchak, whose firm works closely with companies to change their cultures as part of settlement agreements. "But there are ways to add objectivity without reducing the artistic creativity that comes with the job." Standard human resources practices that cut down unconscious discrimination in nonmedia companies are likely to work in newsrooms, too. Rather than allowing one person to decide on a new hire, she tells companies to build in some oversight. Hiring managers should articulate clear reasons for their choices. Instead of tapping promising staffers on the shoulder, she says, post opportunities for committees and plum beats in a timely fashion. Turn promotions, including those that require informal apprenticeship, into an open, competitive process. Make sure there's a way for staff members to make their ambitions known. Create procedures that offer everyone an equal chance to be groomed for top positions.

These practices limit unconscious stereotyping and go a step further by weakening the dominant group's predictable resistance. "These solutions change the company's personnel practices as they apply to everybody, making them better and more fair for everyone," Demchak says.

The best diversity programs do more than bring many varieties of human beings into the workplace. They embody the conviction that diversity enhances the work environment and the product itself – whether it is a car, pancakes and syrup, life insurance, a newspaper or a news broadcast. Successfully diverse companies find ways to infuse it into the operation until it becomes as unconscious a part of everyday work as implicit stereotyping used to be. ●

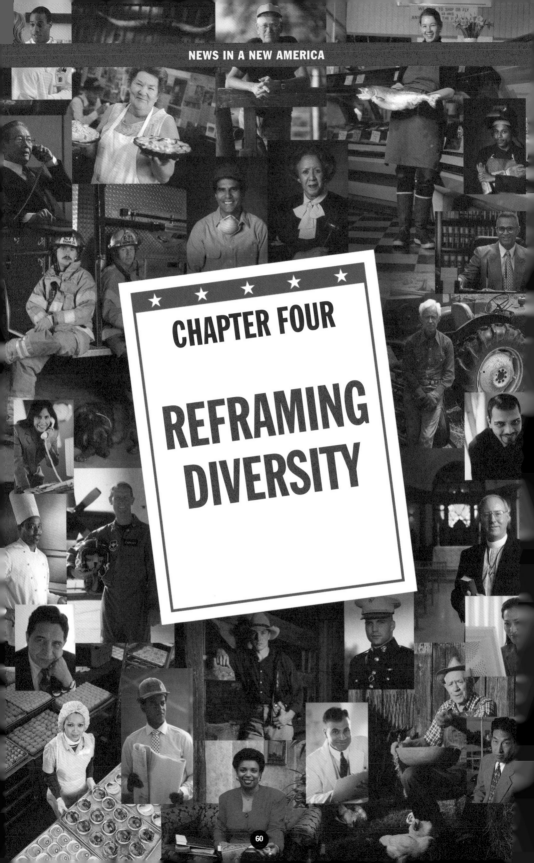

CHAPTER FOUR

REFRAMING DIVERSITY

In May 2003, President George W. Bush declared the military's mission had been accomplished in Iraq. Many Americans thought peace was around the corner, polls showed. But one diverse collection of U.S. residents had misgivings. Immigrants to the United States from many parts of the world said it was too early to claim victory. In particular, those who had come from the Middle East, China and Korea worried about the war's destabilizing effects on the region. Many expected the conflict to increase terrorism. A majority of immigrants from nearly every national background feared that the United States would lose international credibility unless soldiers found nuclear or biological weapons.

These immigrant views emerged in an 11-language, 1,000-person poll by New America Media, which was reported shortly after the president's announcement. (See chart Page 63.) Unfortunately, few outside of the ethnic media heard these cautionary voices.

Public opinion polls typically exclude people who don't speak English well, or at all. Mainstream news outlets, relying on such surveys, reported broad optimism about the war. People in one ABC/Washington Post poll a few weeks before Bush's announcement, for example, fully expected the conflict to help stabilize the Middle East. Only by December 2003 did the English-only U.S. public begin to worry that the invasion might not have eased terrorism at all.

The immigrants' skepticism generally did not result from misgivings about the United States. Three-quarters of Latin Americans and Asians – and half of the respondents from the Middle East – said they believe this country is a positive force in the world. Almost nine out of 10 Vietnamese and Filipino respondents approved Bush's

handling of the war at the time. Nearly two-thirds of those from Latin America felt that way, too. But immigrants may have been more realistic about the conflict's outcome because of what they knew about the world.

Immigrants drew on their personal experience and global connections to family and friends, as well as the news they generally rely on. In a typical news program leading up to the 2004 election, for example, Spanish-language networks devoted at least five more minutes to world affairs than English-language networks, according to a study by the Pew Hispanic Center and the USC Annenberg School for Communication. In a typical local news broadcast, Spanish-language stations offered one minute and 44 seconds of foreign policy. Their English-only counterparts gave the subject just 17 seconds.

New America Media, founded in San Francisco as New California Media, represents more than 700 ethnic and community news organizations. The consortium estimates that 29 million native and foreign-born people of color turn first to ethnic media. These outlets generally cover international news more extensively than their mainstream counterparts. In five case studies for the William and Flora Hewlett Foundation, the consortium found that ethnic media routinely offer analysis by those who live elsewhere in the world. The group's 2005 survey indicated two-thirds of Latinos said they turned first to ethnic media when they wanted information about politics and U.S. government activities.

"Ethnic media simply write and report from a more global perspective," says Sandy Close, executive director of New America Media. "When it comes to understanding the U.S. role in the world, these (news media) are definitely ahead of the curve."

THE ETHNIC MEDIA BOOM

Sandy Close

People look to the news to help them decide what's important – to learn arguments about various aspects of an issue. When journalists offer only the perspective of one demographic group, how can truth emerge? When stories are overlooked that affect large groups of people, how does that serve the democratic process? As America changes, members of a more diverse public will notice coverage that leaves them out. Instead of complaining, people can easily turn to entertaining web sites and blogs. They may try to absorb whatever news they might need from reality TV, comedy and movies. They may or may not disengage from politics and such hotly debated issues as health care, pensions and schools. But they will surely lose interest in traditional news media if they don't find it relevant to their own experience.

Specialized news organizations, especially the ethnic media, are booming. These outlets command loyalty and attention wildly out of proportion to their resources, which come nowhere close to those of mainstream outlets. Such niche media reach more than half of the people in the United States who identify themselves as Hispanic or Latino, African American, Native American, Arab American or Asian American, according to the 2005 New America Media survey of 1,895 individuals across the country. (See chart Page 64.) One quarter of Asian Americans and Native Americans, about 40 percent of Arab Americans and African Americans, and more than one half of the Hispanics

surveyed said they *prefer* ethnic media and use it frequently. Nationally, the black press now includes about 250 publications that reach 11 million readers each week. The Chinese-language juggernauts, the World Journal and Sing Tao Daily, each day reach 350,000 and 180,000 respectively. And, in five cities across the nation, more people ages 18 to 34 watched Univision's early evening news in 2004 than any other local newscast in English or Spanish.

Loyal audiences like these helped inspire Viacom to buy Black Entertainment Television for $3.9 billion in 2000 and make a failed run at Univision two years later. The Washington Post bought El Tiempo Latino for an undisclosed price in 2004, while Time Warner picked up Essence for $170 million in early 2005. The New York Times announced plans that year to start its own African American newspaper in Gainesville, Fla. America Online owns *Africana.com, Blackvoices.com*, and started its own AOL Latino.

Are mainstream outlets smart to buy or start their own ethnic media? Depends whom you ask. In a July 2005 essay, syndicated columnist and editor George Curry pointed out that the black press is a trusted source for alternative news and perspectives. "Rather than trying to supplant black and Latino publications," Curry wrote, "white-owned media companies should show that they can improve their unbalanced coverage and increase African-American presence at all levels within their organizations."

Certainly, the explosion of ethnic news sources does make a point: cover all of America, broaden your audiences and bloom.

Immigrants' Unease About the War

Early in the Iraq war, the mainstream, English-language press
reported that most Americans were optimistic, with many expecting
the conflict to help stabilize the Middle East. But, as this chart shows,
immigrants who relied on the ethnic media had their doubts.
Among the questions answered by 1,000 immigrants in a 2003 survey:
"Do you think the war with Iraq will improve the relations of the
United States with the Arab and Islamic worlds or do you think
it will create problems?" Their response:

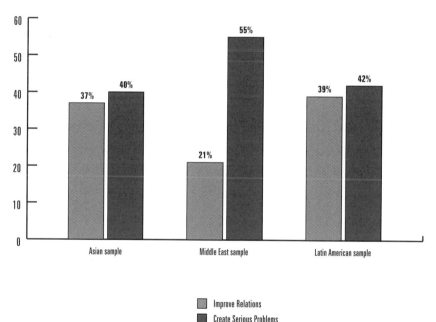

Source: "First Multilingual Poll of Immigrant Opinions on the War in Iraq."
Bendixen & Associates for New America Media, 2003.

63

The Reach of Ethnic Media

When they want the news, a significant percentage of people
who identify themselves as Hispanic, African American, Native American,
Arab American or Asian American turn first to their ethnic media.
This chart shows their preference between
ethnic and mainstream media.

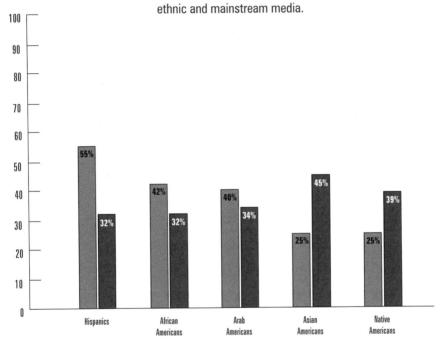

Source: "The Ethnic Media in America: The Giant Hidden in Plain Sight." Study by Bendixen & Associates
for New America Media, 2005. Based on 1,895 phone interviews in 10 languages.

BACK TO BASICS: WHO LIVES HERE?

A news organization that decides to cover its whole community often starts by taking a closer, systematic look at exactly who lives there. This sounds elementary, but it turns out to be a crucial first step. When the American Society of Newspaper Editors asked its members to estimate the demographics of their areas, most got it wrong. Nearly two-thirds of editors had no idea how diverse their cities and towns had become. If journalists don't really know their communities, how can they bring in a full range of voices?

Of course, many reporters and editors do realize that they live in racially mixed places. But that, the staff of The News-Star in Monroe, La., learned, is also only a beginning. "We thought we knew what was what," Kathy Spurlock, the executive editor, wrote in Nieman Reports. Seeking to improve, the paper tried civic journalism techniques. Reporters walked away from their phones and computers. They spent time in barber shops, community centers and coffee shops. They began interviewing in a more conversational manner. An entirely new flow of stories began. The paper discovered how government agencies had been complicit in economic discrimination, Spurlock wrote. A reporter described firsthand the miseries of living downwind from an aging sewage treatment plant. "Familiarity had instilled in us natural biases," Spurlock explained, "blinding us."

The Maynard Institute for Journalism Education in Oakland, Calif., starts its newsroom training by helping journalists find out who lives in the regions they write about. But participants don't just look at race. Dori Maynard, the institute's president, explains how to think about a community in a more complex way. She helps journalists see the many human differences that influence how society sees us and how we see society. These "fault lines" – race, class, generation, gender, geography and, many diversity experts add, ideology – are always there. It's normal to try to ignore them or pretend they don't exist. But the social pressures caused by our differences can build, and, like the tectonic plates whose movement causes earthquakes, make themselves known in overpowering ways.

Robert C. Maynard, the late owner of The Oakland Tribune and the inventor of the fault-lines concept, believed social pressures can ease when people see their concerns reflected in a diverse news stream. A good newspaper, in its fundamental role of supporting democratic debate, was an "instrument of community understanding," he said. People and communities free to express themselves will more easily solve their own problems.

Maynard urged journalists to better understand themselves and how their experiences have changed the way they see the world. Are you a woman or a man? What's your sexual orientation? What race are you? How old? How much do you earn? Do you live in a city, or a suburb, or a rural area? What religious beliefs did you grow up with? Only if you know yourself, Maynard said, can you really know enough to find the sources who will help you tell the whole story.

Today the Maynard Institute works to help journalists see into their "blind spots" and challenge their assumptions. A recent example: Most coverage of the Social Security debate has focused on the question of pension for the primary wage-earner,

A CHALLENGE FOR J-SCHOOLS

Ralph Izard had grown up knowing few African Americans. Then his high school in southern West Virginia was integrated. The young man got a job cleaning up the black campus that was merging into his own. "It really hit me – my school building ... was a palace compared to theirs," he says.

Ralph Izard

Later, when Izard traveled around the globe as a journalism educator, he was stunned at how little he knew about other people's lives.

Tomorrow's journalists shouldn't have to work with such a handicap. But based on the track record of today's colleges and universities, they could very likely start out that way. In most journalism schools and departments, students will meet mostly white people. Their professors will mainly be male. Many students won't experience America's diversity until they step into a professional newsroom or out to report a story.

Newsrooms across the country clamor to hire graduates who can cover a multicultural society. Yet journalism schools themselves frequently fail to meet their own diversity standards. First, only roughly 100 of the nation's 450 journalism and mass communications programs are accredited. Second, of those that are, in accrediting reports over the 15 years leading up to 2003, more than one quarter of those cited for noncompliance missed the mark in diversity.

The Accrediting Council on Education in Journalism and Mass Communications created this standard because it believed the media must reflect and serve the diversity of America. The council requires schools to hire women and faculty members of color. They must seek a wide mixture of students. And in their teaching choices, professors must expose their charges to a spectrum of issues, voices and views.

But the nation's journalism school faculty does not reflect the nation's population. For the past two decades, less than one out of every 12 full professors in journalism and mass communication was someone of color. Journalism and mass communication programs include a smaller proportion of faculty of color than the overall makeup of most four-year colleges nationwide.

Women make up about 40 percent of the teaching staff in journalism and mass communications, although usually at lower ranks and rates of pay than male faculty. Still, two of every three students in these programs are female – taught by a faculty where nearly two of every three teachers is male.

"I wish we were doing a lot better," says Jerry Ceppos, former vice president for news at Knight Ridder and immediate past president of the council. "We kind of know the way to do this: have good critical mass on your faculty, and in every syllabus have specific items that deal with diversity."

Recruiting women faculty should be easy, points out Lionel C. Barrow Jr., immediate past chair of the Commission on the Status of Minorities for the Association for Education in Journalism and Mass Communication. About 60 percent of doctoral graduates in 2003 were women. "Are we ready to hire them?" Barrow asked in his August 2005 chair's report.

The pipeline for professors of color needs more attention, Barrow says. Only about one in five receiving doctoral degrees were students of color, and of those, very few were African American or Latino. "We should, we can and we must do better than that," he wrote. In an interview, Barrow said schools simply aren't actively recruiting these students. "There are a number of places the deans and directors could be looking for minorities and they aren't," he said. If schools don't have funds to do their own recruiting, they could easily identify promising candidates from resources such as the McNair Scholars Program, which prepares low-income, first-generation college students and undergraduates of color for doctoral study.

In her 2003 study of the links between classrooms and newsrooms, Mercedes Lynn de Uriarte described how faculty ratios affect much more than the faces in the hallway. Some schools have managed to change their courses despite a preponderance of white professors. But in most cases, these teachers continue doing things the way they always have.

Even when faculty members start paying attention to diversity, they can inadvertently set up a dichotomy between "us" and the "other." People of color, those who are not Christian or Jewish or those who have disabilities often remain the exception and the outsider.

The Accrediting Council doesn't consider staff diversity of student publications or broadcast outlets. But when Kathleen Woodruff Wickham at the University of Mississippi reviewed demographics in the Southeast Journalism Conference, she found student newspaper staffs there to be overwhelmingly white. The skew matters, because student newspaper alumni often help each other get newsroom jobs after graduation. Student media are indeed important stepping stones, educator and former Washington Post reporter Betty Medsger found in her study of journalism education, *Winds of Change*. In a survey of 500 newsroom recruiters and managers, more than half said they hired three-quarters of their interns from among people who had worked in campus print or broadcast outlets.

The accrediting council tried to give journalism schools some tools for change in a 2003 handbook of best practices. The teaching strategies ranged from bringing in guest speakers to integrating diversity into every part of the school. In the most successful classrooms, all courses – from journalism history to news values to ethics – include ideas about diversity.

"You're going to do a much better job with this if you make it a normal part of everything you do," says Izard, who is now Sig Mickelson/CBS professor at the Louisiana State University Manship School of Mass Communication. He is also professor emeritus at the E.W. Scripps School of Journalism at Ohio University. Newswriting classes should look at word choices that contain buried assumptions, Izard says. Reporting courses ought to underline the value of consulting multiple sources. Ethics seminars can study stereotypes, fairness and unconscious symbolism. And discussions can stop assuming that the white, male, heterosexual experience is the norm.

Many educators agree that teaching diversity well requires depth and intensity. Students can absorb ideas about multicultural reporting more easily through activities than lectures. For instance, they can examine their own stereotypes in classroom exercises. They can learn to identify media bias through collaborating on projects. Story assignments and beats can help students meet people from unfamiliar cultures and communities.

De Uriarte, who is an associate professor at the University of Texas at Austin, recommends changing the learning environment so that it supports intellectual diversity. Readings and discussions should include more writings and research by authors of color. New classes should educate students about the history of race in America and the U.S. power structure, she says. Students could read George Fredrickson's *A Short History of Racism*, for example, or Ronald Takaki's *A Different Mirror: A History of the Multicultural United States*.

Like newsrooms, journalism schools that commit to do it can indeed diversify. The University of Alabama went from no communication professors of color in 1989 to about one in eight in 1998. The University of Florida more than doubled minority faculty from 9.4 percent to nearly 20 percent over the same period. The University of Missouri quadrupled its faculty of color to 12.2 percent and doubled its female faculty to 40.8 percent during that time.

Lee Becker and his colleagues at the University of Georgia studied the reasons behind such successes. All three colleges had targeted hiring and kept job descriptions flexible. They also developed student recruiting and curriculum diversity at the same time.

At LSU, Manship designed its action plan after it received a poor rating on the diversity standard six years ago. The faculty began working harder to recruit doctoral candidates of color, tapping historically black colleges and universities for leads. Professors developed relationships with high schools in Baton Rouge and New Orleans to introduce journalism to the students.

Izard arrived at Manship as an associate dean two years after the wake-up call. Under his leadership and that of Adrienne Moore, director of the Reilly Center for Media & Public Affairs, the school recently founded Mass Communicating: The Forum on Media Diversity (*http://www.masscommunicating.lsu.edu*). The web site, the most comprehensive of its kind, offers a host of resources to support diversity in newsrooms and academia. An impressive collection of research can help reporters and editors improve news coverage on minority issues. The online library features searchable articles on media, gender, religion and race, including directories of scholars, courses and research centers. The site features more than 100 course syllabi.

Izard says he believes that both professional

(Continued on next page)

(Continued from previous page)

journalists and faculty must commit themselves to diversity before much will change. In an audit of 300 journalism and mass communication programs across the country, the Forum found that only about one-third address the subject at all. "It's not a racist attitude," Izard says, "as much as 'This approach was good enough for me, why should I do more?'"

He warns that any new emphasis in a university department, let alone diversity, takes more than lip service. "It's a matter of total dedication and absolute persistence," Izard says. Then, and only then, he says, is it reasonable to expect a little bit of progress.

— Sally Lehrman

who is usually assumed to be male. This seems absolutely right to daily newspaper editors – typically white, middle-aged family men. They can't help but think about the story in relation to their own futures, often that of the main wage-earner. The issue of spousal and survivor benefits rarely gets covered. Yet these make up 14 percent of Social Security payouts and go mostly to women – usually black women. Also cut are discussions about disability benefits, though these account for nearly 17 percent of payouts. And never mind working women, who as a group rely heavily on the benefits. When you add it all up, more than half of those affected by proposed Social Security changes don't find their concerns routinely addressed.

Dori Maynard, Bob's daughter, describes fault lines this way: "These are the prisms through which we view events, ourselves and each other." Journalists who recognize them are able to see stories others may not. Newsrooms using the fault-lines system find they can develop more relevant angles, too. The fault lines provide a practical framework for better reporting and editing. Since everyone is on one side of a social fault line or another, journalists who look at diversity this way see why it's an issue for all of us.

THINKING ABOUT THE JOURNALISM

If individual journalists can do it, can mainstream journalism as a whole get beyond its institutional fault lines? Despite progress in recent years, studies still show that America's mainstream news organizations tilt toward coverage of the group that for the most part still runs both the media and the country: white men. As outlined in Chapter 2, communications research also has found that news media tend to frame stories from this group's general perspective. Are we locked into a way of thinking that makes it harder to cover today's America?

No, we aren't. But change demands rigorous honesty and an ability to look not just at who journalists are but what they do. Embedded in the daily journalistic process are many "fault-lines moments," when people who are operating openly and deliberately can do things differently from those acting internally and instinctively.

Budding journalists learn a set of criteria in school that help them decide what is newsworthy. They weigh the prominence of the people and institutions involved. They consider the event's impact, its timeliness and its proximity to readers and listeners. They evaluate its currency in the public discussion and whether it is surprising or involves conflict.

But these measures are not as neutral as they may seem. Take prominence. Prominence to whom? The whole community? People who have lived there for generations? The readers of that particular newspaper? The editor? If we don't examine this question, we can easily overlook some of the most important people in the communities we cover. Editors who go to church every Sunday morning, for instance, may not know about an influential Muslim leader in town. Reporters may not know the funeral home director who follows the activities of the black community. Younger journalists might never have heard the names of many who led their community's civil or disability rights movements.

Again, it sounds basic. But is it? When actor and racial justice champion Ossie Davis died in February 2005, for instance,

The New York Times ran a short metro story on the funeral. Yet the memorial lasted four hours. Thousands of mourners attended. New York public radio station WBAI offered six and a half hours of live coverage – and created a web page with photos from the funeral and links to tributes. Despite tight space, Jet magazine ran 1,200 words on the event.

The definition of a "credible" source also is worth thinking about. When we want authorities and experts to contribute facts and analysis, reporters routinely call business executives, government officials and others with high-powered titles. But what, exactly, is "high-powered," and who decides?

When the highly anticipated results from the first AIDS vaccine clinical trial came out in 2002, medical reporters turned to the heads of virology departments and national AIDS organizations for comment. The result? They spoke mostly to people who thought of the epidemic the old way – as among white gay men. Most reporters did not realize that the most important target for a vaccine would now be people of color, because both black and Hispanic populations have much higher rates of AIDS than whites. The New York Times and other papers pronounced the vaccine a complete flop. The San Francisco Chronicle reported, "AIDS vaccine mostly a failure: Doesn't help whites but may help some minorities." When they saw the headlines, "the African American community heaved a big, collective sigh ... this isn't for us or about us," said Dan Hlad, communication associate for the Black Coalition on AIDS in San Francisco at the time.

The sources we consult influence the "truth" we learn and the story we tell. In a nine-month analysis across all news media types, the Project for Excellence in Journalism found that reporters were more than three times as likely to quote more than one man in a story than more than one woman. (See chart Page 71.) Three-quarters of news stories contained at least one male source. But only one third included at least one woman. Media Tenor analysts studied nearly 19,000 news reports on ABC World News Tonight, CBS Evening News and NBC Nightly News in 2001. They found that 92 percent of news sources on the network news were white, and 85 percent were men. When people of color and women were included, they usually served as "ordinary people," rather than as experts or authorities.

People of color fared far worse as story subjects. Media Tenor researchers looked at 170,212 reports in The Wall Street Journal, two news magazines and on three network news shows over two years. They counted just 322, or less than one percent, that featured one or more U.S. ethnic minority groups as the main subject.

Yet in the real world, the demographics are far more diverse. For example, during the past eight years, native Hawaiians and Pacific islanders alone increased their business ownership by 67 percent – compared to 10 percent across the full population. Companies owned by women and every racial and ethnic group other than whites grew at higher rates than the average, the U.S. Census announced in July 2005.

If journalists define the only "authorities" in business or politics as the big-company CEOs or the men who dominate Congress, well, we're oversimplifying. Our country is more complicated than that. Journalists who really want to tell the story of today's

America, should, as Kevin Merida, an associate editor at The Washington Post, puts it, "cross-pollinate the 'experts' with the lived experience."

Just plugging people in like colors in a numbered painting doesn't work, either. *How* people are quoted is important. Who usually provides the analysis and authority? Are women, people of color, gays and lesbians, and people with disabilities treated as an emotional supporting cast? Look at the follow-up stories when Harvard President Lawrence Summers said early in 2005 that women's brains just might not naturally be as capable in math and science. WTNH Channel 8 in New Haven, Conn., interviewed several female high school seniors. The girls, all calculus students, said, "It's scary," "I was ... shocked," and "I'm really upset." Instead of asking what the young women thought of the math or science of the issue (or even what they thought of Harvard), the interviews went right for what they felt.

The routine use of terms offered up by sources also gets journalists into trouble. Think of the assumptions conveyed by language such as "underprivileged minority" (when most of the nation's poor are white); and "ethnic cleansing" (a more correct phrase is genocide). Why does an "inner-city" group "threaten," while rich people make up a group that "cautions"?

Journalists make many decisions on the fly. It is simply impossible, under extreme deadlines, to thoroughly reflect. Newsrooms can shape answers in seconds. In a fast-moving, high-pressure climate like this, social psychologists have found, unconscious belief systems come to the fore. Scholars who track news choices, such as Hemant Shah, a media analyst and expert on race

70

Who Do We Talk To? Men or Women?

As sources for their news stories, reporters in all media are more than three times as likely to quote more than one man than more than one woman, an analysis in 2005 found. This chart reflects the percent of all stories in which the source's gender could be determined. The numbers suggest that news sourcing has a long way to go to reflect the actual proportion of women in the work force, management, politics and other societal roles.

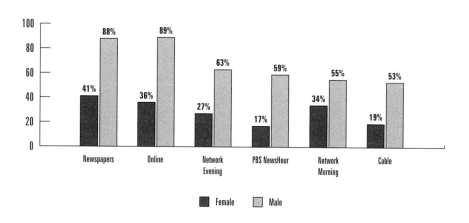

Source: Project for Excellence in Journalism (2005).

REZNET: AN OUTLET, A MENTOR FOR NATIVE AMERICAN STUDENTS

Denny McAuliffe Jr., who worked at The Washington Post for 16 years, began his journalism career at age 15. In his first job, he earned $5 a story covering high school sports for the local paper. "The way I learned was sitting next to my editor and watching my editor rip my stories apart," recalls McAuliffe, who is a member of the Osage tribe of Oklahoma.

Now McAuliffe provides the same intensive, hands-on training for young Native American journalists through Reznet, an online student newspaper (*www.reznetnews.org*) launched in 2002. A grant from the John S. and James L. Knight Foundation funds the project through the University of Montana School of Journalism and the Robert C. Maynard Institute for Journalism Education. McAuliffe edits and mentors through the Internet and on the telephone, reaching across long distances as if students were in his office.

The approach is working. As Reznet enters its fourth year of publication, more than 60 of 73 participating students have so far landed intern-ships at publications including The Washington Post, Minneapolis Star Tribune, Associated Press, Arizona Daily Star, Lincoln (Nebraska) Journal Star and Great Falls (Montana) Tribune. Reznet photographer Tetona Dunlap (Eastern Shoshone) became the first Native American intern at The Post in the summer of 2005. The paper liked her work so much that editors asked her to stay an extra month.

During the past two years, 10 graduates have moved into full-time journalism jobs. That's signi-ficant, at a time when daily newsrooms employ fewer than 300 Native Americans.

One writer, Dalton Walker, became a special corres-pondent for The Post after the shootings at the Red Lake Chippewa reservation, where he is a tribal member. The day after the tragedy, Walker flew back home from Mesa Community College in Arizona and contributed to stories written by Post staff writers. "I returned to the reservation as a voice. I was on the Red Lake Reservation as a messenger for my people," Walker wrote in an essay about his experiences.

McAuliffe says the key to Reznet's success is continuity, combined with attentive mentoring. "This particular setup puts me in close contact with students, and I'm shoving opportunities down their throats," he says. Students usually apply after they've completed the Freedom Forum American Indian Journalism Institute, a three-week boot camp that McAuliffe also helped create. They may have first learned about journalism careers in high school at the Freedom Forum Native American Newspaper Career Conference, held each spring in Crazy Horse Memorial, S.D. And each year, many of them go on to become Chips Quinn Scholars, joining a Freedom Forum program that offers students of color hands-on training in journalism and mentoring by news veterans.

Denny McAuliffe Jr.

For the 2005-2006 school year, McAuliffe hired 24 staffers to write at least two stories a month, working under the direction of three editors. Another 16 Reznet veterans contribute occasionally. The students earn $50 per story or photo shoot. They have produced news and features on issues such as mascots for sports teams, diabetes in rural areas, the war in Iraq and the portrayal of Native Americans in the media.

"The success is just that they're writing," McAuliffe says. With just a single program like a boot camp or training, he laments, "We got them all fired up about journalism then, well, it's 'Have a nice life!'"

With Reznet, McAuliffe builds a long-term support system. He edits stories with intensity and keeps after students to make sure they apply for intern-ships. While this is a condition of working for Reznet, he has found that he can't just tell students about these opportunities and leave it at that. "You have to ask, beg, order and threaten," he says. Other-wise, students will let a lack of self-esteem and con-fidence talk them out of their ambitions. McAuliffe also expects to have to prod and cajole when it comes time to searching for a job. "Once they're in, they're fine," he points out.

McAuliffe thought up Reznet when he was trying to figure out how to get American Indian kids interested in journalism. The obvious answer? Give them a chance to write. Some 25,000 Native American students from 550 recognized nations attend 32 tribal colleges in "Indian Country."

Only one college has a printed newspaper, though – and it does not have any journalism classes. But all tribal colleges have Internet access. So McAuliffe created Reznet, which alows students to get journalism experience with a Native American-oriented publication. During one peak period in March 2005, the Reznet site attracted 16,600 unique users. Reznet writers come from tribal colleges, journalism schools, reservations and urban areas. Their ages range up to 40.

"Reznet allows them to build clips, to be engaged in journalism, whether or not their school has a journalism program or a student newspaper," says Jack Marsh, executive director of the Freedom Forum's Al Neuharth Media Center and founding director of the American Indian Journalism Institute.

Without these programs, Marsh says, Native Americans simply wouldn't be going into media jobs. In 2005, the American Society of Newspaper Editors said their members employed 295 Native American journalists, or about 0.5 percent of 54,000 newspaper journalists in all. With such a large gap to fill, Marsh says, "We measure success one journalist at a time."

McAuliffe really works the Reznet stories, sometimes calling students about them several times in one day. If necessary, he'll mail a phone card to make sure the student can stay in touch. "I'm a pretty heavy-duty editor," McAuliffe says. "Other editors of Native American students are worried about damaging fragile psyches. I don't buy that." He edits a lot like he did in The Washington Post newsroom. He may bounce a piece back a couple of times for rewrites, asking for more quotes, more sources or more evidence to back up claims.

"A lot of my stories for Reznet I consider my best clips," says Sarah Moses, a senior at Syracuse University in 2005 who interned at The Observer-Dispatch in Utica, N.Y., as a Chips Quinn Scholar. McAuliffe teaches while he edits, Moses explains. He is straightforward about the realities of the business, but also very encouraging. She is especially proud of a pair of articles that she wrote after author Vine Deloria Jr. (who died in 2005) visited campus. In a question and answer session, he challenged the identity of people who are not enrolled in a tribe and did not grow up on reservations. Moses felt hurt by Deloria's attack on what he called "frauds," but wrote a fair story

anyway. Then she responded in an essay, using her own heritage as an example. Her father is full-blood Onondaga and her mother is English. Since the Onondaga Nation defines membership through the mother, according to Deloria she would not be a "real Indian," she wrote.

Moses wasn't particularly interested in writing for her college paper. White students dominate it and, especially with her desire to write about Native Americans and other people of color, she felt that she wouldn't fit in very well. "I jumped on Reznet because it was a place I could write the kind of stories I want to write," she says. Even better, "people know what Reznet is, and that's just the greatest!" ●

– Sally Lehrman

TIPS FROM JOURNALISTS WHO BUILD STAFF DIVERSITY BY WORKING WITH HIGH SCHOOL AND COLLEGE PROGRAMS

Find out if there's a summer high school journalism program in your area. The Dow Jones Newspaper Fund web site lists them all by state (*http://djnewspaperfund.dowjones.com*). The American Society of Newspaper Editors holds regional training as well.

Visit English, art, marketing, design, writing and social studies classes and let the students and teachers know about the program. Recruit students who applied to freelance or intern for you. Go to the clubs that focus on ethnicity, culture and gender at local campuses. Ask the students what's wrong with the newspaper and tell them they can help change it by joining.

Encourage local journalism teachers to let students report on the communities that they live in. Have them tell their stories, their parents' stories and their friends' stories. It may not be hard news, but editorials and features are vital to a publication.

Assign students to work in teams of two with someone completely different from themselves, or someone whom they do not normally hang out with. They will learn from working with each other that they probably have more in common than not. Find out if there is a local chapter of one of the ethnic journalism organizations (Asian American Journalists Association, National Association of Black Journalists, National Association of Hispanic Journalists, Native American Journalists Association) or the National Lesbian and Gay Journalists Association in your area. Ask representatives to visit. Invite students from other classes. Those who are not interested in journalism because they think it doesn't represent them may change their minds.

When covering so-called "ethnic issues," don't cover them just during a cultural event, such as Native American Heritage Month. Often, people complain that their cultures make it into the pages only during a special event or when a crime occurs.

Work with English teachers. Ask them to assign students to write editorials; promise to publish the

(Continued on next page)

and mass communication at the University of Wisconsin, find compelling evidence of a "white" point of view in mainstream coverage. Yet as the U.S. population changes and we become a nation of multiple "minorities" – no single point of view can dominate and still be relevant. "There needs to be a readiness and a willingness to rethink the whole process of journalism," Shah says.

HOW WE COVER COMMUNITIES

If the routine leads us astray, then the traditional newsroom beat system is its Pied Piper. Let's say there's a protest. If the City Hall reporter is on duty, it might seem more of a story about disrupted government business. If the police reporter is on it, street violence might be the focus. If it's the community reporter, then we'll learn about the leaders of the unrest and their demands. It doesn't happen on every story. But it happens often enough that experienced editors know that their reporters are not interchangeable. Who you assign affects what you get back.

When a new crop of Baby Boom-generation editors began to take over in the mid-1980s, some started to replace the old-school beat systems. Editors created a "youth" beat, for instance, and found that reporters would cover teens from more varied perspectives. No longer did young people show up only as gangs (according to the crime beat), fad machines (business pages) or test-takers (education beat).

But the new reporting teams weren't enough. Sometimes the stories they produced had a hard time finding their way into the paper. Sometimes the same old sources showed up in new wrappers. Editors also found that the system can cut both ways.

The women and gender team, the urban affairs desk and the aging beat can end up being the place where other reporters dump story ideas they don't want or understand.

In 1988, David Lampel, then senior vice president of Inner City Broadcasting, complained: "The black community is covered (by the mainstream media) as though you were covering a foreign country." The Kerner Commission's famous 1968 report on the urban uprisings of the 1960s chided reporters for relying almost entirely on information from police and local officials. As a result, the commissioners wrote, the news media exaggerated the scope, damage, and even the nature of the disturbances. Journalists didn't just badly cover the riots, the commission found. Their incomplete coverage of urban America contributed to the riots.

Alas, journalists again made many of the same mistakes when they went out to cover the more recent interethnic conflicts in Washington, Miami and Los Angeles, according to studies by Shah and fellow researcher Michael C. Thornton. Mainstream news reporters asked city officials for statements, for instance, and usually didn't also get residents' voices and views. Their stories ended up oversimplifying the events and their causes. They buried underlying issues such as racism and economic disparities. Their reports suggested that individual acts caused the conflicts – and so the best solutions, one might surmise, would take place at an individual level, too.

In contrast, Shah and Thornton found, the ethnic media more often pointed to institutional and societal underpinnings to the disputes. Reporters for these outlets tended to talk to ordinary people. They detailed each group's history of grievances

(Continued from previous page)

best ones. Encourage teachers to discuss student writing in class. Often, once students see their bylines they get excited. Discussing the writing makes it real, makes it matter.

Sponsor a high school journalism day. Show up. Talk about why journalism matters and how the students are the type of people needed in newsrooms.

Encourage students and teachers to talk to their school's career counselors about the need for journalists of color at news organizations. Get them to help encourage students to think about the profession.

Work with the ethnic media in your area. Often, these organizations are interested in youth voices, and your students can get published off campus. It also shows the students that their voices count in many ways that mainstream media may not consider. Ethnic media reporters, photographers and copy editors can serve as role models and mentors.

Set up a coaching program between your news organization and local students. To find out more about this, write *ciij@sfsu.edu* to get a copy of its coaching manual, "One-on-One, One-by-One." Although geared toward college students, it can work for high school journalism programs too.

**– By Cristina L. Azocar, director
Center for Integration and Improvement of Journalism, San Francisco State University**

and the conflicts between them. "The general circulation press seems more thoroughly bound than the ethnic minority press to a model of reporting that seems to result in misunderstanding interethnic conflict," the authors concluded. Such experiences have led groups like the National Association of Hispanic Journalists to include the Spanish-language and community press in their annual conventions. English-language sessions include translators. Some panels take place in Spanish. The Society of Professional Journalists has begun encouraging and honoring collaborations between ethnic and mainstream media with its New America Award.

GETTING TO THE UNDERLYING ISSUES

While it is fashionable for general-circulation news reporters to dismiss niche outlets as less professional, the ethnic media does know its territory. Sure, some in the ethnic press have a narrow focus. Many don't hesitate to include an explicit point of view in news reports. But the way ethnic media frame stories, select sources and include context and history suggests lessons for other journalists who want to make their work more relevant. "They treat the issues as a process, not as an event," Shah says. "They want to be a press that allows the community to understand itself."

Ethnic news media are winning accolades that once were the province of general audience journalists. Univision, for instance, ranked alongside other major networks in the Radio and Television News Directors Association's 2004 Edward R. Murrow Awards. The Spanish-language media giant picked up two of the 11 honors in network television. In its winning series, Univision

producers detailed child abuse in Mexico. Another award went to an hour-long Univision special that focused on religious miracles, including the Catholic Church's process for determining sainthood. The National Black Programming Consortium won two 2003 Peabody Awards for news documentaries it helped produce. One explored the racial divide in Jasper, Texas, where James Byrd Jr. was dragged to his death in 1998. The other described conflicts between two marginalized groups, gays and blacks, in the Olde Towne East district of Columbus, Ohio. These pieces, which clearly meet traditional standards of journalism excellence, touch on fresh coverage areas. They reach a depth of insight that producers for general audience outlets rarely attain.

These can be global, general interest stories anchored here at home: Siddharth Srivastava, reporting for Siliconeer, a monthly magazine for the Asian Indian community, reached beyond the usual outsourcing story angles to describe the subcontracting of Roman Catholic Masses to India. U.S. and Western European dioceses pass paid requests for "intentions" to congregations in Kerala, India, where priests offer the desired Mass in the local language. Sing Tao Daily and The Filipino Express described how strict new rules to identify customers could put small community banks out of business and block immigrants from sending money back home.

Niche media journalists often have a deep knowledge of community and a great interest in providing social and historical context. Their stories about education, health care and crime, for instance, typically provide background on past inequities that underpin revelations about disparities today. A piece about the rising incidence of AIDS in the black community might well mention a historic distrust of the public health system by African Americans – because of its long-standing failure to serve them. This level of context can serve mainstream media, too: It trans-formed a Minneapolis Star Tribune story about soul food into an engaging educa-tional essay on black history in America. It turned The Orange County Register's "The Boy Monk" into an intimate picture of Vietnamese-Americans' cultural history. That series told the story of Donald Pham, a child from Laguna Niguel, Calif., whose parents felt he was destined to become a learned monk. Both works ranked among the 2004 award winners at the "Let's Do It Better!" Workshop on Race, Ethnicity & Journalism at Columbia University.

No matter their topic, nearly all the Columbia Workshop winners emphasized the time they had spent building trust and getting to a complicated story's heart. They described being open to surprising ideas. They said they had to truly observe and follow up. Inclusive coverage means more than going to different parts of a city, participating in cultural activities or building a comprehensive source list. It takes time to build trust, notes New America Media's Sandy Close: "You can't do this like a drive-by. You really have to embed yourself."

Anh Do

NEW PARTNERSHIPS IN A NEW AMERICA

Hoping to widen their own awareness and access, some mainstream news operations are collaborating with ethnic and community outlets. Anh Do, who led the reporting

on "The Boy Monk" for The Register, is an Asian affairs columnist there and also vice president of business for her family's paper, Nguoi Viet (Vietnamese People) Daily News. The two papers partner on stories, a weekly bilingual radio show and on joint town hall meetings. Both the San Jose Mercury News and the Los Angeles Times bring in anchors from non-English television outlets to broadcast a sampling of budget lines and stories. At the Columbia Workshop, reporters and editors envisioned content swaps, newsroom exchanges and informal meetings to talk stories and solve problems.

The results can transcend coverage that either outlet might accomplish alone. SPJ gave the top New America Award prize for 2005 to an outstanding series that combined the skills of investigative journalists at The Chicago Reporter with the knowledge and contacts of editors at the Residents' Journal. Together they revealed the deadly, unforeseen consequences of the city's effort to relocate people from deteriorating public housing projects into mixed-income neighborhoods. Second-place winners Alyssa Katz of City Limits and Abu Taher of Bangla Patrika also combined investigation techniques with deep community connec-tions. They conducted interviews jointly in Bangla and English. Together they uncovered the exploitation of Bangladeshi push-cart food vendors in Central Park under city contracts. Eleven months after publication, the workers won a $450,000 settlement for labor law violations.

Such collaborations work best when both partners benefit from the relationship, suggests Sandip Roy, who hosts *UpFront*,

New America Media's weekly radio show. The ethnic journalist gains little by simply serving as a conduit into the community for the mainstream outlet. But if the larger organization contributes resources and enterprise, coverage improves for everyone. In the Chicago public housing story, for instance, Roy says, "the two sides, a paper with investigative reporting capabilities and one with on-the-ground connections, really complemented each other."

These new partnerships work because of the different institutional perspectives on the part of both mainstream and ethnic outlets. Our news organizations' priorities and traditions lead us to certain coverage choices. Assignments and the stories that result reflect the people who work there. The New America Media case studies showed this in the coverage of Severe Acute Respiratory Syndrome (SARS). The Chinese-language press, reporting for people for whom the disease struck close to ancestral home and family, generally focused on solutions. Journalists covered an engaged citizenry "intent on prevention, helping others and defusing the panic," wrote New America Media editor Pueng Vongs. News outlets concentrated on dispelling rumors, educating the public and fighting discrimination. In contrast, Vongs concluded, The New York Times and Los Angeles Times described a frightening problem arising from Asia. In episodic coverage that relied on case counts and official comments, these journalists conveyed the image of an American populace helpless against a worldwide health threat.

In another case study, mainstream journalists writing about the outsourcing of jobs to India focused on the losses to American workers. The emphasis on displaced employees and explanations by company executives conveyed a sense of inevitability. Indian-American outlets brought in a wider array of sources affected by the trend. They more commonly described the practice as a two-way street, explaining its economic roots and describing benefits to workers and companies. Both depictions could be seen as equally true. Each also reflects an understanding based on a particular frame of reference.

If we are to think more about our biases, what do we do when we are ready to admit that we have them? University of Washington professor David Domke thinks news outlets should actively acknowledge the viewpoints and decisions that drive the news. And, he urges us to consider shaking off some of the constraints of "objectivity."

"This notion binds journalists in a straight-jacket I'd love them to be freed from – and I think it would be good for the public, too," he says. If journalists could sometimes write about the subjects they were really passionate about, their work might provoke more interest and debate, Domke suggests. This isn't as hard as it seems – writers express their opinions all the time in columns clearly labeled as analysis or commentary.

Recall the uproar when a lesbian couple covering the gay marriage story for the San Francisco Chronicle decided to get married themselves in a private civil ceremony. The paper took them off the beat. But many journalists argued that these two, one of whom was the City Hall reporter, had access and insight that no one else could match. Instead of declaring the wedding an insurmountable conflict, the newspaper could have simply disclosed it in regular taglines on news stories and photos, some journalists said. Others thought opinion columns would be a better idea.

Venise Wagner

"Knowledge and interests always intersect," wrote Theodore Glasser, director of the journalism program at Stanford University, who criticized the Chronicle's decision on the Grade the News web site. "The pretense of a disinterested and detached press, an 'objective' press, doesn't dissolve interests or distance the press from them; it only makes journalists less aware of their personal and institutional interests and unprepared to acknowledge and examine them." By being more open about who we are, journalists may create room to be more honest and fair.

Civic journalism techniques championed in the 1990s suggested comparable ways to get closer to stories. Trainers at the Pew Center for Civic Journalism taught reporters at daily newspapers things known for generations at community weeklies. They urged journalists to hang out in "third places," or informal gathering places like cafes, parks or beauty salons, to find out what people care about. They told reporters to search out "connectors" within the community, instead of just leaders with titles, and to converse with them instead of simply getting "both" sides of a story.

By its nature, civic journalism puts reporters in touch with lots of different kinds of people, says Venise Wagner, an assistant professor at San Francisco State University. But Wagner warns that another layer of

work is necessary. "That does increase diversity, but if you're not prepared for it, you're not going to be able to deal with it. If you don't check in with yourself, it can be a disaster." Wagner sent her students out to report on a primarily black neighborhood in San Francisco, but they came back empty-handed. After the group discussed the outcome, she realized that the white students felt uncomfortable talking about race.

Now Wagner helps students think about their own cultural autobiography – and discuss their fault lines – before they venture out.

THE MAJORITY'S UNEASE

Wagner uses a "diversity wheel" developed by Poynter Institute photojournalist Kenny Irby that expands on the core fault lines of race, class, gender, generation and geography as described by Maynard. Students mark down aspects of themselves that make them feel "different," say, in their school, in their own neighborhood or on their beat. Among other things, their choices include religion, nationality, physical abilities and intellect, and education and cultural heritage. As with fault lines, the tool sidesteps defensiveness. Using it, we all can see ourselves as part of the equation. Wagner's students can more quickly notice their tendency to make assumptions. And when they feel uncomfortable, they may resist the inclination to retreat.

Both Maynard's framework and the Poynter diversity wheel are especially valuable now, as journalists try to cover a dramatically changing nation. Some wonder, will the declining majority's needs and contributions no longer be important? Concerns like this spark reactions ranging from tongue-in-cheek proposals to serious petition drives. The College Republicans at Roger Williams University in Rhode Island offered a "whites-only" scholarship as a parody. And some residents of the Cardinal Valley area of Lexington, Ky., began organizing against a proposed Hispanic center.

CAN DIVERSITY BE DIVISIVE?

In his book, Coloring the News, which won a National Press Club Award in 2002, Manhattan Institute Fellow William McGowan argued that diversity initiatives were corrupting journalism. He said they promoted an orthodoxy of coverage favorable to people of color, women, and gays and lesbians.

And in the medical arena, some physicians have complained that training doctors to interact with other cultures takes too much time away from other parts of the curriculum. Stanford University School of Medicine clinical professor Wallace Sampson told The Chronicle of Higher Education that doctors can easily respond to people's differences. "Students don't want to be lectured on how to be a human being," he said. "It's insulting and demeaning."

Perhaps the greatest advantage of Maynard's fault-lines concept is that it allows McGowan, Sampson and others a place at the table. Any human being willing to be honest and self-aware has a place. Rather than demanding agreement, the fault-lines concept sets up a structure of integrity for every point of view, a basis for civil debate and understanding.

In one training session, Dori Maynard recalls, newspaper reporters went out into various communities and asked how they could cover people better. "They said you could stop looking at us from your middle-class point of view," Maynard says. "You see two families in one house, with one car, and you say we're poor. We say we have a house. We have a car. We're not poor."

When we recognize the historical, social and cultural roots that shape our own world, we can see how they both limit and enhance our understanding.

In their report on the ethnic media, researchers Rufus Browning, Holley Shafer, John Rogers and Renatta DeFever from San Francisco State University sum up the importance of a vibrant, inclusive press that knows how to report across fault lines:

> "Discourse in a democracy does not require agreement; rather, it requires debate and the willingness to hear real disagreement. There must be some common ground – some shared democratic values and some confidence in democratic institutions – but beyond that, there must be vigorous assertion of interests, vigorous competition for attention, vigorous argument about important issues."

Most journalists take our professional duties quite seriously. We see ourselves as digging out the facts that shed light on inequities, offer insight on social and political issues, and inform public debate. As the Society of Professional Journalists outlines in its mission statement, we believe we ought to be government watchdogs, advocates of free speech and instruments of communication.

Today, as the population we serve grows ever more diverse, we must learn to cross the boundaries of our own history and upbringing in order to report fully and completely not just on events, but on the issues and ideas that shape society. Only then do we have a chance of covering a truly extraordinary story, the central story of our era: the rapid demographic change sweeping the United States. And only then can we reveal and record the conflicts and joys of the American people as our nation enters its third century of striving toward an inclusive, equitable society for all. ●

AFTERWORD

BY JOHN L. DOTSON JR.

When I was a 17-year-old high school senior, my grandmother offered to pay my first year's college tuition if I chose to go to nearby Temple University. She also promised a back bedroom in her ancient row house in the Little Harlem section of North Philadelphia. All she knew about Temple was that it was within walking distance of her home.

Several months later, when I told her that I had been admitted to Temple – the only school I applied to – she asked what I planned to study.

"Journalism," I said proudly.

"Journalism," she sniffed incredulously. "You'll never make a dime in 'journalism.'"

That was 1954 and, for all intents and purposes in those days, she was right. There were so few "Negroes" in journalism that no one in my family could conceive of actually making a living in that field. Indeed, I doubt that many blacks in the country could name a journalist outside of the local black newspaper or Ebony and Jet magazines.

Much has changed in the 50-odd years from that day. Today there are blacks, Latinos and Asians working at newspapers, magazines, television and radio in most of the larger cities in America. But the pace of change has slowed from the days when integration and diversity were in vogue back in the late 1960s and '70s.

As the first of those integration pioneers prepare to retire, they are leaving a business that is in such a state of turmoil that racial, ethnic and gender diversity are far down on the list of concerns. Mainstream media are fighting for survival in a society that is in technological transition. There is no way to predict the forms of media a half century from now, let alone to suggest how diverse they will be.

The biggest diversity these days is in the outlets for news, information and entertainment. What started as a trickling decline in newspaper readers and network broadcast audience has turned into a gusher as more Americans seek their news and information online and through wireless devices. Movie and music producers are crying foul as more and more of their product turns up free on the Internet.

Like other American institutions, mainstream media have been forced by circumstances and confrontation to adopt new ways of doing things. They hired blacks to cover urban disturbances and Latinos to cover the burgeoning Hispanic population, just as today they are hiring Arabs and Asians to cover the Middle East. Where newspapers, radio and TV had a virtual lock on news in former decades, it has become a commodity today, dispensed in myriad forms and myriad ways. In response, traditional media have joined the fray.

Out of such turmoil in a country as diverse as the United States, one would think that lots of new voices would be heard. But, for the most part, that has not been the case thus far. It is true that there are now more Spanish-language television and radio stations and more ethnic newspapers, but the preponderance of media are still English-speaking and mostly white. And, certainly, the online and wireless worlds are dominated by whites.

Clearly, our media world is in such a state

of change that no one can predict what the landscape will look like 40 or 50 years from now. And so how can we predict what its racial, gender and sociological diversity will be? What we do know is that, compared with many other institutions, the media in general have been slow to change.

Racism is so much a part of the fabric of America that it will be nearly impossible to rid the country of it altogether. America was settled as a white, Eurocentric nation and for the most part, white males have fought mightily to maintain it as such. Even some European immigrants had trouble fighting their way into the society when they arrived. And once again, immigration is a flashpoint in America. So, there is little question that the nation will still be fighting bigotry in 2050.

Throughout most of our history, white men have clung to the levers of power as tightly as Charlton Heston clutches his rifle – until it is pried from his "cold, dead hand." Like government and business, media have been one of the levers of power. All the statistics about changing demographics and all the rationales about society's need to be inclusive haven't undermined the basic human drive: to stay "in," to get what you want for your family, your children, grandchildren and their progeny. It is a basic need.

There is some potential promise in the tumult brought on by the electronic media. As more readers and viewers turn to the Internet for their news and commentary, many seek outlets that cater to their viewpoints. In that way, the Internet is more like the dawn of American newspapering, when most of the writers were polemicists, arguing their points of view on every

subject they reported. Indeed, we may not be too far away from the wide-open days of muckraking and yellow journalism.

That kind of turmoil sets the stage for entrepreneurs to sweep in with new ideas and new ways of doing business. But, that does not necessarily bode well for demographic diversity. Though it doesn't take much funding to start a web site or blog, it does take know-how and, often, funding to make a splash. And people of color are not at the forefront of the nascent efforts. Furthermore, the one startling fact that can't be corrected easily or quickly is that 80 percent of poor households, many of them made up of people of color, don't even own a computer.

Just as newspapers and network broadcasting companies were merged and gobbled up by conglomerates in past decades, they could get caught up in the globalization of world business. Already, more viewers than ever are reading foreign newspapers and watching foreign TV on the 'Net and satellite TV. By the middle of this century, American news outlets may not even be owned by American companies, so the very nature of "diversity" may be entirely different.

It has taken some time for the large, mainstream media companies to get fully into the Internet game, but as they do, they will move aggressively to regain dominance. They are expanding their platforms to include every other medium. Newspapers now have online outlets, bloggers and TV operations; network broadcasters have 24/7 online offerings of text and video. The question is whether they can hold onto their readers, viewers and advertisers and thus their news staffs while they build a sizeable audience in the new media.

Like any new technology bubble, many of the new ventures will fail because they won't make enough money to keep going. However, those that succeed will be mighty challengers to the current media conglomerates. Regardless of the media structure, as mass audiences form of people with similar interests, advertising is sure to follow. And, make no mistake, the big guys will move decisively to follow the money.

As new media are becoming established, diversity won't be of much concern in employment or reach unless there is a market to be exploited. Thus far, beyond Spanish-language outlets, there aren't many large-scale efforts to reach citizens of color. That does not bode well for media multiculturalism in the short run.

Government can have a tremendous impact on the future of diversity. In the years immediately following the black riots and the civil rights movement, integration was a front-burner issue in America. But, for decades now, ever since Ronald Reagan led conservatives to the presidency, the federal government has pulled on the reins of diversity. It hasn't halted progress, but it has slowed the pace of change. As the nation's demographics continue to be transformed, however, diversity is inexorable.

Newspapers, with their large local reporting and editing staffs, are still the gorillas of local news, just as network TV still dominates the way most people get their national and international news. It's important to keep the pressure on these large organizations to hire and promote journalists of color and women and to diversify their coverage because they will dominate the news landscape for many years to come. Further, it is mainly in the mainstream media that young journalists are trained in the traditional methods and ethics of the profession.

People of color and women are in a better position than they were when newspapers, television and radio were considered the new media. Until the amorphous, new electronic media take a definite form, as will inevitably happen, people of color, women and those whites concerned about diversity must broaden their interests to stump for changes in all aspects of the media. They must become bloggers and citizen journalists alongside their white male counterparts, learning and experimenting and investing in all forms of the new media. Only in that way will the nation's multiculturalism be reflected, as it should be, in our news media of the future. ●

John L. Dotson Jr. is publisher emeritus of the Akron Beacon Journal, a co-founder of the Robert C. Maynard Institute for Journalism Education and a member of Knight Foundation's Journalism Advisory Committee. Under his leadership, the Beacon Journal won a Pulitzer Gold Medal for Meritorious Public Service in 1994 for its series on race relations and the launch of Coming Together, a community organization dedicated to improving race relations in Akron. He also won the diversity award for lifetime achievement by the National Association of Minority Media Executives and the president's award of the National Association of Black Journalists. The Beacon Journal is one of just 24 large newsrooms nationally that has attained racial parity with the community it covers.

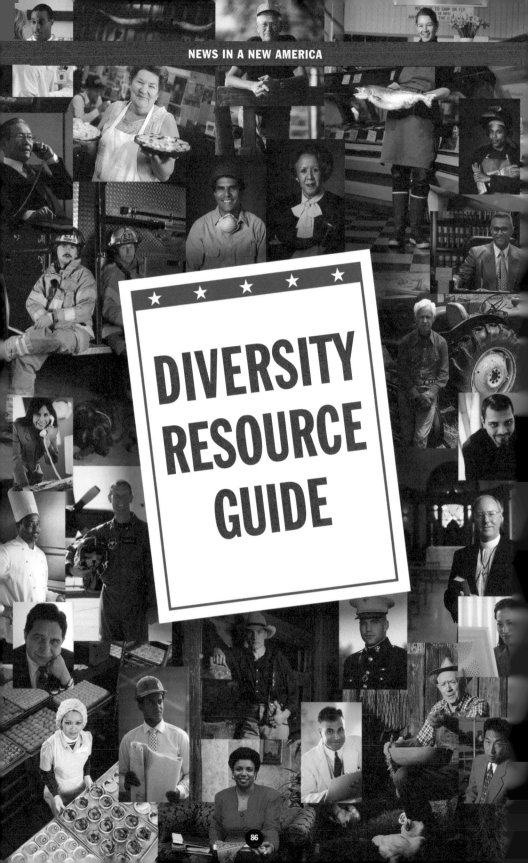

DIVERSITY RESOURCE GUIDE

This guide is designed to help everyone from high school students to professionals to recruiters find programs that suit their needs. Information may vary from year to year. The Robert C. Maynard Institute for Journalism Education developed this guide with the support of the McCormick Tribune Foundation.

If there is a program that should be included, contact the Maynard Institute, which maintains the guide on its web site, *www.maynardije.org*. Phone: (510) 891-9202. E-mail: *mije@maynardije.org*

TRAINING PROGRAMS FOR PROFESSIONALS

Asian American Journalists Association
1182 Market St., Suite 320
San Francisco, CA 94102
Phone: (415) 346-2051
Fax: (415) 346-6343
E-mail: *National@aaja.org*
http://www.aaja.org

Executive Leadership Program is an annual AAJA leadership-development seminar for Asian American journalists. The two-day seminar focuses on an array of topics and issues with a different theme each year. For more information about the program, contact Albert Lee at *albertl@aaja.org* or visit *http://www.aaja.org/programs/professional/executive_leadership*.

Freedom Forum
1101 Wilson Blvd.
Arlington, VA 22209
Phone: (703) 528-0800
Fax: (703) 284-3770
E-mail: *news@freedomforum.org*
http://www.freedomforum.org

Diversity Institute, a state-of-the-art educational facility adjacent to the Freedom Forum's First Amendment Center at Vanderbilt University in Nashville, Tenn., works with daily newspapers, newspaper groups and others to identify and develop new journalists of color, many of whom come from different careers. For more, go to *http://www.diversityinstitute.org*.

Maynard Institute for Journalism Education
1211 Preservation Park Way
Oakland, CA 94612
Phone: (510) 891-9202

Fax: (510) 891-9565
E-mail: *mije@maynardije.org*
http://www.maynardije.org

Maynard Management @ Kellogg was created to increase the number of media managers of color in both editorial and business departments. The four-week program at Northwestern University's Kellogg Graduate School of Management immerses participants in financial management, budgeting, organizational behavior, human resources, advertising, marketing, business operations, editorial process and technology and its effects on news. The total fee is $12,000 and covers on-campus tuition, lodging, breakfast and lunch. For more, go to *http://www.maynardije.org/programs/mtc*.

Maynard Media Academy training is broken into two nine-day sessions during the year. This program is open to news professionals and supervisors from other industries looking to make a career change. Like all Maynard programs, it is open to people of all races, though the emphasis is on training people of color. The total fee is $2,500. For more, go to *http://www.maynardije.org/programs/mediaacademy*.

Maynard Editing Program has nearly 20 years experience producing top quality copy editors. The six-week session immerses participants in everything from the basics of headline writing, grammar, page design and story organization to interpersonal skills that enable editors to work successfully with reporters and other editors. The $6,000 fee includes lodging, meals and access to all campus student facilities. This program gives participants hands-on experience handling daily deadline pressure along with producing for both print and the web. They make the tough judgments editors face every day. The curriculum was developed by veteran newspaper editors and includes classroom work, daily skills-building drills, evening seminars and practical experience working at an area newspaper. For more, go to *http://www.maynardije.org/programs/editing*.

National Association of Hispanic Journalists
1000 National Press Building
529 14th St. N.W.
Washington, DC 20045-2001
Phone: (202) 662-7145 / (888) 346-NAHJ
Fax: (202) 662-7144
E-mail: *nahj@nahj.org*
http://www.nahj.org

The Parity Project: The goal of the project is to double the percentage of Latinos employed by daily newspapers and to boost the percentage of Latinos working for local English-language television stations. NAHJ identifies cities where Latinos are underrepresented in the newsrooms but make up a significant portion of the population. In those cities, NAHJ works jointly with print and broadcast outlets, area journalism schools, foundations and Latino community leaders to develop comprehensive model programs that will increase Latino newsroom presence and influence. NAHJ's first partner on the project was the E.W. Scripps Co. Since its inception, the Parity Project has gained two more partners, Lee Enterprises Inc. and Pulitzer Inc. For more, go to *http://www.nahj.org/parityproject/parityproject.shtml.*

National Association of Minority Media Executives
1921 Gallows Road, Suite 600
Vienna, VA 22182
Phone: (888) 968-7658
Fax: (703) 893-2414
E-mail: *info@namme.org*
http://www.namme.org

McCormick Tribune Fellowship Initiative: This executive development program for senior managers and executives in the news media is administered by NAMME. Each year, eight fellows are selected (four from newspapers and four from television) to attend two foundation-funded executive development programs (Advanced Executive Program and Management Development Seminar for Television Executives, both conducted at the Media Management Center at Northwestern University in Evanston, Illinois). For more, go to *http://www.mccormicktribune.org/journalism/fellowship.htm.*

Leadership Development Institute is a leadership development workshop for managers of color. The three-day, hands-on program for new and middle managers of color is offered twice a year, in the spring and fall, in partnership with different media organizations and associations. For more, go to *http://www.namme.org/programs/ldi.*

Newspaper Association of America
1921 Gallows Road, Suite 600
Vienna, VA 22182-3900
Phone: (703) 902-1600
Fax: (703) 917-0636
http://www.naa.org/

Midcareer newspaper professionals of color are paired with senior-level executives for the Newspaper Association of America's annual **Breakthrough: James K. Batten Leadership Program**. In this year-long program, senior executives serve as mentors to junior colleagues and offer guidance and advice to help them develop leadership skills and broaden their knowledge of the newspaper industry.

The Minority Fellowship program of NAA is a scholarship program for mid-level management. The program is designed to widen opportunities for professionals of color to enter or advance in newspaper management. Newspaper executives and journalism educators are asked to nominate candidates who demonstrate managerial potential. The supervisors' recommendations play a key role in the selection of fellows. For more information, contact Angela Winters at (703) 902-1727, or e-mail *angela.winters@naa.org.*

The Poynter Institute
801 Third Street S.
St. Petersburg, FL 33701
Phone: (888) 769-6837
http://www.poynter.org

Four seminars are being offered in 2006 to help journalists deepen their understanding of diversity: "Beyond Schiavo: Reporting on End-of-Life Issues," Jan. 9; "Reporting and Writing the Untold Stories," Feb. 26; " Diversity Across the Curriculum," May 21; and "Beat Reporting: Covering Race Relations," Sept. 10. For more information, go to the web site and click on Diversity. The site also provides excellent tip sheets, discussions, resources and diversity reports.

TRAINING PROGRAMS FOR HIGH SCHOOL, COLLEGE STUDENTS AND ADVISERS

American Society of Newspaper Editors
11690B Sunrise Valley Drive
Reston, VA 20191-1409
Phone: (703) 453-1122
Fax: (703) 453-1133
E-mail: *asne@asne.org*
http://www.highschooljournalism.org/

The High School Journalism Institute is an intensive two-week summer newspaper journalism training program for high school teachers. Teachers who have never advised a school newspaper but want to are encouraged to apply. Experienced teachers seeking to update their journalism skills are also welcome. Most expenses are paid by the High School Journalism Program. For more information, contact Diana Mitsu Klos, ASNE Senior Project Director, at (703) 453-1125 or dmk@asne.org.

ASNE Partnership Program works to establish links between daily newspapers and the high schools in their communities. Its immediate goal is to create high school newspapers where none exist or to dramatically improve existing papers; grant money is available, if needed, to fund technology purchases to help realize this goal. Partnerships are initiated by the daily newspaper.

Asian American Journalists Association
1182 Market St., Suite 320
San Francisco, CA 94102
Phone: (415) 346-2051
Fax: (415) 346-6343
E-mail: National@aaja.org
http://www.aaja.org

J Camp is a free six-day training camp that brings together a multicultural group of high school students from across the nation to sharpen their journalism skills and work together in a learning environment. The curriculum consists of interactive workshops, hands-on training and field trips. For any questions or inquiries about student-related programs, contact Brandon Sugiyama, student programs coordinator, at (415) 346-2051, ext. 102, or e-mail: brandons@aaja.org.

Detroit Free Press High School Journalism Program
Joe Grimm
600 W. Fort St.
Detroit, MI, 48226
Phone: (313) 222-6490, ext.600
E-mail: grimm@freep.com
http://www.freep.com

Specially prepared high school pages are part of Free Press editions. Those editions are delivered to high schools and their feeder middle schools (about 72,000 copies per month). In the summer of 1991, the Free Press inaugurated an annual five-week summer apprentice program for high school journalists. High school juniors and seniors from the Detroit and Flint areas receive intense journalism instruction at the University of Michigan and Oakland University before starting their Free Press

apprenticeship. While at the Free Press, students receive four weeks of hands-on experience working with Free Press staffers who serve as their mentors. For information, e-mail Pat Hartley, high school journalism coordinator, at pchartley@freep.com.

Freedom Forum
1101 Wilson Blvd.
Arlington, VA 22209
Phone : (703) 528-0800
Fax: (703) 284-3770
E-mail: news@freedomforum.org
http://www.freedomforum.org/diversity/
http://www.usd.edu/press/news/
news.cfm?nid=153&uid=user

American Indian Journalism Institute, South Dakota. AIJI gives Native American college journalism students the opportunity to train as newspaper reporters, editors and photographers at the Al Neuharth Media Center at the University of South Dakota. AIJI teaches journalism fundamentals in a four-credit course. Students attend classes, receive practical experience in journalism labs, go on field trips and produce two editions of an institute newspaper, The Native Journal. Follow-up programs for institute graduates include paid internships at three daily newspapers, further schooling and assistance with eventual job placement. For more information, contact Jack Marsh at (605) 677-6315 or jmarsh@freedomforum.org.

Chips Quinn Scholars program offers students of color mentoring and hands-on training in journalism. The aim is to provide support and encouragement that will open doors to news careers and bring greater diversity to the nation's newspaper newsrooms.

George Washington University School of Media and Public Affairs
Prime Movers Project
Dorothy Gilliam
805 21st St. N.W.
Washington, DC 20052
Phone: (202) 994-0761
E-mail: dgilliam@gwu.edu

This project brings experienced journalists, particularly people of color and women, into high school classrooms to help students launch school newspapers, web sites, and television and radio broadcasts. The program enables veteran journalists, or

"Prime Movers," to share their knowledge and experiences with junior colleagues and high school students interested in creating student media in high schools in underserved communities in the Washington, D.C., area. Four urban high schools have been selected to participate in the program during the 2005–2006 school year. This project is funded by the John S. and James L. Knight Foundation.

Hispanic Link Journalism Foundation
1420 N St. N.W.
Washington, DC 20005
Phone: (202) 234-0280
http://www.hispaniclink.org/foundation/
fellowshipinternship.htm

The Hispanic Link Journalism Foundation offers reporting fellowships on a continuing basis. They include a one-year fellowship for an aspiring Hispanic print journalist to train as a reporter in the nation's capital. It offers a stipend of $20,800, plus benefits. Other paid and unpaid internships, including work-study, are available throughout the year. Each placement is designed to provide a challenging work environment in which individuals can expand their expertise and develop new skills.

National Association of Hispanic Journalists
1000 National Press Building
529 14th St. N.W.
Washington, DC 20045-2001
Phone: (202) 662-7145 / (888) 346-NAHJ
Fax: (202) 662-7144
http://www.nahj.org/educationalprograms/
educationalprograms.shtml

Creating Future Journalists is built around a full day of activities held in conjunction with annual conventions of the NAHJ. Over the past three years, the program has helped 300 middle school and high school students and their journalism advisers explore the benefits of media careers. It includes post-convention events such as essay contests and field trips.

Los Angeles Times Student Journalism Program
Student Journalism Program Hotline
Phone: (213) 237-5195
http://www.latimes.com/extras/studentjournalism/

This program is designed to support the education of high school and college students in the greater Los Angeles area who exhibit talent and interest in journalism. The program helps prepare participants for print media careers, with an emphasis on cultivating journalists of color who will reflect the diverse communities of Southern California in the newsroom. For information about specific events, call the Student Journalism Program Hotline at (213) 237-5195.

Native American Journalism Association
High School Project - Project Phoenix
555 N. Dakota St.
Vermillion, SD 57069
Phone: (605) 677-5282
Fax: (866) 694-4264
E-mail: info@naja.com
http://naja.com/phoenix/

Project Phoenix meets in the host city of the Native American Journalists Association's annual convention. Each year, 10 to 15 students gather to find out what it takes to put together their own newspaper. The students of Project Phoenix learn the basics of newswriting and photojournalism. During the course of about a week they produce a 12-page newspaper called Rising Voices.

The Poynter Institute
801 Third Street S.
St. Petersburg, FL 33701
Phone: (888) 769-6837
http://www.poynter.org/seminar/
seminar_view.asp?int_seminarID=3170

Florida High School Writers Workshops are designed for high school students and teachers in the Tampa Bay area. This program is modeled after Poynter's highly successful National Writers Workshops for professional journalists. Each daylong workshop will be on a Saturday and will offer intensive sessions on writing, reporting and editing taught by Poynter faculty and visiting professionals. Contact: Jeanne Nissenbaum, jnissenbaum@poynter.org.

Radio and Television News Directors Foundation
1600 K Street N.W., Suite 700
Washington, DC 20006-2838
Phone: (202) 659-6510
Fax: (202) 223-4007
E-mail: rtnda@rtnda.org
http://www.rtnda.org/resources/highschool.shtml

The RTNDF High School Journalism Project,
funded by a grant from the John S. and James L.
Knight Foundation, seeks to identify, inspire, train
and challenge the next generation of diverse radio
and television journalists and First Amendment
advocates. Its mission is to develop scholastic
broadcast journalism programs and to strengthen
existing projects through collaborations with the
professional journalists who are members of the
Radio and Television News Directors Association.

SUMMER JOURNALISM WORKSHOPS FOR HIGH
SCHOOL STUDENTS OF COLOR

ALABAMA

University of Alabama
207 Student Media Building
Box 870172
Tuscaloosa, AL 35487
Contact: Ed Mullins
Phone: (205) 348-8592
E-mail: *emullins13@netscape.net*

ARIZONA

University of Arizona
Department of Journalism
Tucson, AZ 85721
Phone: (520) 621-7556
Contact: Kathy D'Assis
E-mail: *dassis@u.arizona.edu*
http://journalism.arizona.edu

This serious, but fun, intensive summer journalism
workshop is intended to help high school students
of color understand the demands of today's and
tomorrow's journalism, the opportunities for a
higher education and the possibilities for success
in the newspaper field. The workshop covers
reporting, interviewing, writing, editing, layout,
design, photojournalism and visual communication.
Students will be introduced to state-of-the-art
digital imaging and design. Each student will
construct a web page.

CALIFORNIA

**California Chicano News Media Association/San
Diego**
Leonel Sanchez
The San Diego Union-Tribune

P.O. Box 120191
San Diego, CA 92112-1023
Phone: (619) 293-1023
E-mail: *leonel.sanchez@uniontrib.com*
http://www.ccnmasd.org/

Students spend two weeks each summer at a
journalism boot camp, guided by professional
journalists in the classroom and in the field. That
field experience in a student's journalism career is
commonly reserved for junior and seniors at the
university level. The students produce a
newspaper, a television newscast and a radio
newscast. They also attend classes on writing and
grammar and participate in panel discussions on
ethics in journalism and interviewing techniques.
The workshop is open to high school junior and
seniors from San Diego, Riverside, San Bernardino
and Imperial counties. Applications are available
in January and the workshop is usually held in
June at a local university.

**California Chicano News Media Association/San
Jose**
Daniel Vasquez, director
San Jose Mercury News
750 Ridder Park Drive
San Jose, CA 95190
Phone: (408) 920-5406
http://www.mosaicworkshop.org

Bay Area Multicultural Media Academy
San Francisco State University
Doris Y.S. Owyang, Program Manager
Center for Integration and Improvement of
Journalism
1600 Holloway Ave.
San Francisco, CA 94132-4082
Phone: (415) 405-0727
www.ciij.org

The Bay Area Multicultural Media Academy is a
two-week residential program built around developing journalism skills and careers for Bay Area high
school students. The Center for Integration and
Improvement of Journalism at San Francisco State
University has sponsored BAMMA since 1990. Its
graduates work in print, radio, television and
online journalism. BAMMA is dedicated to providing
opportunities to youth from underserved communities to develop skills as journalists that will open
doors for them in media careers and help the profession do a better job covering news for everyone.

DISTRICT OF COLUMBIA

Howard University
Department of Journalism
525 Bryant St. N.W.
Washington, DC 20059
Phone: (202) 806-7855
http://www.howard.edu/schoolcommunications/

FLORIDA

Florida A & M University
Professor Diane Hall, director
School of Journalism
Tallahassee, FL 32308
Phone: (904) 599-3357
E-mail: *dhall@sjgc.net*
http://www.sjgc.net/index1.html

Florida International University
North Campus
Professor Don Sneed, director
School of Journalism and Mass Communication
3000 N.E. 151st St.
North Miami, FL 33181
Phone: (305) 940-5625
http://jmc.fiu.edu/sjmc/

University of Miami
Professor Tsitsi Wakhisi, director
School of Communication
P.O. Box 248127
Coral Gables, FL 33124-2030
Phone: (305) 284-6493
E-mail: *communication@miami.edu*
http://www.miami.edu/com/

ILLINOIS

Eastern Illinois University
Professor Joseph Gisondi
Department of Journalism
600 W. Lincoln Ave.
Charleston, IL 61920
http://www.eiu.edu/~journal/

Youth Communication/Chicago
Phil Costello
Columbia College and Roosevelt University
600 S. Michigan Ave.
Chicago, IL 60605
Phone: (312) 922-7150
http://www.uiowa.edu/~journal/faculty/

KENTUCKY

Western Kentucky University
Dr. Pam Johnson, director
School of Journalism and Broadcasting
1 Big Red Way
Bowling Green, KY 42101-3576
Phone: (270) 745-5837
E-mail: *james.highland@wku.edu*
http://www.geocities.com/wkumjw

University of Kentucky
Dr. Beth Barnes
School of Journalism
107 Grehan Building
University of Kentucky
Lexington, KY 40506-0042
Phone: (859) 257-4275
Fax: (859) 323-3168
E-mail: *bbarnes@uky.edu*
http://jat.uky.edu/indexALL.html

MASSACHUSETTS

New England High School Journalism
Professor Carole Remick, director
University of Massachusetts
Regis College
100 Morrissey Blvd.
Boston, MA 02125-3393
Phone: (617) 287-7932
E-mail: *carole.remick@umb.edu*
http://www.mijohn.com/hsjc/index.htm

MISSISSIPPI

University of Mississippi
331 Farley, P.O. Box 1848
University, MS 38677
Contact: Beth Fitts
Phone: (662) 915-7146
http://www.olemiss.edu/depts/journalism/

MISSOURI

University of Missouri
Dr. Anna Romero
School of Journalism
76-K Gannett Hall
Columbia, MO 65211-1200
Phone: (573) 882-2422
E-mail: *journalism@missouri.edu*
http://www.journalism.missouri.edu/contact.html

NEW JERSEY

Monmouth University
Dr. Eleanor Novek, director
Communications Department
400 Cedar Ave.
West Long Branch, NJ 07764
Phone: (732) 571-4427
http://www.monmouth.edu/academics/deptlinks/
comm.asp

NEW YORK

New York University
Professor Pamela Newkirk
Department of Journalism
10 Washington Place
New York, NY 10003
Phone: (212) 998-7980
E-mail: pamnewkirk@nyu.edu
http://journalism.nyu.edu/ujw/

OHIO

Kent State University
Gene Shelton, director
School of Journalism and Communication
P.O. Box 5190
Kent, OH 44242-0001
E-mail: eshelto1@kent.edu

PENNSYLVANIA

The Pennsylvania State University
Joseph M. Selden, Director/Assistant Dean and
Lecturer
Office of Multicultural Affairs, College of
Communications
208 Carnegie Building
University Park, PA 16802-5101
Phone: (814) 863-6081
http://my.highschooljournalism.org/pa/
universitypark/mhsjw

SOUTH DAKOTA

Native American Journalists Association
Kim Baca, Interim Executive Director
University of South Dakota
414 E. Clark St..
Vermillion, SD 57069-2390
Phone: (605) 677-5282
Fax: (866) 694-4264

E-mail: info@naja.com; kim@naja.com
http://www.naja.com/news.html

TEXAS

San Antonio College
Irene Abrego, director
Journalism Department
1300 San Pedro Ave.
San Antonio, TX 78212-4299
Phone: (210) 733-2870
http://www.accd.edu/sac/j-p/jlsm.html

Texas Christian University
Elizabeth Faulk, director
Department of Journalism
294 Moudy South
Fort Worth, TX 76129
Phone: (817) 257-6274
E-mail: e.faulk@tcu.edu
http://www.jou.tcu.edu/

University of Texas at El Paso
Zita Arocha, director
Department of Communication Studies
500 W. University Ave., Room 202
El Paso, TX 79968-0550
Phone: (915) 747-6287
E-mail: zarocha@utep.edu
http://www.utep.edu/comm/

VIRGINIA

Virginia Commonwealth University
June Nicholson, director
School of Mass Communications
901 W. Main St.
P.O. Box 842034
Richmond, VA 23284
Phone: (804) 367-1260
E-mail: jonichol@vcu.edu
http://www.has.vcu.edu/mac/

WASHINGTON

Seattle University
Tomas Guillen, director
Communication Department
Casey Building, Room 232
900 Broadway
Seattle, WA 98122-4340
Phone: (206) 464-2045
E-mail: tomasg@seattleu.edu
http://www.seattleu.edu/artsci/communication/

WISCONSIN

Marquette University
Rose Richard
College of Communication
1131 W. Wisconsin Ave.
Milwaukee, WI 53201
Phone: (414) 288-5227
http://www.marquette.edu/dept/comm/

MULTI-STATE PROGRAMS

Hispanic Link Journalism Foundation
1420 N St. N.W.
Washington, DC 20005
Phone: (202) 234-0280
http://www.hispaniclink.org

Reporting Fellowships: For 20 years, Hispanic Link has been the training host of 25 full-year fellows and provided shorter-term internships for more than 100 aspiring journalists. Participants cover national news in Washington alongside correspondents, with emphasis on how current events affect Hispanics. Their work is published in Hispanic Link Weekly Report and distributed to subscribers nationally. Dozens of still-connected, Link-trained journalists continue to work and advance at major dailies and broadcast outlets throughout the country.

Freedom Forum Grants for Native American High School Journalism Students
Dr. Richard W. Lee
Department of Journalism and Mass Communication,
South Dakota State University
Brookings, SD 57007
Phone: (605) 688-4171
Fax: (605) 688-5034
E-mail: Richard_Lee@sdstate.edu

Native American high school students may apply for grants to attend the South Dakota State University summer journalism institute held in mid-June. Grants cover transportation and workshop costs.

The Poynter Institute
801 Third Street S.
St. Petersburg, FL 33701
Phone: (888) 769-6837
http://www.poynter.org/content/
content_view.asp?id=9260

Poynter College Fellowships

Newswriting and reporting: Poynter is looking for the best graduates in the arts and sciences and journalism who will become leaders in tomorrow's newsrooms. It seeks people who can write with clarity and flair, who have the education and insight to understand the world they report on, who recognize the important role the profession plays as a public service, and who have great ambition to succeed in life.

Visual journalism: Fellows will learn (or relearn) the fundamentals of visual journalism from Poynter faculty and guest experts. This is a visual boot camp where students will explore typography, color and architecture for news and feature page design; information graphics; traditional and photo illustration; documentary photojournalism; online design; and interactivity.

The Washington Post
1150 15th Street N.W.
Washington, DC 20071-0002
http://washpost.com/community/education/yjdp/
index.shtml

The Post's **Young Journalists Development Program** provides a range of services to local high school journalism programs. They include equipment donation, printing services, technical assistance, seminars and workshops, and scholarships. For more information, contact director Athelia Knight, (202) 334-7132 or knighta@washpost.com.

COLLEGE PROGRAMS

The following is an abbreviated list of colleges and universities that serve primarily students of color. For a complete list of the historically black colleges and universities that have communications programs, go to the Black College Communication Association web site, www.bccanews.org.

California State University, Fresno
Mass Communication and Journalism
McKee Fisk Building, Room 238
2225 E. San Ramon Ave. M/S MF10
Fresno, CA 93740-8029
Phone: (559) 278-2087
Fax: (559) 278-4995
http://www.csufresno.edu/MCJ/

Forty percent of the student population is Latino and Asian American. Graduates of the mass communication and journalism program have gone on to careers at The Washington Post, The Bakersfield Californian and The Record in Stockton, Calif.

Florida A&M University
Professor Diane Hall, director
School of Journalism
Tallahassee, FL 32308
Phone: (904) 599-3357
E-mail: *dhall@sjgc.net*

In 1982, FAMU's Division of Journalism became the first journalism program at a historically black university to earn accreditation by the Accrediting Council on Education in Journalism and Mass Communications. It was reaccredited in 1988, 1994 and 2000.

Florida International University
University Park Campus
11200 S.W. Eighth Street
Miami, FL 33199
Biscayne Bay Campus
3000 N.E. 151st St.
North Miami, FL 33181
http://jmc.fiu.edu/sjmc/

Master's Program in Spanish-Language Journalism
This program is designed for those who want to work at the professional level in the Spanish-language media in the United States, Latin America or Europe. The program focuses on the development of the writing, critical thinking, analytic and ethical skills necessary for a professional journalism career.

Hampton University
School of Journalism and Communication
Department of Mass Media Arts
Armstrong 117
Hampton University
Hampton, VA 23668
Phone: (757) 727-5405
http://www.hamptonu.edu/arts_edu/arts_humn/mass_media/

This journalism and communications program trains students in print and broadcast journalism, public relations, advertising and media management.

Howard University School of Communications
525 Bryant St. N.W.
Washington, DC 20059
Phone: (202) 806-7690
http://www.howard.edu/schoolcommunications/

Students gain critical, hands-on work experience at WHUR-FM/WHBC (Howard University Radio) and WHUT-TV (Howard University Television), the only African American-owned public television station in the United States.

Lehman College
Multilingual Journalism Program @ Lehman College
Prof. Patricio Lerzundi
Phone: (718) 960-8161
Fax: (718) 960-8218
http://www.lehman.cuny.edu/depts/langlit/mlj/

At this City University of New York campus in the Bronx, students of color comprise more than 80 percent of the student population. Lehman emphasizes multilingual media, a reflection of the diversity on campus and in the community. The Bronx Journal, the campus newspaper, is written in 11 languages.

Norfolk State University
Mass Communications and Journalism
700 Park Ave.
Norfolk, VA 23504
Phone: (757) 823-8330
Fax: (757) 823-9119
http://www.nsu.edu/mcjr/contact.htm

About half of the students in the mass communications program at this historically black university in Virginia are men, a surprise given that women outnumber men in many communications programs. The Spartan Echo, the student newspaper, was named best biweekly in 2001 by the Black College Communications Association.

HISTORICALLY BLACK COLLEGES AND UNIVERSITIES SCHOLARSHIPS

Knight Ridder
Director, Corporate HR Services
50 W. San Fernando St., Suite 1500
San Jose, CA 95113
http://www.knightridder.com/career/internships.html

Knight Ridder provides scholarships in advertising, business and journalism at two major historically black colleges: Howard University, located in Washington, D.C., and Florida A&M University in Tallahassee, Fla. The scholarships are awarded to outstanding students entering their junior year. The scholars are awarded $2,500 for their junior year and work at a Knight Ridder company as a summer intern. The scholarship continues into the senior year if the student maintains a 3.0 GPA. If you are a student at one of these institutions, contact your college placement office.

University of North Dakota
School of Communication
O'Kelly Hall 7169
P.O. Box 7169
Grand Forks, ND 58202
Phone: (701) 777-6388
Contact: Paul Boswell, Director, Native Media Center
E-mail: *paul.boswell@und.nodak.edu*

The **Native Media Center Program** is designed to increase communication skills of Native Americans, the number of native people working in the media and the quantity and quality of coverage of Native Americans. Programs include Red Nation News, an online news magazine and Native Community Studio, a weekend during the school year when Native American high school students come to the Native Media Center to work with professional journalists on developing skills and gain exposure of the profession.

University of Texas, El Paso
College of Liberal Arts
500 W. University Ave.
El Paso, TX 79968
Phone: (915) 747-5129
http://www.utep.edu/comm/

The UTEP program in communication is a contemporary blend of the humanistic and applied directions of the field as the profession is challenged by a changing world order, new media and information technology, and the new realities of the information-based society. UTEP's Department of Communication has partnered with the National Hispanic Press Foundation to bring exposure and recognition to university students' research and writing abilities and increase the number of Hispanic professionals in communication fields.

University of Texas-Pan American
1201 W. University Drive
Edinburg, TX 78541
http://www.panam.edu/

About 88 percent of the student population is Hispanic. Students at this lower Rio Grande Valley campus get newspaper experience at the Pan American, which comes out twice weekly. The Pan American web site is located at *http://www.panam.edu/dept/panamerican*.

Wayne State University
Department of Communication
585 Manoogian Hall
Detroit, MI 48201
Phone: (313) 577-2943
http://www.comm.wayne.edu/

Wayne State University's **Journalism Institute for Minorities** trains high-achieving students of color for communication careers. Exceptionally talented students are recruited for the intensive four-year career preparation program. Institute members receive fully paid scholarships and gain professional experience through internships with such local newspapers as the Detroit News and Detroit Free Press, as well as The New York Times, USA Today and the Chicago Tribune. Institute graduates are employed at the Los Angeles Times, The Wall Street Journal, the Detroit Free Press and other news organizations throughout the country. Institute students have received numerous awards, including the Community Journalism Award of the Michigan Press Association.

Wilberforce University
1055 N. Bickett Road
Wilberforce, OH 45384-1001
Phone: (937) 376-2911
http://www.wilberforce.edu/opencms/export/ bulldog/home/home.html

This private, four-year historically black university requires internships and practicums for graduates, who can study journalism as a communications major in the Humanities Division. Students can get experience at the biweekly campus paper, The Mirror. Wilberforce students have interned at the local Xenia Daily Gazette and the nearby Dayton Daily News. Five Wilberforce students have had internships at The Philadelphia Inquirer.

AWARDS, FELLOWSHIPS AND SCHOLARSHIPS

Asian American Journalists Association
1182 Market St., Suite 320
San Francisco, CA 94102
Contact: Albert Lee, professional programs coordinator

Phone: (415) 346-2051
Fax: (415) 346-6343
E-mail: *albertl@aaja.org*

AAJA supports and encourages the advancement of mid-career journalists in the newsroom. It offers several fellowships to provide members the opportunity to attend career-building programs.

AAJA Fellowships help members attend short-term professional training and development programs. Grants of up to $1,000 are offered to provide assistance with tuition, travel, food, lodging and other program-related expenses. Applicants must be full or associate members wth at least three years of professional experience. Applications are accepted throughout the year.

AAJA/Poynter Institute Fellowships help two midcareer journalists attend selected management training courses at the Poynter Institute in St. Petersburg, Fla. Applicants should be full-time employees of a print, broadcast or online news organization or journalism educators. Tuition and hotel costs are covered by Poynter, while transportation costs are covered by AAJA.

AAJA/Newspaper Association of America Fellowship helps newspaper journalists attend the annual Executive Leadership Program. Applicants should be full-time employees of a newspaper organization. The fellowship covers seminar registration fees, travel, meals and hotel expenses.

AAJA Business Fellowship offers members a chance to develop a better understanding of the challenges of running a newspaper or media company. Participants can expect to observe and learn about the operations in production, marketing, advertising, circulation and distribution. Previous fellowships took place at the St. Paul Pioneer Press and The New York Times.

American Society of Newspaper Editors
11690B Sunrise Valley Drive
Reston, VA 20191-1409
Phone: (703) 453-1122
http://www.asne.org

Robert G. McGruder Awards For Diversity Leadership: ASNE, in partnership with the Associated Press Managing Editors and the Freedom Forum, accepts nominations for the Robert G. McGruder Awards for Diversity Leadership. Two awards are given annually – one for newspapers with a circulation of up to 75,000 and one for newspapers with more than 75,000 circulation. Each award is $2,500. The awards go to individuals, newsrooms or teams of journalists who embody the spirit of McGruder, a former executive editor of the Detroit Free Press and a relentless champion of diversity. McGruder died of cancer in April 2002.

Columbia Scholastic Press Association
http://www.columbia.edu/cu/cspa/index.html

Services provided by the CSPA include written evaluations of student publications (annual critiques) as well as the planning and conducting of four conferences and workshops. In addition, the CSPA publishes a quarterly magazine called SPR, Student Press Review. The highest awards given to publications by the CSPA each year are its Crown Awards. The association also judges more than 10,000 individual entries in its annual Gold Circle Awards for student journalists. More than 500 college students and 500 high school students receive awards in the 75 categories of this competition.

Detroit Free Press Scholarships for High School Seniors
Joe Grimm
600 W. Fort St.
Detroit, MI, 48226
Phone: (313) 222-6490, ext.600
E-mail: *grimm@freep.com*
http://www.freep.com

The Detroit Free Press High School Journalism Program was conceived by former Free Press executive Jerry Tilis in 1985 after budget woes forced the school district to eliminate the journalism program from most schools. Once a month, from October through May, each of 22 participating public schools produces one full-size newspaper page.

Independent Press Association
65 Battery Street, Second Floor
San Francisco, CA 94111
Phone: (415) 445-0230, ext. 116 or 117
Fax: (415) 445-0231
E-mail: *gww@indypress.org*
http://www.indypress.org

The George Washington Williams Fellowship was created to encourage journalists with diverse backgrounds to pursue important social issues. Named for the 19th century African American journalist who wrote the first history of African Americans from their own point of view, the fellowship funds magazine stories about such issues as environment, global trade policy, health care, race and education. Fellows receive access to some research support, consultants, advanced professional training and a large network of journalists working in the public interest sector. Any journalist with at least three years of solid professional reporting and writing experience may apply.

Knight Ridder Scholarship for High School Seniors
http://www.knightridderscholars.com/index.html

$40,000 Minority Scholarship Program: Each year, Knight Ridder offers four college scholarships to outstanding high school graduates of color. Two scholars are chosen for their interest in journalism; two are chosen for their interest in business-side departments such as marketing, technology and advertising. The scholarships are for $5,000 a year for four years. In addition, KR Scholars will work at a KR company each summer beginning after high school, and continuing through their college years. After graduation, the scholars will work at a Knight Ridder company for at least one year. The scholarships are intended for students in communities served by Knight Ridder papers, and applicants must win at the local level to go on to national judging. As local winners are chosen in January, local deadlines tend to be in December and January.

National Association of Black Journalists
Scholarships for Undergraduate and Graduate Students
University of Maryland
8701-A Adelphi Road
Adelphi, MD 20783-1716
Phone: (301) 445-7100
Fax: (301) 445-7101
E-mail: *nabj@nabj.org*
http://www.nabj.org/media_institute/fellowships/index.html

Ethel Payne Fellowships: NABJ annually seeks to award $5,000 fellowships to journalists wanting international reporting experience through self-conceived assignments in Africa. The fellowships bear the name of the woman known as the "first lady of the Black Press." Ethel Payne (1911 – 1991) covered seven U.S. presidents as a journalist and was a war correspondent for The Chicago Defender and Sengstacke Newspapers. In 2002, the U.S. Postal Service honored Payne – who reported on

the civil rights movement during the 1950s and 1960s and in 1972 became the nation's first black female network commentator – with a commemorative 37-cent stamp. It was Payne's work in Africa as a foreign correspondent that prompted NABJ to create the fellowships.

Ida B. Wells Award: Given annually by NABJ and the National Conference of Editorial Writers *(http://www.ncew.org/)* to a media executive or manager who has made outstanding efforts to make newsrooms and news coverage more accurately reflect the diversity of the communities they serve. The award is named for the 19th century journalist who crusaded against lynching. It is administered by Northwestern University's Medill School of Journalism. Contacts: Lisa Goodnight, NABJ communications manager, (301) 445-7100, or *lisa@nabj.org;* and Wendy Leopold, Medill School of Journalism, *w-leopold@ northwestern.edu*.

NABJ Scholarships: Annually, NABJ awards deserving students interested in pursuing a career in journalism awards of more than $30,000 in scholarships. Each scholarship is worth up to $5,000. Scholarships are open to any foreign- or American-born students, currently attending an accredited four-year college or university in the U.S. or those who are candidates for graduate school.

National Association of Hispanic Journalists
1000 National Press Building
529 14th St. N.W.
Washington, DC 20045-2001
Phone: (202) 662-7145 / (888) 346-NAHJ
Fax: (202) 662-7144
E-mail: *nahj@nahj.org*

The Rubén Salazar Scholarship Fund program offers scholarships designed to encourage and assist Latino students to pursue journalism careers. NAHJ offers scholarships to college undergraduates and graduate students pursuing careers as print, photo, broadcast or online journalists. Applicants must plan to attend a college or a university in the United States or Puerto Rico as a full-time student for the entire academic year to be eligible.

ñ Awards: Awards are presented in these categories – Leadership, Emerging Journalist, Frank del Olmo Print Journalist of the Year, Broadcast Journalist of the Year, Photographer of the Year. The leadership award is open, through nomination, to any individual, organization or institution that has demonstrated an outstanding commitment to Latino concerns and is actively working toward promoting a better understanding of Latino issues or culture. The other awards are open through a nomination process to Hispanic journalists who have made a significant contribution to the Latino community and brought awareness to issues affecting Latinos, or Hispanic journalists who have achieved excellence through their chosen media.

New America Media
275 Ninth St., Third floor
San Francisco, CA 94103
Phone: (415) 503-4170
Fax: (415) 503-0970
E-mail: *sandip@pacificnews.org*
http://www.newamericamedia.org

The **NAM Awards** recognize journalistic excellence in ethnic media. They showcase news stories and the people and media outlets that report them. Journalists from print, broadcast and online ethnic media are nominated by colleagues. Journalists can also nominate their own work.
Contact: Sandip Roy.

Radio and Television News Directors Foundation
RTNDA/RTNDF
1600 K St. N.W., Suite 700
Washington, DC 20006-2838
Phone: (202) 659-6510
Fax: (202) 223-4007
E-mail: *rtnda@rtnda.org*

N.S. Bienstock Fellowship: A $2,500 award established in early 1999 by N.S. Bienstock Inc. owners, Richard Leibner and Carole Cooper. Bienstock is a longtime member of RTNDA. This award recognizes a promising journalist of color in radio or television news management.

Michele Clark Fellowship: RTNDF's first fellowship is named for a CBS News correspondent who was killed in a plane crash while on assignment in 1972. Her family and colleagues at CBS created a fund in her name, endowing a permanent $1,000 award for young, promising professionals of color in television or radio news.

Society of Professional Journalists
Eugene S. Pulliam National Journalism Center
3909 N. Meridian St.
Indianapolis, IN 46208
Phone: (317) 927-8000

Fax: (317) 920-4789
http://www.spj.org/awards_NAA.asp

New America Award: To encourage and honor collaborations between ethnic and mainstream media. This award honors collaborative public service journalism by ethnic and mainstream media working together to explore and expose an issue of importance to immigrant or ethnic communities in the United States. The competition is open to any ethnic media organization or journalist and a mainstream media organization or journalist based on the quality and impact of their collaborative work. SPJ welcomes nominations from media outlets, journalists, community and issue advocacy groups, individuals and others concerned with ethnic and immigrant issues. Each entry must include a letter explaining the significance of the issue, why it was chosen and how the collaboration between ethnic and mainstream media came to be, including obstacles encountered and benefits gained.

The New America Award winner is honored at the annual Sigma Delta Chi Awards banquet in Washington, D.C.

Sponsors for Educational Opportunity
SEO Scholars Program
126 E. 31st Street
New York, NY 10016
Phone: (212) 532-2454
http://www.seo-usa.org

The SEO Scholars Program (formerly the College Preparation or Traditional Program) is an out-of-school academic enrichment program for promising students of color in New York City public schools. It works with motivated students from under-resourced communities and has provided consistent, targeted services over several years. The Scholars Program offers a rigorous four-year plan of academic enrichment and standardized test preparation, college counseling, mentoring and summer learning experiences.

Thomson Fellowships
Jim Jennings, Vice President and Editorial Director
Thomson Newspapers
Metro Center
1 Station Place
Stamford, CT 06909
(203) 435-2515
http://journalism.berkeley.edu/jobs/
details.php?cat=newswire&ID=1997

Thomson Newspapers offers several paid three-month working fellowships for university juniors, seniors and graduate students who plan to pursue careers in newspaper journalism. These fellowships are available to members of racial or ethnic minority groups in the U.S. and Canada. Each fellow works at a daily newspaper as a member of its editorial staff with training and evaluation. Applicants should send a résumé, a one-page essay on the role of newspapers in their communities, nonreturnable samples of their work, three references and a cover letter describing what they hope to gain from the fellowship and what they can bring to the newspapers.

INTERNSHIPS, PROFESSIONAL PROGRAMS AND FELLOWSHIPS FOR JOURNALISTS OF COLOR

Asian American Journalists Association
Albert Lee, professional programs coordinator
1182 Market St., Suite 320
San Francisco, CA 94102
Phone: (415) 346-2051
Fax: (415) 346-6343
E-mail: albertl@aaja.org
http://www.aaja.org

AAJA Broadcast Mentor Program: Mentoring for those who work in front of the camera or behind the scenes in television.

Cox Reporting Internship: Cox Newspapers offers a Washington, D.C., reporting internship to an AAJA member. The interns works for the summer as general assignment reporter in the Cox Washington Bureau, helping cover all aspects of Washington, from Capitol Hill to the White House. Cox will provide the intern with airfare and a furnished apartment in the DuPont Circle area of Washington, as well as a $300 weekly stipend. Contact: Lila Chwee at AAJA.

Siani Lee Broadcast Internship for Television is held during the summer at CBS affiliate KYW-TV in Philadelphia. Interns must be at least 18 years of age and enrolled in a post-secondary program that gives academic credit for internships. Qualified AAJA members are preferred. AAJA awards a stipend of $2,500 to help defray internship costs of travel and housing. AAJA created the internship to honor the late Siani Lee, a Philadelphia television news anchor who died in 2001.

Black College Wire
c/o National Association of Black Journalists
University of Maryland
8701-A Adelphi Road
Adelphi, MD 20783-1716
(301) 445-7100
E-mail: bcwire@hotmail.com
http://www.blackcollegewire.org

Black Newspaper Internship: Students work as reporters, copy editors, photographers, graphic artists or page designers at participating black newspapers. Interns are responsible for their own housing and transportation; placements will take into consideration the student's summer living plans.

Black College Wire Internship: Interns work as reporters for the Black College Wire. They will report, write and file from their summer homes as correspondents under the supervision of the wire's editors. A telephone and Internet-accessible computer are required.

Institute for Justice and Journalism
University of Southern California
Annenberg School for Communication
1 California Plaza
300 South Grand Ave., Suite 3950
Los Angeles, CA 90071
Phone: (213) 437-4410
Fax: (213) 437-4424
http://www.justicejournalism.org/index.htm

The institute provides professional fellowships, reporting tools and a network of colleagues and justice experts to support in-depth coverage of complex justice issues.

National Public Radio Internship
Human Resources Department
635 Massachusetts Ave. N.W.
Washington, DC 20001
Fax: (202) 513-3047
E-mail: internship@npr.org
http://www.npr.org/about/jobs/intern/

NPR offers internships at its national headquarters in Washington and at its NPR West office in Los Angeles. The internship program is designed to provide students and recent graduates with an opportunity to learn about broadcasting and the supporting areas of NPR. A candidate must be a graduate student, an undergraduate student or have graduated from college within 12 months of beginning the internship. Interns are expected to work between 20 and 40 hours a week during an 8-to-10 week period. Internships are offered during the summer, fall and winter-spring semesters. Interns may receive academic credit if an agreement is made between the NPR Human Resources Department and the intern's college or university. More than two dozen internships are offered. See web site for details.

Kaiser Media Fellowships Program
Penny Duckham, Executive Director
The Henry J. Kaiser Family Foundation
2400 Sand Hill Road
Menlo Park, CA 94025
Phone: (650) 234-9220
Fax: (650) 854-4800 or (650) 854-7465
E-mail: pduckham@kff.org
http://www.kff.org/about/mediafellowships.cfm

The **Kaiser Media Fellowships** is a summer program for young journalists of color interested in specializing in urban public health reporting. There is no application form. Applicants should submit a detailed letter describing their reasons for applying, a resume, examples of recent work and one or more letters of support. Please refer to the specific program area for complete application instructions.

Knight Ridder Newsroom Internships
http://www.knightridder.com/career/internships.html
This is a guide to newsroom internships at Knight Ridder newspapers. Apply directly to the newspapers. Each newspaper acts independently, so mass applications are not possible.

Minorities in Broadcasting Training Program
Patrice Williams
P.O. Box 39696
Los Angeles, CA 90039
Phone: (818) 240-3362
E-mail: mibtp@pacbell.net
http://www.thebroadcaster.com

This nonprofit organization provides training opportunities to college graduates of color in radio and television news reporting and news management.

National Association of Black Journalists Internships
University of Maryland
8701-A Adelphi Road

Adelphi, MD 20783-1716
Phone: (301) 445-7100
Fax: (301) 445-7101
E-mail: nabj@nabj.org
http://www.nabj.org/programs/internships/

NABJ provides internships to African American journalism students. Students are placed in 10-week paid internships with newspapers, television and radio stations and online news services across the country. NABJ internships give students hands-on reporting, editing, photography and design experience in professional settings. Interns have worked at news outlets such as Bloomberg News, The Associated Press, The Seattle Times, The News & Observer in Raleigh, N.C., CBS, National Public Radio and The Atlanta Journal-Constitution.

The Philadelphia Inquirer
P.O. Box 8263
Philadelphia, PA 19101
Phone: (215) 854-4975
Fax: (215) 854-2578
E-mail: recruiting@phillynews.com
(only for questions)
http://www.philly.com/mld/philly/contact_us/2480089.htm

Art Peters Program: Seven college students of color are selected for 10-week internships, four in copyediting and three in reporting. After an orientation period, reporting interns are assigned to the metropolitan, business, features or sports desks. Students from all college classes are eligible. Applicants should submit five to seven clips, a resume and cover letter, and references.

Minority Graphic Arts Internship: One person is chosen to work in the art department. Applicants should submit five to seven samples of their work (published or unpublished), a resume and cover letter, and references.

Minority Photojournalism Internship: One person is chosen to work in The Inquirer's photo department. Applicants should submit 20 to 40 images of news, features, sports, environmental portraits or a photo story, a resume and cover letter, and references. Contact Ed Hille, Inquirer director of photography, E-mail: ehille@phillynews.com

Acel Moore Minority Career Development Workshop: This program for high school students

of color seeks to introduce them to journalism. They are taught reporting, writing, editing and photography by Inquirer editors. The program runs for four Saturdays in February at The Inquirer. The students help write, edit and produce their own newspaper, First Take, and create a web site of their stories on philly.com. To receive an application contact Acel Moore, *amoore@phillynews.com*
Phone: (215) 854-4975
Fax: (215) 854-2578

St. Louis Post-Dispatch Summer Internship Program
Cynthia Todd, director of newsroom recruitment
900 N. Tucker Blvd.
St. Louis, MO 63101
Phone: (314) 340-8282
E-mail: *ctodd@post-dispatch.com*

Thirteen-week, paid internships in all areas of the newsroom are available on the metro, business, sports, features, design, graphics, photography and copyediting staffs.

The salary is $393 per week. Applicants must be seniors or graduate students enrolled in a degree program at the time the internship begins. Students also must have taken basic journalism courses as well as any specialized courses in the students' areas of interest.

To apply for a reporting or copyediting internship, send six clips; an autobiographical essay; a resume; and the names, telephone numbers and titles of four references. To apply for other internships, submit a portfolio of work (20 images for photography); an autobiographical essay; a resume; and the names, telephone numbers and titles of four references. Applicants also must submit official transcripts, but those may be sent under separate cover.

Times Mirror Minority Editorial Training Program (METPRO)
Los Angeles Times
202 W. First St.
Los Angeles, CA 90012
Phone: (800) 283-6397, ext. 77397
Fax: (213) 237-4749
E-mail: *john.hernandez@latimes.com*
http://www.metpronews.com/

The Minority Editorial Training Program offers 18 aspiring journalists an opportunity to train for two years at Times Mirror newspapers. The paid program

requires little or no experience. METPRO provides training as reporters, photographers and copy editors at daily newspapers. Reporting and photography trainees spend the first year at the Los Angeles Times; editing trainees spend the first year at Newsday, Melville, N.Y. The second-year trainees are assigned to newsrooms of Times Mirror newspapers.

Send an e-mail to receive an application packet. Applications for both METPRO/Editing and METPRO/Reporting are available beginning in October. For reporting and photography applications, e-mail *john.hernandez@latimes.com*
For editing applications, e-mail *jobs@newsday.com*

UNITY: Journalists of Color
http://www.unityjournalists.org/Fellowships/fellowships.html

A resource guide for a variety of internships, fellowships and scholarships for journalists of color.

DIVERSITY TOOLS

Center for Integration and Improvement of Journalism
San Francisco State University
Humanities 307
1600 Holloway Ave.
San Francisco, CA 94132
Phone: (415) 338-2083
Fax: (415) 338-2084
E-mail: *ciij@sfsu.edu*

Extensive lists of organizations and resources can be found at *http://www.ciij.org/resources/*

Journalism Institute for Minorities (JIM)
Wayne State University
191 Manoogian Hall
Detroit, MI 48201
Phone: (313) 577-6304
E-mail: *anails@wayne.edu*
Web site: *http://www.comm.wayne.edu/JIM.html*

Latinos and Media Project
6304 Colina Lane
Austin, TX 78759
Phone: (512) 250-0487
E-mail: *subervi@latinosandmedia.org*
http://www-new.latinosandmedia.org/resources/index.html

Information and resources about a variety of issues

related to Latinos and the media.

Mass Communicating: The Forum on Media Diversity
Manship School of Communication
Reilly Center for Media & Public Affairs
Baton Rouge, LA 70803
Phone: (225) 578-2223
Fax: (225) 578-2125
E-mail: *adrienn@lsu.edu*
http://www.masscommunicating.lsu.edu/about

Provides information about diversity in higher education and professional journalism and mass communication.

Radio and Television News Directors Foundation
1600 K St., N.W. Suite 700
Washington, D.C. 20006-2838
Phone: (202) 659-6510
Fax: (202) 223-4007
Get a copy of RTNDF's "Diversity Toolkit" at
http://www.rtnda.org/diversity/toolkit.shtml

Society of Professional Journalists Rainbow Sourcebook
http://www.spj.org/diversity_search.asp

The SPJ Rainbow Sourcebook, a searchable database of experts compiled by and for journalists, makes it easy to step beyond the narrow demographic band usually seen in stories. The sourcebook, searchable by common news topics, features background and contact information on qualified experts from demographic groups historically underrepresented in the news.

SPJ Diversity Toolbox
http://www.spj.org/diversity.asp

The SPJ Diversity Toolbox offers essays and links to valuable resources to help journalists broaden the perspectives in their work.

STYLE GUIDES

National Association of Black Journalists
http://nabj.org/newsroom/stylebook/index.html

Asian American Journalists Association
http://www.aaja.org/resources/apa_handbook/

National Association of Hispanic Journalists
Manual de Estilo ($14.95 plus shipping and

handling) and "Latinos in the United States: A Resource Guide for Journalists" ($8.50 shipping included) can be ordered at
http://nahj.org/nahjproducts/nahjproducts.shtml,
or call NAHJ at (202) 662-7483;
fax, (202) 662-7144.

Native American Journalists Association
Red Report 2002, a content analysis on coverage of Native Americans by the largest U.S. newspapers, and Red Report 2003, a report about recognizing racism in sports team nicknames and mascots, can be found at
http://www.naja.com/resources/publications/. In addition, two books can be ordered: "The American Indian and the Media" and "Pictures of our Nobler Selves: A History of Native American Contributions to the Media."

National Lesbian and Gay Journalists Association:
http://www.nlgja.org/pubs/style.html

JOB FAIRS

Journalism Opportunities Conference
http://www.ccnma.org
E-mail: *ccnmainfo@ccnma.org*

This annual job fair, organized by the California Chicano News Media Association, is the largest on the West Coast for journalists of color. It is held every October. The conference annually attracts more than 100 news media recruiters representing about 75 companies. Interviews for jobs and internships are a combination of scheduled sessions and walk-up interviews. Workshops on video tape critiques, and resume-writing and interviewing tips are held during the conference.

PSI (Personnel Strategies Inc.)
1809 S. Plymouth Road, Suite 350
Minnetonka, MN 55305-1977
http://psijobfair.com/

Working with such groups as the NAACP and Urban League, PSI conducts a number of diversity job fairs throughout the year and across the country.

Spirit of Diversity
http://www.freep.com/jobspage/toolkit/spinfo.htm

The Spirit of Diversity job fair is designed to connect newspaper recruiters with African American,

Hispanic, Asian-American and Native American job candidates. Most of the job seekers are college students seeking internships and newer professionals seeking full-time jobs. The Spirit of Diversity has been held annually since 1993. It is hosted by the Detroit Free Press, The Detroit News and Detroit Newspapers. Hotel accommodations for one night are provided for students who live more than 75 miles from Detroit.

JOURNALISM DIVERSITY ORGANIZATIONS

American Press Institute
http://www.americanpressinstitute.org/

Associated Press Managing Editors
http://www.apme.com/index.shtml

American Society of Newspaper Editors
http://www.asne.org/

American Women in Radio and Television
http://www.awrt.org/

Asian American Journalists Association
http://www.aaja.org/

Association for Women in Communications
http://www.womcom.org/

California Chicano News Media Association
http://www.ccnma.org/

Center for Integration and Improvement of Journalism
http://www.ciij.org/

Coloring the News
http://www.cmpa.com/

Emma L. Bowen Foundation for Minority Interests in Media
http://www.emmabowenfoundation.com/

Freedom Forum
http://www.freedomforum.org/diversity/

International Women's Media Foundation
http://www.iwmf.org/

Journalism and Women Symposium
http://www.jaws.org/

Journalismnext.com
http://journalismnext.com

Journalism.org
http://www.journalism.org/resources/tools/newsroom/diversity/online.asp

Maynard Institute for Journalism Education
http://www.maynardije.org

Media Awareness Network
http://www.media-awareness.ca/english/index.cfm

Minorities in Broadcasting Training Program
http://www.cwire.com/pub/orgs/Minorities.in.Broadcasting/default.asp

National Association of Black Journalists
http://www.nabj.org/

National Association of Hispanic Journalists
http://www.nahj.org/

National Association of Minorities in Cable
http://www.namic.com/

National Association of Minority Media Executives
http://www.namme.org/

National Center on Disability in Journalism
http://www.ncdj.org/index.php

National Diversity Newspaper Job Bank
http://www.newsjobs.com/

National Federation of Press Women
http://www.nfpw.org/

National Lesbian & Gay Journalists Association
http://www.nlgja.org/

Native American Journalists Association
http://www.naja.com/

News and Views by Native American Students
http://www.reznetnews.org/

News Watch – Center for Integration and Improvement of Journalism
http://www.ciij.org/newswatch

Newspaper Association of America
http://www.naa.org/

New Voices in Independent Publishing
http://www.indypress.org/programs/nvip.html

Northwestern University Media Management Center
http://www.mediamanagementcenter.org/

Pacific News Service
http://news.pacificnews.org/news/

Poynter Institute for Media Studies
http://www.poynter.org/default.asp

Radio and Television News Directors Foundation
http://www.rtnda.org/diversity/index.shtml

Society of Professional Journalists
http://www.spj.org

South Asian Journalists Association
http://www.saja.org/index.html

UNITY: Journalists of Color
http://www.unityjournalists.org/

Women in Journalism
http://www.leisurejobs.net/wij/

OTHER RESOURCES

American Journalism Review
http://www.ajr.org/

Ball State (J-IDEAS)
http://www.jideas.org/

Provides materials for high school journalism programs nationwide, aimed at revitalizing journalism and First Amendment education in high schools, particularly city schools with a majority enrollment of students of color.

Center for Media and Public Affairs
http://www.cmpa.com/

Columbia Journalism Review
http://www.cjr.org/

Columbia School of Journalism
http://www.jrn.columbia.edu/

Editor and Publisher
http://www.editorandpublisher.com

New America Media
http://news.ncmonline.com/news/

National Lesbian and Gay Journalists Association
http://www.nlgja.org/

PBS
http://www.pbs.org/

University of Missouri Television & Radio News Research
http://web.missouri.edu/%7Ejourvs/index.html

University of Missouri School of Journalism
http://journalism.missouri.edu/

APPENDICES

On the Road to a Diverse Work Force, Most Newspapers Have Stumbled

Report for Knight Foundation shows trends at 1,410 U.S. newspapers

By Bill Dedman and Stephen K. Doig

Newsroom diversity has dropped from its peak levels at most of the country's daily newspapers, including three-fourths of the largest, according to a study of newspaper employment from 1990 to 2005 for the John S. and James L. Knight Foundation.

While the newspaper industry may be slowly adding journalists of color overall, the gains have been uneven. In most newsrooms, large and small, the share of journalism jobs held by people of color has receded from its high-water mark.

Among the 200 largest newspapers, 73 percent employ fewer people of color, as a share of the newsroom jobs, than they did in some earlier year from 1990 to 2004. Only 27 percent of these large dailies were at their peak as 2005 began.

Looking more broadly at all daily news-papers, only 18 percent were at their peak, while 44 percent have slipped. And those are the papers that employ any people of color at all. The remaining 37 percent of the daily newspapers that divulged their employment figures reported all-white newsrooms.

This third annual report for Knight Foundation adds context to an annual survey by the American Society of Newspaper Editors. Each year ASNE surveys its members, and each year the editors bemoan the industry's slow progress in employing journalists of black, Hispanic, Asian or Native American descent as newsroom supervisors, reporters, copy or layout editors, or photographers.

But ASNE shows neither the year-by-year changes for individual newspapers, nor which newspapers are meeting ASNE's goal of parity between newsroom and community.

That gap is filled by this report, done for Knight Foundation by journalists Bill Dedman and Stephen K. Doig. Their report traces the historical record of nonwhite employment at 1,410 newspapers and compares the employment at each with the racial makeup of the area it serves.

LARGEST NEWSPAPERS SLIP

The nation's four largest newspapers have fallen from their peak: Gannett, the company with the best overall record on diversity, has seen nonwhite employment at its flagship USA Today slide since the 1994 report (employment at year-end 1993). The Wall Street Journal peaked in 2000, The New York Times in 2003 and The Los Angeles Times in 2000.

THE BIGGEST NEWSPAPERS: HOW DIVERSE?

The charts on these pages trace nonwhite employment at America's four largest newspapers as a percentage of newsroom staffs since 1990.

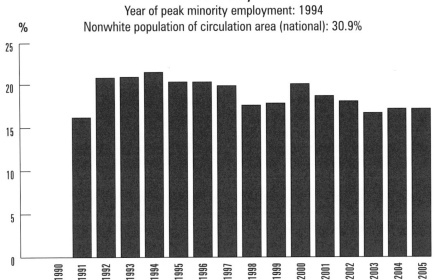

USA Today
Year of peak minority employment: 1994
Nonwhite population of circulation area (national): 30.9%

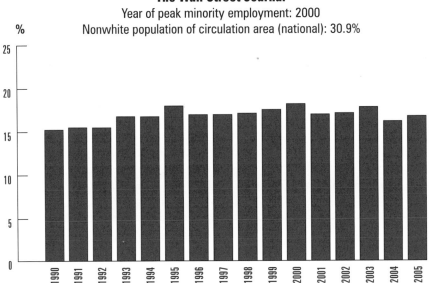

The Wall Street Journal
Year of peak minority employment: 2000
Nonwhite population of circulation area (national): 30.9%

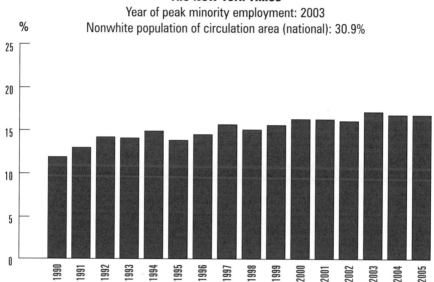

The New York Times
Year of peak minority employment: 2003
Nonwhite population of circulation area (national): 30.9%

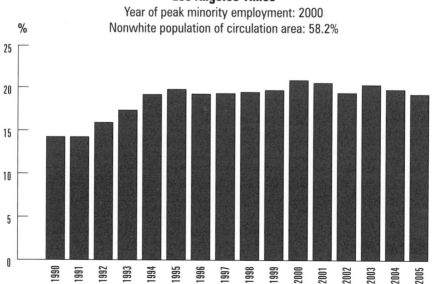

Los Angeles Times
Year of peak minority employment: 2000
Nonwhite population of circulation area: 58.2%

Other papers in the top 25 that are below their peak level of employing journalists of color are New York Daily News (peaked in 1995), The Washington Post (2004), The Dallas Morning News (2004), San Francisco Chronicle (1998), Newsday, Long Island (2002), The Star-Ledger, Newark (1998), Star Tribune, Minneapolis (2001), The Philadelphia Inquirer (2004), The Plain Dealer, Cleveland (1995) and The Miami Herald (1999).

Papers in the top 25 that reached their peak employment of nonwhites in 2005 are the Chicago Tribune, Houston Chronicle, The Boston Globe, The Arizona Republic (Phoenix), The Atlanta Journal-Constitution, Detroit Free Press, The Oregonian (Portland), St. Petersburg Times and The San Diego Union-Tribune. (Papers in the top 25 that did not respond to the 2005 ASNE survey were the New York Post and Chicago Sun-Times.)

FEW REACH PARITY

Comparing newspapers with their communities, only 13 percent of those responding to the survey have reached ASNE's goal of parity between newsroom and community. That's the same share as 2004.

Even that figure gives an optimistic portrait, because the researchers use figures from the 2000 Census. The nonwhite population has continued to grow rapidly, putting ASNE's goal of parity farther out of reach each year. In most communities, a newspaper maintaining the same percentage of nonwhite staff would be losing ground each year.

COMPANY MATTERS

Ownership is a large factor in determining a newspaper's newsroom diversity. Gannett Co. continues to be the leader, measured by a Newsroom Diversity Index that compares the share of jobs held by journalists of color with the nonwhite share of the population in the newspaper's circulation area. Gannett's index is 89 (100 equals parity with the circulation area).

Among the larger newspaper groups, the average index of all their newspapers (weighted by circulation) is:

Rank	Newspaper Company	Average Newsroom Diversity Index (100 =parity)
1	Gannett Co. (Va.)	89
2	Knight Ridder (Calif.)	76
3	McClatchy Co. (Calif.)	71
4	New York Times Co. (N.Y.)	69
5	Cox Enterprises (Ga.)	66
6	Advance (Newhouse) (N.Y.)	63
7	Freedom Communications (Calif.)	59
7	Pulitzer (Mo.)	59
9	Scripps (Ohio)	56
10	Tribune Co. (Ill.)	55
11	Dow Jones (N.Y.)	52
12	Washington Post (D.C.)	48
13	Lee Enterprises (Iowa)	47
13	MediaNews Group (Colo.)	47
15	Hearst Newspapers (N.Y.)	45
16	Copley Press (Calif.)	43
17	Community Newspaper Holdings (Ala.)	41
18	Belo (Texas)	40
19	Media General (Va.)	39
20	Liberty Group Publishing (Ill.)	32
21	Journal Register (N.J.)	24
22	Hollinger International (Ill.)	22
23	Morris Communications (Ga.)	21
24	Horizon Publications (Ill.)	19
25	Paxton Media Group (Ky.)	18
26	Ogden Newspapers (W.Va.)	12

(How the index is calculated: The Newsroom Diversity Index is the percentage of non-white newsroom staff divided by the percentage of nonwhite residents in the circulation area. Parity equals 100.)

The list is led by companies with well-known programs that reward managers—with bonuses – for the recruitment of journalists of color.

Some of the larger chains appear to have a farm team of journalists at their smaller newspapers, ready to move up to the larger newspapers. Leaving out USA Today, Gannett's other newspapers have a combined score of 103 – greater nonwhite employment than the nonwhite share of their circulation areas.

IT COULD BE WORSE

How can the industry generally show improvement in the ASNE surveys, even though many papers are falling behind?

It is clear that the increase in the employment of journalists of color at some newspapers is masking a decline at others.

And some papers that are below their historic peaks have made small gains in recent years. Fifty-seven percent of the largest 200 papers increased their percentage of nonwhite staff in 2004, while 32 percent of the broader list of all newspapers increased. (These figures reflect only those responding to the surveys.)

Another factor is that ASNE does not divulge the raw number of nonwhite journalists. It reports only the percentage of a newspaper's staff that is nonwhite. So it is difficult to know whether a paper truly increased the number of its journalists

of color, or whether the percentage increased as white journalists left.

Many newsrooms have downsized in recent years through involuntary layoffs, voluntary buyouts or attrition. Those cuts would tend to affect an older, and therefore more white group of journalists. If the newsroom shrinks, and whites leave, the nonwhite percentage can increase without a single additional journalist of color being hired. In 2005, ASNE reported that newsrooms have lost more than 2,200 journalists since 2001, a 4 percent decline, while the number of journalists of color has increased by 700, or nearly 11 percent.

Without the industry contraction, presumably the records on nonwhite hiring would look worse at many newspapers. Even with the contraction, most newspapers are below their peak nonwhite employment, as a share of the staff.

ALL-WHITE NEWSROOMS

The number of newspapers reporting an all-white newsroom declined a bit. There were 346 such newspapers in 2005 and 374 the year before. Their editors reported no journalists of color. As a share of all newspapers responding to ASNE's survey, the all-white papers were 37 percent in 2005, down from 40 percent in 2004.

Although many of these all-white newspapers are small, they have a combined weekday circulation of 3,337,478 – about the total of USA Today and The New York Times combined.

That all-white list doesn't include the 486 daily newspapers that ignored the annual ASNE survey. Of those, 275 papers reported an all-white newsroom on their latest report in a previous year. So the latest evidence from 44 percent of all newspapers (621 out of 1,410) showed entirely white newsrooms.

Many of these all-white papers are in relatively white communities, but not all: What do Greenwood, Miss., and Rocky Ford, Colo., have in common with Plainview, Texas,

Sumter, S.C., and Liberal, Kan.? These five communities have a majority of nonwhites in the newspapers' circulation areas, and all their editors reported having an entirely white newsroom. Another 40 all-white newsrooms serve communities where at least a quarter of the population is nonwhite.

Here are the top five U.S. daily newspapers reporting no journalists of color, ranked by nonwhite population in their circulation areas:

Rank	Circulation area nonwhite percentage	Newspaper, State	Ownership	Staff nonwhite percentage	Weekday circulation	Source for circulation area
1	66.2	The Greenwood Commonwealth, Mississippi	Emmerich Newspapers (Miss.)	0.0	7,607	ZIP Codes
2	59.7	Rocky Ford Daily Gazette, Colorado	Rocky Ford Publishing	0.0	3,013	Home City
3	54.9	Plainview Daily Herald, Texas	Hearst Newspapers (N.Y.)	0.0	6,481	Home County
4	54.3	The Item, Sumter, S.C.	H.D. Osteen Jr.	0.0	21,389	ZIP Codes
5	50.6	Southwest Daily Times, Liberal, Kan.	Lancaster family	0.0	4,250	Home County

Nor are all the all-white newsrooms in tiny communities. The all-white newsrooms with the largest daily circulation are:

Rank	Weekday circulation	Circulation area nonwhite percentage	Newspaper, State	Ownership
1	47,105	10.8	Billings Gazette, Montana	Lee Enterprises (Iowa)
2	47,083	9.5	The Pantagraph, Bloomington, Ill.	Pulitzer (Mo.)
3	42,463	8.2	The Macomb Daily, Mount Clemens, Mich.	Journal Register (N.J.)
4	33,714	5.1	Observer-Reporter, Washington, Pa.	Northrop family
5	32,745	4.0	The Scranton Times and The Tribune, Pennsylvania	Times-Shamrock (Pa.)

WHY THIS REPORT?

Since 1978, the American Society of Newspaper Editors has urged editors to improve news coverage by employing at least enough journalists of color to reflect their diverse communities. ASNE asks papers to report the percentage of editors, reporters, copy and layout editors, and photographers who are black, Hispanic, Asian or Native American. In 2005, ASNE again reported slow progress in total nonwhite employment, as a result falling further behind the growing nonwhite population of the nation.

Although ASNE's report shows each newspaper's nonwhite employment, it does not disclose how close that paper is to ASNE's goal, nor which papers are moving closer to the goal.

The Knight Foundation report builds on the ASNE survey by showing which newspapers, and newspaper chains, are closer to the ASNE goal than others. It compares the newsroom staffing, as reported to ASNE, with the circulation area population, using figures from the Audit Bureau of Circulations and the U.S. Census.

The report – on the web at *http://powerreporting.com/knight* – includes a separate web page for each of 1,410 daily newspapers, showing its history of nonwhite employment from 1990 to 2005; a Diversity Index comparing the newsroom nonwhite employment with its circulation area's population; a company-wide Diversity Index; a role model (another newspaper of similar size and circumstance with a higher Diversity Index) and details on the race and ethnicity of the circulation area and the home county. In addition, for the 866 papers that file audited sales

reports by ZIP code, the report shows the racial and ethnic breakdown in each ZIP code, the household income, and sales per household.

The Knight Foundation report is intended to help journalists, newspaper readers and community leaders discuss such questions as:

➤ In which communities and neighborhoods does our newspaper sell well? Or poorly?
➤ Are the low-sales neighborhoods explained by household incomes? By competition from other papers? Do race, ethnicity and language play a role?
➤ Does our newspaper have more readers in nonwhite areas than we had thought? Or fewer?
➤ Is our newspaper missing a business opportunity? Would having more reporters and editors of color help the paper get more news of interest to readers of color? Even with the current staff, what steps can the newspaper take to raise its awareness of news of interest to all readers?
➤ When did our newspaper's nonwhite staffing reach its peak? What has happened since? What are the barriers to hiring and retaining journalists of color?
➤ What explains the persistent number of all-white newsrooms, even in communities with many readers of color?

DISCUSSION TOPICS

1. How close are most newspapers to parity with their circulation areas?

The rarities are still the dailies reaching ASNE's goal. Only 13 percent of newspapers responding to the survey have reached parity between the newsroom and community, unchanged since the 2004 report and up slightly from the 11 percent in 2003.

Only 36 percent of newspapers are even halfway to the goal, up from 34 percent 2004.

Here's how newspapers were dispersed by Newsroom Diversity Index, which compares the newsroom nonwhite percentage with the community nonwhite percentage. (100 = parity.)

	Percent of Newspapers reporting			Number of Newspapers Reporting		
	2003	2004	2005	2003	2004	2005
100 percent parity or better	11%	13%	13%	101	123	120
75 to 99 percent	7%	7%	8%	61	61	74
50 to 74 percent	14%	14%	15%	129	132	136
25 to 49 percent	21%	18%	21%	195	169	191
1 to 24 percent	8%	8%	6%	75	73	57
All-white newsrooms	40%	40%	37%	372	374	346

2. How many newspapers are at their high-water mark?

For a historical perspective, the study looked at ASNE surveys from 1990 through 2005.

Of the 200 largest papers, 176 reported their employment figures for the latest year. Each of these reported at least one nonwhite employee. Of those 176 papers:

➤ 48 papers (27 percent) were at their peak.
➤ 128 papers (73 percent) were below their peak.

Of all 1,410 papers, 924 reported their employment for the latest year. The picture for those papers is more complicated because so many had all-white newsrooms, and many of those had never reported a nonwhite employee.

Of those 924 papers:

➤ 168 papers (18 percent) were at their peak, and reported at least one nonwhite journalist.
➤ 410 papers (44 percent) were below their peak, and reported at least one nonwhite journalist.
➤ 187 papers (20 percent) had at some point employed a nonwhite journalist, but fell back to an all-white newsroom in 2005.
➤ 159 papers (17 percent) reported an all-white newsroom, and have not reported a nonwhite employee for any year since 1990.

Here are the peak years of nonwhite employment for the 75 largest newspapers, along with their peak nonwhite staff percentage and their latest percentage. The 2005 ASNE report, issued in April 2005, reflects employment at the end of the previous year.

Rank by size	Peak year of nonwhite staffing	Newspaper, State	Community nonwhite population %	Peak nonwhite staffing (% of staff)	Latest nonwhite staffing (% of staff)	Latest year reporting
1	1994	USA Today (Va.)	30.9	21.4	17.2	2005
2	2000	The Wall Street Journal (N.Y.)	30.9	18.2	16.7	2005
3	2003	The New York Times (N.Y.)	30.9	17.1	16.7	2005
4	2000	Los Angeles Times (Calif.)	58.2	20.6	19.0	2005
5	1995	Daily News (N.Y.)	65.0	20.9	17.2	2005
6	2004	The Washington Post (D.C.)	43.2	22.6	21.4	2005
7	1994	New York Post (N.Y.)	40.3	17.3	13.9	2001
8	2005	Chicago Tribune (Ill.)	28.5	17.7	17.7	2005
9	2005	Houston Chronicle (Texas)	51.2	21.3	21.3	2005

Rank by size	Peak year of nonwhite staffing	Newspaper, State	Community nonwhite population %	Peak nonwhite staffing (% of staff)	Latest nonwhite staffing (% of staff)	Latest year reporting
10	2004	The Dallas Morning News (Texas)*	40.9	20.2	14.8	2005
11	1998	San Francisco Chronicle (Calif.)	46.8	20.7	16.8	2005
12	2002	Newsday, Long Island (N.Y.)	33.9	26.1	25.7	2005
13	2005	The Boston Globe (Mass.)	16.9	20.0	20.0	2005
14	2005	The Arizona Republic (Phoenix, Ariz.)	32.8	24.2	24.2	2005
15	1996	Chicago Sun-Times (Ill.)	50.3	23.0	23.0	1996
16	1998	The Star-Ledger (Newark, N.J.)	36.8	23.4	19.8	2005
17	2005	The Atlanta Journal-Constitution (Ga.)	38.1	23.0	23.0	2005
18	2001	Star Tribune (Minneapolis, Minn.)	14.6	14.6	14.5	2005
19	2004	The Philadelphia Inquirer (Pa.)	22.3	18.5	17.2	2005
20	1995	The Plain Dealer (Cleveland, Ohio)	24.5	17.9	14.8	2005
21	2005	Detroit Free Press (Mich.)	28.1	29.2	29.2	2005
22	2005	The Oregonian (Portland, Ore.)	18.2	18.8	18.8	2005
23	2005	St. Petersburg Times (Fla.)	15.8	16.5	16.5	2005
24	1999	The Miami Herald (Fla.)*	70.1	46.8	29.9	2005
25	2005	The San Diego Union-Tribune (Calif.)	45.5	17.1	17.1	2005
26	2005	The Orange County Register (Santa Ana, Calif.)	48.8	27.4	27.4	2005
27	2004	The Sacramento Bee (Calif.)	35.0	30.4	29.2	2005
28	2005	St. Louis Post-Dispatch (Mo.)	21.4	16.4	16.4	2005
29	2004	The Kansas City Star (Mo.)	20.4	17.9	17.3	2005
30	2005	The Denver Post (Colo.)	27.5	18.5	18.5	2005
31	2005	Rocky Mountain News (Denver, Colo.)	25.0	14.1	14.1	2005
32	1991	The Sun (Baltimore, Md.)	33.9	19.6	15.9	2005
33	2003	San Jose Mercury News (Calif.)	52.6	33.2	32.1	2005
34	1992	Orlando Sentinel (Fla.)	32.0	20.5	18.9	2005
35	2005	The Times-Picayune (New Orleans, La.)	43.6	17.1	17.1	2005
36	2005	The Indianapolis Star (Ind.)	20.0	14.4	14.4	2005
37	1991	The Columbus Dispatch (Ohio)	17.8	5.5	5.5	1991
38	1995	Boston Herald (Mass.)	24.1	11.2	5.5	2003
39	2005	Milwaukee Journal Sentinel (Wis.)	22.5	19.2	19.2	2005
40	1993	Pittsburgh Post-Gazette (Pa.)	13.2	10.8	9.6	2005
41	2005	South Florida Sun-Sentinel (Fort Lauderdale)	36.1	28.3	28.3	2005
42	1998	The Seattle Times (Wash.)	24.7	23.6	20.9	2005

*The diversity numbers do not include the journalists working for the newspaper's separate Spanish-language publication.

Rank by size	Peak year of nonwhite staffing	Newspaper, State	Community nonwhite population %	Peak nonwhite staffing (% of staff)	Latest nonwhite staffing (% of staff)	Latest year reporting
43	2005	The Tampa Tribune (Fla.)	32.4	9.8	9.8	2005
44	2004	San Antonio Express-News (Texas)	57.9	31.2	30.6	2005
45	2001	The Charlotte Observer (N.C.)	27.2	17.1	16.3	2005
46	2005	The Detroit News (Mich.)	21.6	26.2	26.2	2005
47	2004	Fort Worth Star-Telegram (Texas)	32.8	22.5	21.0	2005
48	2005	The Courier-Journal (Louisville, Ky.)	15.7	13.8	13.8	2005
49	2000	The Virginian-Pilot (Norfolk, Va.)	39.1	14.0	13.7	2005
50	2005	The Oklahoman (Oklahoma City)	24.4	25.5	25.5	2005
51	2003	The Buffalo News (N.Y.)	16.5	12.1	10.9	2005
52	2003	Omaha World-Herald (Neb.)	12.1	6.8	6.5	2005
53	1999	Hartford Courant (Conn.)	21.1	16.3	11.1	2005
54	2002	St. Paul Pioneer Press (Minn.)	13.9	18.0	17.9	2005
55	2005	Richmond Times-Dispatch (Va.)	36.6	12.9	12.9	2005
56	1993	The Cincinnati Enquirer (Ohio)	15.6	16.2	11.8	2005
57	2005	The Press-Enterprise (Riverside, Calif.)	49.4	25.0	25.0	2005
58	2005	Contra Costa Times (Walnut Creek, Calif.)	39.0	19.9	19.9	2005
59	1991	Arkansas Democrat-Gazette (Little Rock)	21.7	14.1	8.5	1992
60	1999	Los Angeles Daily News (Calif.)	52.3	17.8	16.7	2005
61	2005	Austin American-Statesman (Texas)	37.9	23.6	23.6	2005
62	2003	The Record (Hackensack, N.J.)	34.9	16.5	15.5	2005
63	1994	The Tennessean (Nashville, Tenn.)	19.5	20.9	20.2	2005
64	2004	The Palm Beach Post (West Palm Beach, Fla.)	30.9	19.0	17.6	2005
65	1997	The Providence Journal (R.I.)	17.3	9.4	5.4	2001
66	1998	Rochester Democrat and Chronicle (N.Y.)	17.9	16.7	15.3	2005
67	1997	The Florida Times-Union (Jacksonville)	29.6	18.8	10.4	2004
68	2005	The News & Observer (Raleigh, N.C.)	30.8	21.0	21.0	2005
69	2000	The Commercial Appeal (Memphis, Tenn.)	48.1	14.8	10.6	2005
70	1997	Asbury Park Press (Neptune, N.J.)	15.3	13.3	11.2	2005
71	2003	The Fresno Bee (Calif.)	57.6	30.6	25.0	2005
72	1993	Las Vegas Review-Journal (Nev.)	39.3	8.2	8.2	1993
73	2004	The Des Moines Register (Iowa)	8.3	12.5	12.3	2005
74	2005	Daily Herald (Arlington Heights, Ill.)	22.6	7.7	7.7	2005
75	1995	Seattle Post-Intelligencer (Wash.)	27.0	15.3	14.0	2005

3. How many newspapers are increasing their employment of journalists of color?

More than half of the largest newspapers employed a higher percentage of journalists of color in 2005 than a year earlier.

Looking at the raw ASNE figures for the top 200 newspapers, there were 164 reporting employment for those two years. Their trend:

➢ 57 percent improved, raising newsroom nonwhite percentages in the previous year
➢ 39 percent declined, lowering nonwhite percentages
➢ 4 percent stayed the same

Among newspapers of all sizes, gainers and losers were about even. There were 777 newspapers reporting employment for both 2005 and 2004. Their trend:

➢ 32 percent improved, raising nonwhite journalist percentages
➢ 22 percent declined, lowering nonwhite percentages
➢ 46 percent stayed the same

Taking a longer view, newspapers can be compared on their trends over one year, three years, five years and 10 years:

Largest 200 daily papers
A steady one-third of the large newspapers are not improving, even over 10 years.

One-year trend (164 papers reporting in both 2005 and 2004):

➢ 57 percent moved higher, increasing their nonwhite staffing percentage
➢ 39 percent moved lower
➢ 4 percent stayed the same

Three-year trend (163 papers reporting in both 2005 and 2002):

➢ 69 percent moved higher
➢ 29 percent moved lower
➢ 2 percent stayed the same

Five-year trend (165 papers reporting in both 2005 and 2000):

➢ 67 percent moved higher
➢ 30 percent moved lower
➢ 2 percent stayed the same

Ten-year trend (152 papers reporting in both 2005 and 1995):

➢ 68 percent moved higher
➢ 32 percent moved lower
➢ 0 percent stayed the same

All newspapers
Improvement has been slower among smaller newspapers, with fewer than half of all the papers showing gains, even over a decade.

One-year trend (777 papers reporting in 2005 and 2004):

➢ 32 percent increased their nonwhite staffing percentage
➢ 22 percent moved lower
➢ 46 percent stayed the same

Three-year trend (730 papers reporting in both 2005 and 2002):

➢ 43 percent moved higher
➢ 25 percent moved lower
➢ 32 percent stayed the same

Five-year trend (715 papers reporting in both 2005 and 2000):

➢ 46 percent moved higher
➢ 28 percent moved lower
➢ 26 percent stayed the same

Ten-year trend (691 papers reporting in both 2005 and 1995):

➢ 45 percent moved higher
➢ 27 percent moved lower
➢ 29 percent stayed the same

A final way of examining the pattern is a statistical analysis of the data, which does offer evidence that many newspapers are sensitive to building newsrooms that look something like the communities they serve. The analysis shows a moderately strong relationship between the percentage of nonwhite employees in the newspapers' circulation areas and the percentage of nonwhite journalists. In other words, the greater the nonwhite percentage of the community, the more likely a newspaper is to have a larger proportion of nonwhite journalists.

But the analysis shows that the pattern across the industry does not come near the ASNE ideal of parity. Of the newspapers that reported to ASNE, the analysis shows that every 10-point increase in community nonwhite percentage is accompanied by only about a 4 point increase in newsroom percentage. But this is an overall view; there is a great deal of variation from newspaper to newspaper. The outliers are the few newspapers that have reached the goal of parity and the many others still stuck at zero nonwhite journalists.

The analysis also shows that about 41 percent of the variation in newsroom percentage across newspapers can be predicted by the corresponding community percentage, but that means that other factors figure

heavily as well. Ownership of the newspaper clearly is one. But some other factors that can't readily be measured play a role, such as desire to meet the goal, desirability of the community as a place to live, racial change in the community, the reputation of a newspaper, the supply of nonwhite journalists in that area, and the extent of the newspaper's recruiting.

4. How many of the largest newspapers have staffs that are as diverse as their communities?

As this chart shows, there was some improvement at the top for the largest 100 newspapers in 2005, with three more newspapers reaching at least 75 percent of parity, for a total of 28. But more than one out of every four large newspapers remained below half of parity.

Among the top 100, the Newsroom Diversity Index at these 14 newspapers reached or exceeded parity:

Rank	Name	Newsroom Diversity Index (100=parity)
1	The Akron Beacon Journal	177
2	The Knoxville News-Sentinel	160
3	The Des Moines Register	148
4	St. Paul Pioneer Press	129
5	The Post-Standard (Syracuse, N.Y.)	127
6	The Detroit News	121
7	The Boston Globe	119
8	The Oklahoman (Oklahoma City)	105
9	St. Petersburg Times	104
10	Detroit Free Press	104
11	The Tennessean (Nashville)	103
12	The Oregonian (Portland)	103
13	Pittsburgh Tribune-Review	102
14	Lexington Herald-Leader	102

ABOUT THE RESEARCHERS

Bill Dedman *is managing editor for The Telegraph in Nashua, N.H. He is a former correspondent for The Boston Globe, where he wrote investigative articles, helped other reporters and editors, and trained the staff in computer-assisted reporting. While at The Atlanta Journal-Constitution, he received the 1989 Pulitzer Prize in investigative reporting for "The Color of Money," a series of articles on racial discrimination by mortgage lenders. His Power Reporting site on the web is used by many journalists as a starting point for research, and he has led seminars in more than 100 newsrooms. E-mail him at* Bill@PowerReporting.com.

Stephen K. Doig *holds the Knight Chair in Journalism, specializing in computer-assisted reporting at Arizona State University. Before joining ASU in 1996, he was research editor of The Miami Herald, where he worked for 19 years. Various computer-assisted projects on which he worked at The Herald have won the Pulitzer Prize for public service, the Investigative Reporters and Editors Award, the Goldsmith Prize for Investigative Reporting, and other awards. He is on the board of directors of Investigative Reporters and Editors. E-mail him at* Steve.Doig@ASU.edu.

Where to find more information

The full report is on the web at
http://powerreporting.com/knight/

Minority Broadcasters: No Progress in TV; Falling Behind in Radio

By Bob Papper

SUMMARY

Television news departments are holding steady in their employment of minorities, according to a 2005 survey of broadcast journalists. But radio news is falling behind, the annual survey by the Radio and Television News Directors Association and Ball State University shows.

In television, the minority work force remained largely unchanged at 21.2 percent, compared with 21.8 percent in the 2004 survey.

At non-Hispanic stations, the minority work force also remained largely steady at 19.5 percent, compared with 19.8 percent the year before.

After a jump in the 2004 minority radio numbers, the percentage fell for 2005. The minority work force in radio news came in at 7.9 percent, compared with 11.8 percent the year before. Except for last year, minority numbers in radio news have generally slipped since stringent Equal Employment Opportunity rules were eliminated in 1998.

The numbers for news directors were mixed, with the percentage of minority TV news directors down slightly to 12 percent (from 12.5 percent for 2004), while minority radio news directors rose substantially to 11 percent (from 8 percent).

The bigger picture remains unchanged. Over the past 15 years, the minority work force in TV news has risen 3.4 percent. At the same time, the minority population in the United States has increased 7.3 percent. Overall, the minority work force in TV has been at 20 percent – plus or minus 3 percent – for every year in the past 15. Some years it edges up, sometimes down, but there has been no consistent change. Radio is worse, with the minority percentage in news down from 15 years ago.

Minority Population vs. Minority Broadcast Work Force

	2005	2004	2000	1995	1990
Minority Population in U.S.	33.2%	32.8%	30.9%	27.9%	25.9%
Minority TV Work Force	21.2	21.8	21.0	17.1	17.8
Minority Radio Work Force	7.9	11.8	10.0	14.7	10.8

Source for population data: U.S. Census Bureau

Broadcast News Work Force

Television	2005	2004	2000	1995
Caucasian	78.8%	78.2%	79.0%	82.9%
African American	10.3	10.3	11.0	10.1
Hispanic	8.7	8.9	7.0	4.2
Asian American	1.9	2.2	3.0	2.2
Native American	0.3	0.5	<1.0	0.6
Radio	**2005**	**2004**	**2000**	**1995**
Caucasian	92.1%	88.2%	90.0%	85.3%
African American	0.7	7.3	5.0	5.7
Hispanic	6.0	3.9	3.0	7.5
Asian American	0.7	0.2	1.0	0.6
Native American	0.5	0.4	1.0	1.0

The minority TV news work force is down slightly – 21.2 percent for 2005 compared with 21.8 percent the year before. African Americans remained the same, but all other minority groups dropped slightly. Among non-Hispanic stations, the minority percentage was essentially unchanged at 19.5 percent, down slightly from the previous year's 19.8 percent.

The percentage of minorities in radio news dropped from 11.8 percent to 7.9 percent. That puts the number more in line with past minority percentages since the elimination of the strict EEO guidelines. The employment of Hispanics, Asian Americans and Native Americans in radio news increased over 2004, but African-American employment all but disappeared. Unfortunately, even as the number of radio stations contacted for the survey goes up each year, the number returning the survey continues to fall. That means the radio numbers tend to fluctuate, depending on which stations return the surveys and where those stations are located. And radio consolidation makes year-to-year comparisons even more difficult.

Broadcast News Directors

Television	2005	2004	2000	1995
Caucasian	88.0%	87.5%	86.0%	92.1%
African American	3.9	3.2	3.0	1.6
Hispanic	5.8	6.7	9.0	3.8
Asian American	1.3	1.3	2.0	1.5
Native American	1.0	1.3	<1.0	1.0
Radio	**2005**	**2004**	**2000**	**1995**
Caucasian	89.0%	92.0%	94.0%	91.4%
African American	0.0	2.7	3.0	5.4
Hispanic	8.8	2.7	2.0	2.4
Asian American	0.0	0.0	0.0	0.0
Native American	2.2	2.7	1.0	0.8

The percentage of minority TV news directors slid to 12 percent from 12.5 percent in 2004, although it's still the third highest ever. The percentage of African-American news directors rose and Asian-American news directors held steady, but the percentage of Native American and Hispanic news directors dropped.

At non-Hispanic stations, the minority percentage actually rose from 8.1 percent in 2004 to 8.4 percent. Excluding Hispanic stations, Hispanic news directors make up 2.8 percent of TV news directors. That's up 0.4 percent from last year. African-American TV news directors rose even more, from 3.2 percent to 3.9 percent. Asian-American news directors held steady at 1.3 percent, but Native American news directors fell from 1.3 percent to 1 percent.

Minority news directors were most likely to work in the biggest markets but were also most likely to be in the smallest news departments. CBS affiliates were the most likely to have minority news directors, and minorities were most likely to be news directors in the South and West.

In radio, the percentage of minority news directors rose from 8 percent in 2004 to 11 percent the next year. Minorities in radio were a little more likely to be news directors at noncommercial than commercial stations and more likely to be in the biggest markets and in the Northeast. They were less likely to be at group-owned stations.

Women in the Local Broadcast Work Force

TV News	News Staffs With Women	Women News Directors	Women as Percentage of Work Force	Average Number of Women on Staff
All Television	99.0%	21.3%	39.3%	14.3
Network affiliates	99.1	20.8	38.9	15.1
Independents	100.0	17.6	39.4	11.9
DMA* 1-25	96.8	39.0	39.0	22.7
DMA 26-50	100.0	19.2	40.0	21.5
DMA 51-100	100.0	18.0	38.0	14.2
DMA 101-150	98.6	17.1	40.7	11.3
DMA151+	· 98.2	18.2	39.0	7.3
Staff 51+	100.0	26.4	40.0	31.5
Staff 31-50	100.0	16.9	37.7	14.9
Staff 21-30	100.0	17.2	38.1	9.6
Staff 11-20	100.0	24.4	42.1	6.7
Staff 1-10	91.2	19.4	47.8	3.3
Radio News	**News Staffs With Women**	**Women News Directors**	**Women as Percentage of Work Force**	**Average Number of Women on Staff**
All Radio	47.6%	24.7%	27.5%	1.1
Major Market	90.0	30.8	33.7	2.9
Large Market	80.0	35.3	32.3	2.0
Medium Market	40.7	25.0	23.8	0.7
Small Market	23.3	16.1	18.6	0.4

*Designated Market Area, the term A.C. Nielsen uses to rank the country's television markets. The numbers refer to the size of the market, with DMA 1-25, for example, indicating the largest market in the nation.

Major markets are those with one million or more listeners. Large markets are from 250,000 to one million; medium markets are 50,000 to 250,000; and small markets are fewer than 50,000 listeners.

The numbers for women in TV news were little changed from 2004, although women news directors dropped for the second year in a row (from 25.2 percent to 21.3 percent in 2005). On the other hand, women were most likely to be news directors in the very largest markets and at the largest news departments. NBC affiliates were the most likely to have women news directors, and they were most likely to be in the Northeast.

Radio news numbers were also little changed. Generally, the bigger the market, the greater the likelihood of finding a woman news director and the higher the percentage of women in the news department. Women in the radio work force were most likely to be in the South and

Minorities in the Local Broadcast Work Force

TV News	News Staffs With Minorities	Minority News Directors	Minorities as Percentage of Work Force	Average Number of Minorities on Staff
All Television	87.2%	12.0%	21.2%	7.4
Network affiliates	87.2	5.3	20.0	7.7
Independents	96.4	20.0	18.6	5.6
DMA* 1-25	90.3	14.3	29.0	16.9
DMA 26-50	100.0	12.0	22.1	11.9
DMA 51-100	93.0	9.4	18.0	6.7
DMA 101-150	85.7	13.6	17.4	4.8
DMA 151+	67.3	7.0	14.7	2.7
Staff 51+	98.2	28.1	21.8	17.2
Staff 31-50	97.8	14.6	19.1	7.5
Staff 21-30	83.3	8.6	16.7	4.2
Staff 11-20	74.5	9.8	22.7	3.6
Staff 1-10	64.7	3.9	33.6	2.3
Radio News	**News Staffs With Minorities**	**Minority News Directors**	**Minorities as Percentage of Work Force**	**Average Number of Minorities on Staff**
All Radio	17.1%	11.0%	7.9%	0.3
Major Market	40.0	7.7	10.5	0.9
Large Market	40.0	11.8	9.7	0.6
Medium Market	7.4	12.9	2.5	0.1
Small Market	6.7	10.0	7.1	0.2

*Designated Market Area, the term A.C. Nielsen uses to rank the country's television markets. The numbers refer to the size of the market, with DMA 1-25, for example, indicating the largest market in the nation.

West; women news directors were less likely to be in the West.

Minorities were most likely to be found in the biggest TV markets, with their numbers dropping as market size fell. That has been the overall pattern in the past. The smallest news departments were also the most likely to have the highest percentage of minorities. Minorities were most likely to be in the South and West, but there was no difference by network affiliation.

There were few consistent trends for minorities in radio news, although minorities were generally most likely to be in larger markets – a pattern that has been true for years.

ABOUT THE SURVEY

The 2005 RTNDA/Ball State University
Annual Survey was conducted in the fourth
quarter of 2004 among all 1,624 operating,
nonsatellite television stations and a
random sample of 1,509 radio stations.
Valid responses came from 1,223 television
stations (75.3 percent) and 103 radio news
directors and general managers representing
417 radio stations. Data for women TV
news directors are a complete census and
are not projected from a smaller sample.

*Bob Papper is professor of telecommuni-
cations at Ball State University and has
worked extensively in radio and TV news.
Data entry and tabulation were done by the
Bureau of Business Research at Ball State.
This research was supported by the
Department of Telecommunications at Ball
State University and the Radio-Television
News Directors Association.*

Where to find more information

The full report is on the web at
http://rtndf.org/news/2005/071105.shtml

The American Journalist in the 21st Century

By David Weaver and G. Cleveland Wilhoit

This survey continues the series of major national studies of U.S. journalists begun in 1971 by sociologist John Johnstone and continued in 1982 and 1992 by David Weaver and G. Cleveland Wilhoit. Much as the U.S. Census does for the general population, these studies provide an important measure of the pulse of U.S. journalism every 10 years.

The latest survey, the fourth, was conducted in 2002 by researchers at Indiana University School of Journalism. Here are some of their key findings:

WOMEN JOURNALISTS: NO GAIN

Women are still one-third of all full-time journalists working for the traditional mainstream media, as they have been since 1982, even though more women than ever are graduating from journalism school and entering the profession. Among journalists with fewer than five years of work experience, 54.2 percent are women, outnumbering men for the first time. Among all journalists, the largest proportion of women work for newsmagazines (43.5 percent) and the smallest for the major wire services (20.3 percent) and radio (21.9 percent). Women compose 37.4 percent of television journalists, 36.9 percent of weekly newspaper journalists, and 33 percent of daily newspaper journalists.

Compared to the U.S. civilian work force in 2000, journalists are considerably less likely to be women (33 percent vs. 46.5 percent) and even less likely when compared to the overall U.S. managerial and professional work force, which included 49.8 percent women in 2000. Retention, then, is an issue.

Gender
Percentage of all journalists

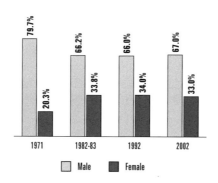

	1971	1982-83	1992	2002
Male	79.7%	66.2%	66.0%	67.0%
Female	20.3%	33.8%	34.0%	33.0%

☐ Male   ■ Female

MINORITY PROGRESS IS LOW

Overall, full-time journalists of color working for traditional news media have increased slightly during the past decade. Still, the percentage of full-time journalists of color working for traditional news media is well below the overall percentage of people of color in the U.S. population (30.9 percent according to the 2000 U.S. Census). A more appropriate comparison may be with the percentage of college degree holders who are people of color (24 percent according to the 2000 U.S. Census), considering that a four-year bachelor's degree is now the minimum educational requirement for U.S. journalists. Among people of color, Asians are the most likely to hold college degrees (43.9 percent), followed by blacks (16.5 percent) and Hispanics (10.6 percent). No separate census figures are reported for Native Americans or Pacific Islanders.

Journalists of color are more likely to be women (50 percent) than are white journalists (31.5 percent). Among all journalists with less than five years experience, 16.9 percent are people of color, suggesting that increased efforts to hire people of color in the past few years have made a difference. Television employs the largest percentage of people of color (14.7 percent) and weekly newspapers the lowest (5.6 percent). Daily newspapers are second with 9.6 percent, followed by the major wire services (8.7 percent), radio (8.6 percent) and newsmagazines (8.2 percent).

JOURNALISTS GROW OLDER

The median age of full-time U.S. journalists is increasing. In 1992, the average age of journalists was 36; in 2002, it was 41. The trend, which applies to journalists at daily and weekly newspapers, radio and television, newsmagazines and wire services, reflects the aging of the baby boom generation. During the 1970s, boomers inflated the 25- to 34-year-old age bracket in the American Journalist Survey. In the 1980s, they inflated the 35- to 44-year-old group. In the 1990s, the boomers moved into the 45- to 54-year-old age group, which increased from 14 percent of all journalists to 28 percent.

Compared to the 2000 U.S. civilian labor force, journalists in 2002 are considerably

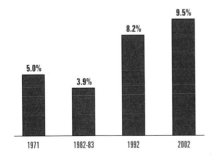

Journalists of Color
Percentage of all journalists

5.0% — 1971
3.9% — 1982-83
8.2% — 1992
9.5% — 2002

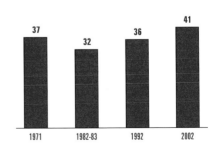

Age
Median for all journalists, in years

37 — 1971
32 — 1982-83
36 — 1992
41 — 2002

less likely to be younger than 24 years of age (4.4 percent vs. 16.1 percent), more likely to be 25 to 34 (29.3 percent vs. 22.5 percent), about as likely to be 35 to 44 (27.9 percent vs. 26.9 percent), more likely to be 45 to 54 (28.3 percent vs. 21.6 percent), slightly less likely to be 55 to 64 (7.8 percent vs. 9.9 percent), and about as likely to be 65 and older (2.3 percent vs. 3 percent).

FEWER JOURNALISTS ARE DEMOCRATS

Compared with 1992, the percentage of full-time journalists who claim to be Democrats had dropped 7 percentage points in 2002 to slightly above 37 percent, moving this figure closer to the overall population percentage of 32 percent, according to a July 29-31, 2002, Gallup national telephone poll of 1,003 adults. This is the lowest percentage of journalists saying they are Democrats since 1971.

Slightly more journalists said they were Republicans in 2002 (18.6 percent) than in 1992 (16.3 percent), but the 2002 figure is still notably lower than the percentage of U.S. adults who identified

with the Republican Party (31 percent, according to the Gallup poll mentioned above). About one-third of all journalists (33.5 percent) said they were Independents, which is very close to the figure for all U.S. adults (32 percent). Journalists in 2002 were much more likely than the general public, however, to say that they were something other than Democrat, Republican or Independent (10.5 percent vs. 1 percent).

The survey at Indiana University School of Journalism was funded by the John S. and James L. Knight Foundation. The authors are David Weaver, the Roy W. Howard professor in journalism and mass communication research; G. Cleveland Wilhoit, professor emeritus of journalism; Randal Beam, associate professor of journalism; Bonnie Brownlee, associate professor of journalism; and Paul Voakes, associate professor of journalism.

Democratic Party Affiliation
Percentage of all journalists

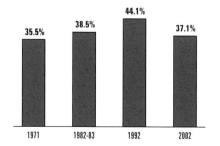

1971	1982-83	1992	2002
35.5%	38.5%	44.1%	37.1%

Study and Discussion Questions

CHAPTER 1: NEWS IN A NEW AMERICA

1. The Society of Professional Journalists asks journalists to seek "truth," not "the Truth" in its ethics policy in the belief that a universal, shared Truth does not exist. How might people have different ideas about the "truth" of an event, situation or idea? To what extent, and with what substantiation, can journalists conclude that something is an impartial truth?

2. Does an increase in newsroom staff diversity always change coverage? What else is necessary for inclusive journalism?

3. Based on trends today, what do you think the news media will look like in 2020? In 2050? What kind of stories will be important, and who will report them?

4. Look up the census data on your state and some of its major cities (See American FactFinder at *http://www.census.gov/main/ www/cen2000.html*). Does it meet your own perceptions of the people who live there? Why or why not?

5. Do you think that the news media in homogeneous communities – where people are almost all the same race or ethnicity, class, religion or age group – need to cover people outside of the prevailing group? Why or why not?

CHAPTER 2: THE HUMAN FACTOR

1. Try going to a neighborhood or community gathering where people are really different from you – because of their race, politics, language or disability, for instance.

Afterward, write or discuss how you felt. Was it hard to strike up conversations?

2. Do you think you have biases? What are they? In what ways do they hinder you? Are they useful to you in some way?

3. If your best sources on a general-interest topic all come from the same demographic group, is it necessary to look for more? Are there times when seeking diverse sources can skew news coverage?

4. Producer Tom Jacobs and media analyst Hemant Shah assert that the news media covers events from a "white" point of view. What do you think? Would we see different types of stories if it did or didn't? What about an "able-bodied" point of view that assumes everyone is nondisabled?

5. If The New York Times' Bill Keller is right, how should large, mainstream newspapers stretch beyond their urban, culturally liberal orientation?

6. Should journalists think about the unconscious biases or viewpoints that they might trigger with their reporting, as documented by David Domke, Franklin D. Gilliam Jr., Shanto Iyengar and others? Or would that be another form of introducing bias into stories?

7. What do you think of the term *refugee* to describe the evacuees from New Orleans? Based on Mahzarin Banaji's findings, how do you think the coverage of Hurricane Katrina might affect nonblack people's unconscious perceptions of African Americans?

CHAPTER 3: PRESSURES IN THE NEWSROOM

1. Many newsroom employees feel they do their best to make journalists of color, those with disabilities or those who are gay, lesbian or bisexual feel comfortable. What questions would you ask these reporters and editors to find out if hidden biases are at work?

2. Do you think that white people are ever stereotyped as racist, or men as sexist? How should they respond in that situation? Are there ways for them to ask questions or discuss their thoughts about race, ethnicity, gender, sexual orientation or other social categories without offending others or seeming biased?

3. Most newsrooms are trying to add diversity to their staffs by paying attention to hiring women and people of color. Should they also be working actively to hire gay, bisexual, lesbian or transgender people? What about people with disabilities? Conservatives? Religious people?

4. Look up some of the newsroom staffing data on newspapers in your region in Stephen Doig and Bill Dedman's database *(http://www.powerreporting.com/knight/)*. Do they meet your expectations? Are these outlets' demographics reflected in coverage?

5. Do you worry about being stereotyped? In what ways? What techniques do you use to influence what you think are other people's perceptions about you?

6. Erna Smith and Herbert Lowe emphasize the importance of newsroom culture in fostering creativity and openness. How can students and professors create an open culture in the classroom? How can student publications create a welcoming environment for all types of people?

CHAPTER 4: REFRAMING DIVERSITY

1. Pick up a copy of a publication written for immigrants, a community of color, homeless people, the older generation, people with disabilities, or gay, lesbian, bisexual or transgender people. What differences from general circulation news do you notice? Thinking as a reporter, did you get any story ideas?

2. Describe your own background. How do you think your own personal history – your race, class, gender, generation, ideology or the place you grew up – might limit the stories you see and the ways you report them? As a journalist, how might they help or hurt your reporting? How do you think you might expand your vision?

3. Chapter Four makes the case that standard news values and priorities tilt news coverage toward a white, male, heterosexual and middle-class world. What do you think? Are there fresh ways to think about news values and editorial priorities that might change this?

4. William McGowan worries about a "diversity orthodoxy" in the news media. Is this something to be concerned about? How could it affect coverage? What factors could cause it, and what would the risks be?

5. How could Venise Wagner's white students have asked their sources about race without having firsthand experience with discrimination?

6. Do you agree with David Domke that journalists should stop trying to be fully objective? Where would you draw the line on conflict of interest? How would news coverage change?

7. Do you think there are important issues in society today that are not discussed because of the way the news media chooses to cover or not cover them?

Thank you to professors Cristina Azocar, Beth Haller, Teresa Moore, Erna Smith and Venise Wagner and to author and independent journalist Peter Sussman for their feedback on these questions.

Further Reading

There are many excellent resources, from scholarly to news-based to personal essays, that can broaden journalists' understanding of inclusive news coverage. Many of those consulted for this book are listed here, by chapter.

CHAPTER 1: NEWS IN A NEW AMERICA

American Society of Newspaper Editors. *Newsroom Census. http://www.asne.org/index.cfm?id=5145* (2004). This professional association for newspaper editors each year surveys newspapers' staff counts of journalists of color and women. In 2005, out of 54,000 journalists across the country, 12.94 percent were journalists of color. Only one-third of super-visors, one-third of copy editors and reporters, and one-fourth of photographers were women. ASNE's web site also includes information about its diversity initiatives, including the Time Out for Diversity and Accuracy program.

Asian American Journalists Association.
http://www.aaja.org and
http://www.aaja.org/news/mediawatch/.
AAJA's mission is to encourage Asian Americans and Pacific Islanders to become journalists, to work for fair and accurate coverage of Asian Americans and Pacific Islanders, and to increase the numbers of Asian American and Pacific Islander news managers. The AAJA web site features news about the organization, community news and reports on news coverage of Asian Americans. You'll also find a stylebook for covering Asian Americans and its Media Watch page, which offers AAJA perspectives and action reports on news coverage concerns.

Cole, Yoji. "The Top 10 Companies for Diversity: What Makes Them Exemplary." Diversity Inc. June-July 2004, 56-76, and other articles. The magazine and web site Diversity Inc. says its editorial mission is "to provide information and clarity on the business benefits of diversity." Its readership includes senior management at large companies and smaller companies owned by women and people of color. Diversity Inc. has developed a set of benchmarks to help companies measure their progress in diversity. In 2005, 203 companies participated in its in-depth diversity survey, which laid the foundation for its annual ranking of the most diverse U.S. companies. The magazine also ranks top companies for recruitment and retention and other aspects of a diverse work force, explaining their tactics for success in its pages.

Davey, Monica. "Decades After First Refugees, Readying for More Hmong." The New York Times, April 4, 2004. This article details the anticipated arrival of 15,000 Hmong refugees in St. Paul, Minn., and cities in California, Wisconsin and North Carolina. The Hmong refugees, who had lived for years in a camp in Thailand after being driven from their homes in the final days of the Vietnam War, hoped to integrate into family and communi-ties established in the United States nearly 30 years ago.

Dedman, Bill, and Stephen K. Doig. "Newsroom Diversity Has Passed its Peak at Most Newspapers, 1990-2005 Study Shows." John S. and James L. Knight Foundation (2005). *http://www.powerreporting.com/knight/.* Dedman and Doig take the ASNE diversity numbers and compare them to the diversity in the popula-tion that the newspapers serve. The report includes a separate document on each paper, tracing its staffing history in relation to community composi-tion. The authors also analyze the track record of newspaper companies.

Entman, Robert, and Andrew Rojecki. *The Black Image in the White Mind: Media and Race in America.* University of Chicago Press, 2000. *http://www.raceandmedia.com/.* This influential book documents how news and entertainment broadcast media both reflect and help create the public's perceptions of race. The authors, scholars in communications and journalism, found overwhelm-ingly negative portrayals of African Americans across the media. As the publisher describes their conclusions: "While the authors find very little in the media that intentionally promotes racism, they find even less that advances racial harmony. They reveal instead a subtle pattern of images that, while making room for blacks, implies a racial hierarchy with whites on top and promotes a sense of difference and conflict."

Frey, William. *http://www.frey-demographer.org/ usdata.html.* Demographer and sociologist William Frey follows international and domestic migration in the United States and its implications. His reports include looks at segregation, intermarriage, and the shifting influence of age in the population. His web site features a tool that enables users to get a snapshot of population trends in their chosen city, state or region.

Greenwald, Anthony.
http://faculty.washington.edu/agg/bydate.htm. Greenwald, a social psychologist at the University of Washington, and one of the inventors of the Implicit Association Test, is an expert in social cognition, learning, and unconscious attitudes and associations. The web site lists his many articles and books.

Howard, Ina. "Power Sources: On Party, Gender, Race and Class, TV News Looks to the Most Powerful Groups." Extra (May-June 2002). *http://www.fair.org/extra/0205/power_sources.html.* In this study written for Extra by Media Tenor International, an international media analysis firm based in Germany, researchers reviewed the use of sources in 18,765 news reports from Jan. 1 to Dec. 31, 2001. The scope included 14,632 sources on three network evening news programs: ABC World News Tonight, CBS Evening News and NBC Nightly News. Researchers looked at political tilt as well as gender and race. Women made up 15 percent of the sources and men and women of color made up about 8 percent.

Kerner Commission. "Report of the National Advisory Commission on Civil Disorders." Washington: U.S. Government Printing Office, 1968. *http://historymatters.gmu.edu/search.php?function =print&id=6553.* The American Social History Project on the web (CUNY and George Mason University) offers a rich resource of American history, from original documents to course syllabi. In its section on the Kerner Commission, the authors explain: "President Lyndon Johnson formed an 11-member National Advisory Commission on Civil Disorders in July 1967 to explain the riots that plagued cities each summer since 1964 and to provide recommendations for the future. The Commission's 1968 report, informally known as the Kerner Report, concluded that the nation was 'moving toward two societies, one black, one white – separate and unequal.'"

Mattessich, Paul (Wilder Research Center), and Kate Parry (St. Paul Pioneer Press). "Speaking for Themselves: A Survey of Hispanic, Hmong, Russian and Somali Immigrants in Minneapolis-Saint Paul."

2000. *http://www.wilder.org/research/reports.* This 20-page report summarizes the findings of a survey of 1,119 immigrants from a random sample of more than 12,000 households in Twin Cities areas known to have a high portion of immigrants. It offers rare insight into how and why they came to Minnesota, how they work and play there, and their hopes and feelings of stress. The survey was part of a seven-week series on immigration that ran in the St. Paul Pioneer Press. For the Pioneer Press projects page, which includes several series on immigrants, see *http://www.twincities.com/mld/twincities/news/ special_packages/special_projects/.*

McGruder, Robert. Acceptance Speech, Helen Thomas Diversity Award. Detroit Free Press (Jan. 26, 2002).
http://www.freep.com/mcgruder/bgm_thomas.htm. The Helen Thomas Spirit of Diversity Award is given annually by Wayne State University to honor leadership in promoting diversity in the news media and coverage of the issues of race in America. Recent winners include former New York Times managing editor Gerald M. Boyd in 2003, retired Detroit Free Press publisher Heath Meriwether in 2004 and Poynter Institute dean Keith Woods in 2005. In his speech, McGruder introduced listeners to three strong black women who "taught me what I know about diversity," and explained the Detroit Free Press diversity initiatives. In conclusion, he pointed out, "It's something you have to fight for each day to be successful."

Media Tenor. "It's a Man's World – Even More in the Media." Media Tenor Quarterly 4 (September 2003), 36-37. *http://www.mediatenor.com.* This Media Tenor analysis looked at the portrayal of women and their use as sources in international broadcast news. In his summary of the findings, Roland Schatz, chief executive of Media Tenor, concluded, "Female politicians, scientists, entrepreneurs and bishops only appear in one out of six news stories. Thus U.S., British, German and South African news formats do not even remotely reflect the real power distribution in their respective parliaments, governments and universities; let alone the question of the effects that this type of news selection has on the perception of the developments inside and outside of these countries."

Mock, Ray. "Gays on TV – Commercially Viable, But Not Newsworthy?" Media Tenor Quarterly. (October, 2003). *http://www.mediatenor.com.* This study of gays on television news broadcasts found that "before the nomination of the first openly gay Episcopal bishop in New Hampshire and the same-sex marriage debate, there was no coverage of any issues surrounding homosexuality on the news at all, neither in the U.S. nor in the U.K.," Mock wrote.

Morrison, Peter.
http://www.rand.org/news/experts/bios/expert_morrison_dr_peter_a.html. Morrison, founding director of RAND Population Research Center, is a sociologist who tracks demographic trends and envisions their consequences. You can find his research and contact information on his web site. The RAND Population Matters Program focuses on population policy issues.
http://www.rand.org/labor/popmatters/index.html.

Moy, Patricia, David Domke and Keith Stamm.
"The Spiral of Silence and Public Opinion on Affirmative Action." Journalism and Mass Communication 78:1 (2001). 7–19.
http://www.com.washington.edu/Program/Faculty/Faculty/moy.html. Moy, an associate professor of communication at the University of Washington, and her colleagues evaluated attitudes about affirmative action using the "spiral of silence" theory developed by Elisabeth Noelle-Neumann. This theory holds that people are less likely to express opinions when they believe themselves to be in the minority. The team collected surveys from Washington state ferry riders to find out their willingness to speak on a controversial issue such as affirmative action, then explored how it was associated with their use of the news media. The team's research suggested that by giving people the information necessary to articulate their ideas and answer objections, "the news media have the potential to encourage more open and widespread participation in political discussion."

National Association of Black Journalists.
http://www.nabj.org. NABJ's 3,300 members make it the largest organization for journalists of color in the United States. NABJ focuses on strengthening ties among black journalists, supporting their work and efforts to climb the newsroom management ladder, and encouraging fairness in newsrooms. The NABJ web site includes news about the organization, information on workshops and awards, and resources including an online stylebook and a code of ethics.

National Association of Hispanic Journalists.
http://www.nahj.org. With its 2,300 members, NAHJ supports the recognition and professional advancement of Hispanics in the news media and media research. It emphasizes fair treatment in the news and in newsrooms, including a greater understanding of Latino journalists' cultural identity, interests and concerns. Its web site includes organization news, the Network Brownout Reports on Latinos in the news, a resource guide for covering Latinos and a stylebook for Spanish-language media.

National Center on Disability and Journalism.
http://www.ncdj.org. This organization strives to improve accuracy and fairness in the coverage of people with disabilities. Visit its web site for information on its educational resources, internship programs and a discussion group for journalists with disabilities. You'll find a style guide on the site and an extensive list of resources related to disability coverage among the links.

National Lesbian and Gay Journalists Association.
http://www.nlgja.org. NLGJA supports gay, lesbian, bisexual and transgender journalists, aiming to enhance opportunities and fairness in the newsroom. The organization also works for fair and accurate treatment of gay, lesbian, bisexual and transgender people in the news, on issues such as same-sex marriage, parenting and adoption, gays in the military, sex education, civil liberties, gay-related ballot initiatives, gay bashing and anti-gay violence. The NLGJA web site includes a stylebook on terminology.

Native American Journalists Association.
http://www.naja.com. NAJA works to improve communication among native people and between Native Americans and the nonnative public. It acts and offers programs to enrich journalism and to promote native cultures. Its web site includes association news, member news, community links and the Reading Red reports on news coverage of Native Americans. "The American Indian and the Media," edited by Mark Anthony Rolo, offers background on native issues and coverage concerns.

Papper, Bob. "Running in Place: Minorities and Women in Television See Little Change, While Minorities Fare Worse in Radio." Communicator (July-August 2005), 26-32.
http://www.rtnda.org/news/2005/071105.shtml (news release and link to the report and its breakdowns by job category and market size). Each year, Bob Papper, professor of communications, leads the Radio and Television News Directors/Ball

State University broadcast newsroom survey. In 2004, all 1,624 operating, nonsatellite television stations and a random sample of 1,509 local radio stations cooperated. He found that journalists of color made up 21.2 percent of television newsrooms, down slightly from 21.8 percent in 2003. Women made up 39.3 percent, about the same as 39.1 in 2003. In local radio, the portion of journalists of color dropped to 7.9 percent from 11.8 percent in 2003. Women in radio rose to 27.5 percent from 22.4 percent. (These proportions include the Spanish-language media.)

Pew Research Center for the People and the Press "Media Credibility Declines: News Audiences Increasingly Politicized." (2004). *http://people-press.org/reports/display.php3?PageID=833* (overview) and *http://people-press.org/reports/display.php3?PageID=838* (credibility data). This report analyzes where people go for news and how they feel about the quality of the information they are getting. News habits have remained fairly steady over the past couple of years, although more people are watching cable television news and consulting the Internet than before. Credibility is slumping in both broadcast and print outlets.

Society of Professional Journalists. The SPJ Code of Ethics. *http://www.spj.org/ethics.asp*. The Rainbow Sourcebook and Diversity Toolbox, a searchable database to make it easier for journalists to broaden perspectives and voices in the news. *http://www.spj.org/rainbowsourcebook*. SPJ is dedicated to a free press, open government and high journalistic standards in the service of democracy. Diversity in journalism is a core mission, along with professional development, freedom of information and ethics.

U.S. Census Bureau. "Census Bureau Projects Tripling of Hispanic and Asian Populations in 50 Years; Non-Hispanic Whites May Drop to Half of Total Population." Press release. 2004. *http://www.census.gov/Press-Release/www/releases/archives/population/001720.html*. The Census projects: "Overall, the country's population would continue to grow, increasing from 282.1 million in 2000 to 419.9 million in 2050. From 2000 to 2050, the non-Hispanic white population would increase from 195.7 million to 210.3 million, an increase of 14.6 million or 7 percent." The Census Bureau provides regular releases on population trends and offers a useful database that can help you identify who lives in your area and some of their charac-

teristics. In American FactFinder you can look up fact sheets on communities down to the size of a census tract, which can range from 1,500 to 8,000 people. Details include race, age, gender, languages spoken, whether people rent or own their houses, how many cars they own and whether they have plumbing.

Weaver, David, Randal Beam, Bonnie Brownlee, Paul Voakes and G. Cleveland Wilhoit. "Journalists of Color Are Slowly Increasing." The American Journalist Survey, Indiana University, 2003. *http://www.poynter.org/content/content_view.asp?id=28787*. The percentage of journalists of color remains well below that of the general U.S. population. Among news operations, television employs the most; weekly newspapers the least. Other parts of the study include information on gender, income, education and political persuasion.

CHAPTER 2: THE HUMAN FACTOR

Allport, Gordon. *The Nature of Prejudice.* New York: Perseus Books Group, 1954, 25th anniversary edition 1979. In this influential book, Harvard social psychologist Allport examined the roots of hostilities, rivalries and hateful ideologies. He explained stereotyping, ethnic division, group behavior and other core aspects of bias both within us and in our social environment.

American Association of Medical Colleges. Diversity Initiatives. 2004. *http://www.aamc.org/diversity/initiatives.htm*. The AAMC says it is working to increase diversity in medical education and advance health care equality through programs for high school and college students considering medical school; medical school students; medical school faculty, staff, and administrators and graduates.

American Medical Association. The AMA Minority Health Consortium monitors both professional issues and public health-care issues. Statistics on the number of female physicians can be found at *http://www.ama-assn.org/ama/pub/category/12928.html*. Statistics on physicians by race/ethnicity are at *http://www.ama-assn.org/ama/pub/category/12930.html*.

Appiah, Kwame Anthony, and Henry Louis Gates Jr., eds. *Africana: Civil Rights, an A-Z Reference of the Movement that Changed America.* Philadelphia:

Running Press, 2004. A rich reference guide to the people, events and places connected to the U.S. civil rights movement.

Astudillo, Rene. "Michelle Kwan Headline Continues to Haunt Us." AAJA News Media Watch, 2002. For more discussions on coverage of Asian Americans, see http://www.aaja.org/news/mediawatch/. Details about AAJA are in the Chapter 1 resources.

Blumrosen, Alfred and Ruth. "Intentional Job Discrimination in Metropolitan America." Rutgers University Law School, 2002. http://www.eeo1.com/index.htm. This report analyzes EEOC data on employees' race, ethnicity and gender to help employers, government and others identify probable intentional employment discrimination. The Blumrosens, professors at Rutgers University Law School, found that two million minorities and women were affected by intentional job discrimination, mainly by what they call hard-core discriminators, while about 75 percent of large establishments did not appear to discriminate.

Briggs, Kara, Tom Arviso, Dennis McAuliffe and Lori Edmo-Suppah. "The Reading Red Report. Native Americans in the News: A 2002 Report and Content Analysis on Coverage by the Largest News-papers in the United States." http://www.naja.com. This report reviewed coverage by the nine largest U.S. newspapers from Feb. 1, 1999, through Feb. 1, 2002. Most news stories about Native Americans fell into three areas, the authors reported: casino gaming by tribes, mascot team names and stories datelined "on the res."

Cunningham, Dwight. "Media Hurricane is Spinning Out of Control." National Newspaper Publishers Association, Sept. 7, 2005. http://www.louisianaweekly.com/weekly/news/articlegate.pl?200509907b. Cunningham, a special contributor to the NNPA, begins: "Watching TV newscasts on Hurricane Katrina's devastation, I am struck by the media's obvious tilt to covering the story of lawlessness, rather than the bigger story of people who had little in the way of material things before Hurricane Katrina – and who now have been reduced to having nothing at all."

Devos, Thierry, and Mahzarin R. Banaji. "American = White?" Journal of Personality and Social Psychology 88 (2005), 447-466. In six studies, the authors tested how closely participants associated three primary U.S. ethnic groups (black,

Asian and white) with the category "American." They asked for people's conscious beliefs about American identity, then checked both implicit and explicit associations with the word.

Dolhun, Eduardo Peña, Claudia Muñoz and Kevin Grumbach. "Cross-cultural Education in U.S. Medical Schools: Development of an Assessment Tool." Academic Medicine 78:6 (2003), 615-622. The authors asked medical schools to submit course materials on cross-cultural medicine and found considerable variation in teaching and content. Most courses emphasized general themes, such as the doctor-patient relationship, socioeconomic status and racism. They also provided specific cultural information about the ethnic communities they served.

Domke, David, Kelley McCoy and Marcos Torres. "News Media, Racial Perceptions, and Political Cognition." Communication Research 26:5 (1999), 570-607. http://faculty.washington.edu/domke/research.html. The authors write, "News coverage of political issues not only influences people's thinking about the issues but also activates associated stereo-types and influences whether these perceptions are applied in politically meaningful ways." To test these ideas, the authors systematically altered the news frame of immigration – as either material or ethical in nature – within a controlled political information environment to see how people process, interpret and use news information when forming political judgments.

Domke, David. "Racial Cues and Political Ideology: An Examination of Associative Priming." Communication Research 28:6 (2001), 772-801. http://faculty.washington.edu/domke/research.html. Domke studies the racial cues – references that call up images tied to particular racial and ethnic groups – in political coverage and political state-ments. In this experiment, he altered the description of crime in a controlled set of news stories to sometimes include these cues and sometimes not in order to examine how they may influence political judgments.

Jack Dovidio. http://dovidio.socialpsychology.org/. Dovidio studies prejudice, stereotyping and intergroup behavior. His books include On the Nature of Prejudice: Fifty Years after Allport (edited with Peter Glick and Laurie Rudman, 2005), Reducing Intergroup Bias (with Samuel Gaertner,

2000) and *The Social Psychology of Helping and Altruism* (with David A. Schroeder, Louis A. Penner and Jane A. Piliavin, 1995).

Entman, Robert. "The American Media and Race Relations in an Interdependent World: A report on the Shorenstein Center Conference on Race and the Press," Joan Shorenstein Center on the Press, Politics and Public Policy. (June 28, 2001). *http://www.ksg.harvard.edu/presspol/Research_Publications/Reports/Entman.pdf.* Entman summarizes a thought-provoking discussion on key issues such as how well the news media covers a progressively more diverse society; if there are deficiencies, how can they be fixed; and if race and ethnicity should be taken into account when choosing and reporting the news.

Fiske, Susan, Amy J.C. Cuddy, Peter Glick and Jun Xu. "A Model of (Often Mixed) Stereotype Content: Competence and Warmth Respectively Follow From Perceived Status and Competition." Journal of Personality and Social Psychology 82:6 (2002), 878–902. *http://fiske.socialpsychology.org/.* Susan Fiske, social psychologist at Princeton University, studies the ways people categorize each other based on perceived warmth and competence, then react accordingly. Fiske has found that reporters follow predictable patterns of group categorization in their writing. In a study of 200 news articles in 35 publications over two years, feminists and black professionals were routinely depicted as stereotypically competent, but cold. This was accomplished through descriptions that emphasized ambition, confidence and independence, but also illustrated insincerity, aggression or intolerance. Portrayals of housewives and elderly people cast them as warm but not competent. Word choices in their case highlighted a lack of competition, ambition, independence or confidence, but also underlined the subjects' sincerity, good nature, altruism or family ties.

Gandy, Oscar H., Jr., and Jonathan Baron. "Inequality: It's All in the Way You Look at It." Communication Research 25:5 (1998), 505-527. This paper looks at the differences in the ways black people and white people perceive inequalities, including their severity and what causes them. The authors performed a secondary analysis of phone survey data on attitudes about race collected by The Washington Post, the Henry J. Kaiser Foundation and Harvard University. They found that exposure to news stories on race and affirmative action had a significant effect on social comparisons, and led to both groups being less likely to blame African Americans for the hardships they endure. Gandy is author of the influential *Communication and Race: A Structural Perspective.* The book explores race by analyzing media institutions and how they operate; symbolism, coverage themes and story lines; and social constructions. In it, Gandy applies behavioral science, political economy and cultural studies to information media.

Gilliam, Franklin D., Jr., and Shanto Iyengar. "Prime Suspects: The Influence of Local Television News on the Viewing Public." American Journal of Political Science 44:3 (2000), 560–573. The authors assessed the impact of the "crime script" on viewers of television news. When racial elements were included in the crime report, white (but not black) viewers expressed more support for punitive approaches to crime and heightened negative attitudes about African Americans.

Global Language Monitor. *http://www.languagemonitor.com/.* Founded by former high-tech marketer Paul JJ Payack, this organization analyzes word use in media, politics and workplaces around the world. The site offers timely updates on buzzwords and a place to report in to the "language police."

Graham, Sandra, and Brian Lowery. "Priming Unconscious Racial Stereotypes About Adolescent Offenders." Law and Human Behavior 28:5, (2004)483–504. In two studies, one with police officers and one with juvenile-probation officers, researchers tested how racial "priming" might influence decisions about punishment. As hypothesized, officers who had been unconsciously alerted to race with words such as *Harlem, homeboy* and *dreadlocks* were more likely to make judgments about negative traits such as hostility, find greater culpability and expect repeat offenses. They endorsed harsher punishment than did officers who hadn't been given racial cues. The effects were unrelated to consciously held attitudes.

Kaiser Family Foundation. "AIDS at 21: Media Coverage of the HIV Epidemic, 1981-2002." (2004) *http://www.kff.org/kaiserpolls/7025.cfm.* This report, conducted with Princeton Survey Research Associates, examines aspects of media coverage, including key events, domestic versus international focus, the portrayal of affected populations, story topics and tone, story length and placement, and consumer education components.

Kaiser Family Foundation and Robert Wood Johnson Foundation. "Why the Difference?" (2002). *http://www.kff.org/whythedifference/*. Recent research and news on disparities in cardiac care with an eye toward educating physicians.

Longmore, Paul. *Why I Burned My Book and Other Essays on Disability*. Temple University Press, 2003. Longmore breaks down the social, political and historical place of disability in U.S. society for readers, revealing both hidden bias and structural discrimination. One essay addresses stereotypes in television and movie imagery, and the discussion throughout exposes the limitations created by framing disability solely as a medical issue. Longmore directs the Institute on Disability Studies at San Francisco State University.

Maass, Anne, Roberta Ceccarelli and Samantha Rudin. "Linguistic Intergroup Bias: Evidence for In-Group-Protective Motivation." Journal of Personality and Social Psychology 71:3 (1996), 512-526. Linguistic intergroup bias refers to our tendency to describe positive behavior in our own group – but negative behavior in a group of "outsiders" – with more abstract terms. Bad behavior in our own group, but good behavior by an outsider, gets more concrete language. As a result, positive actions by someone in one's own group seem a part of their nature, but negative actions seem unusual. The authors tested this tendency among hunters and environmentalists in Italy. When members of one group were presented with hostile statements from the other, the effect intensified. The results were comparable in tests with northern and southern Italians. The authors concluded that when a group felt its identity threatened, their use of biased language that favored their own kind increased.

Mankiller, Wilma, Vine Deloria Jr., Barbara Deloria, Kristen Foehner and Sam Scinta, eds. *Spirit and Reason: The Vine Deloria Jr. Reader.* Golden, Colo.: Fulcrum Publishing, 1999. Deloria wrote many classics on American Indian law, history, politics and spirituality. This book, a series of informative and thought-provoking essays, is an excellent way to introduce yourself to his thinking on philosophy, education, Indian affairs, religion and science.

Media and Disability Resources. *http://saber.towson.edu/%7Ebhalle/disable.html*. A project of the Media & Disability Interest Group of the Association for Education in Journalism and Mass Communication, this web site includes an extensive bibliography and a page of mass media and disability links, including accessibility resources, disability-oriented news outlets, publications by disability organizations and research groups. Compiled by Beth Haller, associate professor of journalism at Towson University.

Media Tenor International. "Coverage of ethnic and racial groups in U.S. Media: 01/02 - 8/04." 2004. *http://www.mediatenor.com/index1.html*. Media Tenor, an independent media analysis institute, analyzed all news reports in five major outlets between January 2002 and August 2004 in which a member of a selected number of ethnic and racial groups was the main protagonist of the story. The survey included Time, Newsweek, The Wall Street Journal, and the NBC, ABC and CBS nightly news shows. The authors reported that coverage of ethnic and racial groups in leading U.S. media presents trends that, more than representing various groups of the society, may help feed stereotypes.

Mosley, Letha J. "Negotiation of Sociopolitical Issues in Medical Education Program Planning That Addresses Racial and Ethnic Disparities." Unpublished dissertation, University of Georgia, 2005. Mosley studied the qualities of successful diversity programs in medical schools and their most challenging – and often hidden – roadblocks.

The New York Times Credibility Group. "Preserving Our Reader's Trust." The New York Times, 2005. *http://www.nytco.com/pdf/siegal-report 050205.pdf*. This 16-page report to the executive editor focuses mainly on developing a dialogue with readers, limiting the use of unidentified sources and reducing factual errors. In a section on the news-opinion divide, the committee recommends holding strong to diversity goals in gender, race and ethnicity, as well as pursuing diversity in other dimensions of life to ensure a broad range of viewpoints.

Nieman Foundation for Journalism at Harvard University. "Covering Indian Country." Nieman Reports 59:3 (Fall 2005), 5-41. *http://www.nieman.harvard.edu/*. A collection of 14 articles and essays that challenge stereotypes, offer practical tips, and introduce journalists off the reservation to the tribal press.

Nosek, Brian A., Mahzarin R. Banaji and Anthony G. Greenwald. "Harvesting Implicit Group Attitudes and Beliefs From a Demonstration Web Site." Group Dynamics 6:1 (2002), 101-115. The researchers tabulated responses by users of their Implicit Association Test Internet site. Over the study period from October 1998 to April 2000, users completed more than 600,000 tasks to measure their attitudes toward social groups and the stereotypes they hold. The researchers break down the data to learn more about the operations of attitudes and stereotypes, including the strength of unconscious attitudes, the association between conscious and unconscious attitudes or the lack thereof, and the effects of feeling part of a particular group.

Noveck, Jocelyn. "Use of Word 'Refugee' Stirs Race Debate." Associated Press. Sept. 7, 2005. *http://news.yahoo.com/s/ap/20050906/ap_on_re_ us/katrina_refugees__hk4*. The Associated Press explains its position on the use of the word refugee in the context of Hurricane Katrina.

Olsson, Andreas, Jeffrey P. Ebert, Mahzarin R. Banaji and Elizabeth A. Phelps. "The Role of Social Groups in the Persistence of Learned Fear." Science 309:5735 (July 29, 2005), 785-787. *http://www.sciencemag.org/cgi/content/abstract/ 309/5735/785*. The authors looked at fear conditioning and how it may apply when humans learn to associate social in-group and out-group members with a fearful event. They concluded, "Our results indicate that individuals from a racial group other than one's own are more readily associated with an aversive stimulus than individuals of one's own race, among both white and black Americans. This prepared fear response might be reduced by close, positive interracial contact."

Plous, Scott, ed. *Understanding Prejudice and Discrimination*. New York: McGraw-Hill Higher Education, 2003. *http://www.understandingprejudice.org*. A compila- tion of readings from a broad range of scholarly disciplines. The web site includes interactive exer- cises and demonstrations, streaming video clips and other resources.

Ragged Edge Magazine. *http://www.raggededgemagazine.com* and

http://www.mediacircus.org. Blogs, libraries and political commentary from a disability rights perspective. Visit the "Language and Usage Guide for Reporters and Editors" in the Media Circus section.

Shah, Hemant. *http://www.journalism.wisc.edu/ faculty/shahhbio.html*. Shah is a professor of communication at the University of Wisconsin- Madison. He specializes in global media and cultural identity, development theory and history, and mass media representation of race and ethnicity.

Smedley, Brian, Adrienne Stith and Alan Nelson. *Unequal Treatment: Confronting Racial and Ethnic Disparities in Health Care*. Washington: National Academies Press. 2003. *http://www.iom.edu/report.asp?id=4475* and *http://www4.nationalacademies.org/onpi/webextra. nsf/web/minority?OpenDocument*. Racial and ethnic minorities tend to receive a lower quality health care than nonminorities, even when access-related factors, such as insurance and income, are controlled.

Smedley, Brian. *http://www.opportunityagenda.com*. Smedley is now research director of The Opportunity Agenda, a policy think tank that describes itself as "devoted to expanding opportunity and human rights in the United States." Its first projects will concentrate on criminal justice and access to health care.

Takaki, Ronald. *A Different Mirror: A History of Multicultural America*. Reissue edition. New York: Back Bay Books, 1994. This important and engaging book takes readers through the story of America from the perspectives of all the peoples who have been part of this country's history. Packed with the authentic voices of the Indian, African American, Mexican, Japanese, Chinese, Irish and Jewish people of America, it's an essential contribution to every journalist's bookshelf. Takaki is a professor of ethnic studies at UC Berkeley.

Watson, Brendan. "Stalemate, Xenophobia and the Framing of the Immigration Debate." Association for Education in Journalism and Mass Communication, Aug. 10-13, 2005, San Antonio, Texas. *http://www.aejmc.org*. This content analysis reviewed newspaper coverage of Hispanic immi- gration from Jan. 7, 2004, to May 14, 2004. The search identified 166 articles, and then reviewed news frames, reporter ethnicity, story and source tone, and source affiliation. The author found significant differences in the ways Hispanics and non-Hispanics report on immigration topics.

Westin, Av. "You've Got to Be Carefully Taught: Racist Encoding in Television Newsrooms." Nieman Reports. 1:55 (Spring 2001), 63. *http://www.nieman.harvard.edu/reports/contents.html*. Based on 120 interviews with broadcast newsroom staffers, Westin's report concluded that while blatantly racial bigotry was absent, news decisions were guided by an understanding about race that played a role in story selection and content, the editorial point of view and who served as expert sources.

CHAPTER 2 CLOSE-UP

Barlow, Andrew. *Between Fear and Hope: Globalization and Race in the United States.* Lanham, Md.: Rowman & Littlefield, 2003. In this book Barlow examines race from a structural and historical perspective, exploring how market global-ization both reinforces and challenges existing social stratification.

Bonilla-Silva, Eduardo. *Racism Without Racists: Color-Blind Racism and the Persistence of Racial Inequality in the United States.* Lanham, Md.: Rowman & Littlefield, 2003. Bonilla-Silva challenges many people's assumptions that racism has been eliminated from U.S. society. He details subtle forms of discrimination that work to maintain white privilege and calls for change.

Brown, Michael, Martin Carnoy, Elliott Currie, Troy Duster, David B. Oppenheimer, Marjorie M. Shultz and David Wellman. *Whitewashing Race: The Myth of a Colorblind Society.* Berkeley: University of California Press, 2003. This book also attacks the idea that racial discrimination and racist ideologies are things of the past. The authors – sociologists, political scientists, economists, criminologists and legal scholars – detail inequities that persist in wages, income, access to housing, health care and the like and describe the ways these have been built into the structure of U.S. society. They close by offering ways to renew America's commitment to social equality.

Hacker, Andrew. *Two Nations Black and White: Separate, Hostile and Unequal.* New York: Ballantine Books, 1992. Hacker tackles the reasons why racial disparities, interracial tensions and segregation continue to exist. He describes the realities of income, employment, education, family life and other aspects of life that separate racial groups and forecasts their ongoing impact.

Thernstrom, Stephen, and Abigail Thernstrom. *America in Black and White: One Nation Indivisible.* New York: Simon and Schuster, 1997. This study of race in the United States takes a historical perspective to make the argument that the United States is becoming a more just and cohesive society. The authors argue against affirmative action and comparable policies that they say heighten racial consciousness and division.

CHAPTER 3: PRESSURES IN THE NEWSROOM

Alwood, Edward. *Straight News: Gays, Lesbians and the News Media.* New York: Columbia University Press, 1996. *http://www.asne.org/index.cfm?id=5145*. Former CNN correspondent Alwood brings a news-man's perspective to the history of coverage of gays and lesbians from World War II to the '90s. He introduces readers to battles both inside and out-side the newsroom as the news media struggled with its own fears and assumptions when represent-ing LGBT issues and lives.

American Society of Newspaper Editors. "Newsroom Employment Drops Again; Diversity Gains." Press release, 2004. See Chapter 1 resource list for full description.

Andrews, Peter. "Virtual Teaming: You Don't Know Me, But ... Executive Technology Report." New York: IBM Advanced Business Institute, 2004. *http://www-1.ibm.com/services/us/index.wss/mp/ imc/xt/a1001285/1?cntxtId=a1000401*. A report on building teams effectively.

Arnold, Mary, Marlene Lozada Hendrickson and Cynthia C. Linton. "Women in Newspapers 2003: Challenging the Status Quo." Media Management Center, Northwestern University, 2004. *http:// www. mediamanagementcenter.org/publications/ win2003.asp*. The 57-page report profiles six women executives, detailing how they benefited from mentors and broke the glass ceiling. It includes an essay on women's leadership styles.

Branch, Gregory, and Claudia Pryor. "Race Plays a Decisive Role in News Content." Nieman Reports, 55:1 (Spring 2001), 65.

http://www.nieman.harvard.edu/reports/contents.html
The story behind Network Refugees, the nonprofit
film and documentary production company
dedicated to telling stories about people of color
and the issues that affect them.

Carney, Susan. "Battling Bias in the Factory:
Automakers Struggle to Stem Harassment." The
Detroit News, 2002.
http://www.detnews.com/2002/autosinsider/0210/
09/a01-605292.htm. Allegations of harassment
remain a fact of life in car and truck assembly
plants, The Detroit News reports. About 500
complaints of racial or sexual harassment and
discrimination were filed to government regulators
each year between 1992 and 2001.

Carstarphen, Meta. "Can We Talk? Racial Discourse
as a Community-Building Paradigm for
Journalists." Paper for the Association for
Education in Journalism and Communication,
Kansas City, Mo., Aug. 2, 2003.
http://web2.unt.edu/news/print.cfm?story=7291.
Carstarphen was a Poynter Research Fellow in
1997-98 and is the author of Writing PR: A Multimedia Approach. Boston: Allyn & Bacon, 2004.

Demchak, Teresa. More information on Teresa
Demchak's civil rights and employment discrimination cases can be found on the web site of her law
firm, Goldstein, Demchak, Baller, Borgen & Dardarian.
Civil rights: http://
www.gdblegal.com/whatwedo.php?menuItem=32.
Employment: http://
www.gdblegal.com/whatwedo.php?menuItem=33.
Media reports: http://www.gdblegal.com/press.php.

Dedman, Bill, and Stephen K. Doig. "Does Your
Newspaper Reflect its Community?" John S. and
James L. Knight Foundation (April 2003 and May
2004).
http://www.powerreporting.com/knight/2003/.
See the web site for newspaper editors' estimates
of the diversity in their communities. For Dedman
and Doig's data on The Greenwood (Miss.)
Commonwealth, go to
http://www.powerreporting.com/knight/ms_the_
greenwood_commonwealth.html. For a description
of the project, see the Chapter 1 resource list.

Dovidio, Jack. http://dovidio.socialpsychology.org/.
Dovidio studies prejudice, stereotyping and intergroup behavior. See Chapter 2 resource list for more
information.

Fiske, Susan, Amy J.C. Cuddy, Peter Glick and
Jun Xu. "A Model of (Often Mixed) Stereotype
Content: Competence and Warmth Respectively
Follow from Perceived Status and Competition."
Journal of Personality and Social Psychology 82:6
(2002), 878–902. http://fiske.socialpsychology.org/.
Susan Fiske, social psychologist at Princeton
University, studies the ways people categorize
each other based on perceived warmth and
competence, then react accordingly. For more
description, see Chapter 2 resource list.

Glick, Peter, and Susan Fiske. "An Ambivalent
Alliance: Hostile and Benevolent Sexism as
Complementary Justifications for Gender
Inequality." American Psychologist 56 (2001),
109-118. Fiske and Glick review research on sexism
that is manifested as hostility toward women, and
sexism that idealizes women. The article shows
how paternalistic attitudes, which are sometimes
embraced by women themselves, help enforce
inequality and conventional gender roles.

The Greenwood (Miss.) Commonwealth.
http://www.zwire.com/site/news.cfm?brd=1838.

Grutter v. Bollinger, U.S. Supreme Court (2003).
3M, et al (Fortune 500 Corporations): Brief for
Amici Curiae.
http://www.umich.edu/~urel/admissions/legal/
gru_amicus. Amicus briefs for these parallel cases
involving affirmative action in law school and
undergraduate admissions at the University of
Michigan. For an overview of Grutter v. Bollinger
and Gratz v. Bollinger, court filings and supporting
research, see
http://www.umich.edu/~urel/admissions.

Haiman, Robert. "Best Practices for Newspaper
Journalists," Freedom Forum (2000).
http://www.freedomforum.org/templates/document.
asp?documentID=12828. A guide to journalistic
fairness for reporters, editors and others; part of
the Free Press/Fair Press Project.

Hammonds, Keith. "Difference is Power." Fast
Company (July 2000), 258. A profile of Ted Childs,
IBM's vice president of global workforce diversity,
who explains why diversity is good business.

Jensen, Ray. An outline of Ford Motor Co.'s work-
force diversity programs.
http://www.ford.com/en/company/about/corporate
Citizenship/report/principlesRelationshipsDiversity.htm.

For an interesting history of diversity programs at Ford, starting with its hiring of immigrants in 1913, see Charles E. Ramirez, "Ford Motor Pioneers Diversity." The Detroit News (June 9, 2003). *http://www.detnews.com/2003/specialreport/0306/09/f18-187024.htm.*

Jones, Charisse, and Kumea Shorter-Gooden. *Shifting: The Double Lives of Black Women in America.* New York: HarperCollins, 2003. *http://www.harpercollins.com/global_scripts/product_catalog/book_xml.asp?isbn=0060090553.* This book is based on the African American Women's Voices Project, an interview and questionnaire study of 400 women across the United States. USA Today staff writer Charisse Jones and psychologist Kumea Shorter-Gooden document the ways black women change inwardly and outwardly as they respond to race and gender expectations. The price can include anxiety, low self-esteem and even self-hatred, the authors say.

Larson, Christine. "2003 Salary Survey: Behind the Numbers." NAFE Magazine (2003). *http://www.nafe.com/ef_fall.shtml.* While the overall gender gap in wages is 76 cents on the dollar, it's wider in some industries.

Lawrence, David. Robert G. McGruder Lecture and Award. Kent State University. 2004. *http://imagine.kent.edu/media/content/press.asp?id=373.* Kent State makes this award to those who share McGruder's passion and commitment to diversity in the news media. While Lawrence was publisher at The Miami Herald, the paper won five Pulitzer Prizes. Before that, he was publisher at the Detroit Free Press. He has won several national honors for his achievements in the diversity area. Lawrence retired in 1999 and began working on early childhood development initiatives.

McGill, Lawrence. "What Research Tells Us About Retaining Newspaper Journalists of Color: A meta-analysis of 13 studies conducted from 1989 to 2000." ASNE and Freedom Forum (2001). *http://www.asne.org/index.cfm?id=1477.* McGill writes, "Across different surveys, between one-fifth and one-third of journalists of color interviewed have indicated that they do not expect to remain in journalism over the long term." Their biggest disappointments are lack of professional challenge and lack of opportunities for advancement.

National Association of Female Executives. *http://nafe.com/.* The largest women's professional association and the largest women business owners' organization in the United States. Owned by Working Mother Media, it provides resources, networking opportunities and public advocacy for members, publishes magazines and runs a conference division.

Papper, Bob. (2005). See the Chapter 1 resource list.

Pease, Edward, Erna Smith and Federico Subervi. "The News and Race Models of Excellence Project – Overview Connecting Newsroom Attitudes Toward Ethnicity and News Content." (2001). *http://www.maynardije.org/resources/industry_studies/.* This 46-page report examines the link between news content and newsroom attitudes toward race and ethnicity. Background on Edward Pease can be found at *http://www.usu.edu/communic/faculty/pease/tpease.html.* For a Q&A with Erna Smith as part of a Stockholm University project, see *http://jolo.jmk.su.se/students/global04/other/plural/ernasmithquestions.htm.* Her San Francisco State University faculty web page is *http://www.journalism.sfsu.edu/departmentinfo/e_smith.htm.* Federico Subervi runs the Latinos and Media Project, which features a database of news media articles on Latinos, research articles, web-site links and other information. *http://www.latinosandmedia.org/contact.html.*

Rendall, Steve and Will Creeley. "White Noise: Voices of Color Scarce on Urban Public Radio." Extra! (September-October 2002). *http://www.fair.org/extra/0209/white-noise.html.* According to this 2002 survey, the voices on public radio in seven major urban markets are overwhelmingly white and male.

Simmons, Debra Adams. "It's a Great Time to Be a Woman Editor." The American Editor (March 2005). *http://www.asne.org/kiosk/editor/tae.htm.* Simmons tells her story in a special issue of The American Editor about women editors. The ASNE magazine also includes stories about "being the only woman in the room," and "the thrill and the nightmare" of being a publisher. The Akron (Ohio) Beacon Journal has an outstanding track record in diversity. Its publisher, Jim Crutchfield, and editor, Simmons, are African American. Under the guidance of former publisher John Dotson Jr., the paper won a Pulitzer Gold Medal for meritorious public service in 1994 for its broad examination of local racial attitudes and its effort to promote improved and ongoing communication about race.

Smith, Anna Deavere. "Performance puts diversity center stage at retreat." Stanford Report (Feb. 2, 2005). *http://news-service.stanford.edu/news/2005/february2/med-retreat-020205.html.* Playwright and actress Anna Deveare Smith interviewed 14 faculty members, alumni and students at the Stanford University School of Medicine on the subject of diversity. She portrayed her findings through a performance of their words, speech patterns and gestures at the school's strategic planning retreat. Medical school dean Philip Pizzo said the idea was to generate questions and discussion, to start a heartfelt conversation about race and class. For more on Smith, see *http://www.scils.rutgers.edu/~cybers/smith2.html*

Steele, Claude. "A Threat in the Air: How Stereotypes Shape Intellectual Identity and Performance." American Psychologist 52:6 (June 1997), 613-629. Stanford University social and experimental psychologist Steele developed the concept of stereotype threat, which is now widely accepted. The term captures the powerful effects of feeling judged negatively, even when the only reason is membership in a group. Steele is now studying how social identity can influence individual choices such as education and career. An overview of Steele's work in the context of standardized testing and affirmative action can be found in his expert report for *Grutter v. Bollinger*: *http://www.umich.edu/~urel/admissions/research/expert/steele.html.* Steele directs the Center for Advanced Study in the Behavioral Sciences at Stanford.

Steele, Claude, and J. Aronson. "Stereotype Threat and the Intellectual Test Performance of African Americans." Journal of Personality and Social Psychology 69:5 (1995), 797-811. For more on African American achievement in schools, see *Young, Gifted and Black: Promoting High Achievement Among African American Students* by Theresa Perry, Claude Steele and Asa Hilliard III. Boston: Beacon Press, 2003.

Truby, Mark. "New Bias Lawsuit Hits Ford, Visteon." The Detroit News (April 14, 2003). *http://www.detnews.com/2003/autosinsider/0304/14/a01-136079.htm.* Details of an age discrimination suit against Ford Motor Co. in which employees say that educational requirements blocked older workers from promotion.

U.S. Census Bureau. "Census Bureau Projects Tripling of Hispanic and Asian Populations in 50 Years; Non-Hispanic Whites May Drop to Half of Total Population." Press release (2003). *http://www.census.gov/Press-Release/www/releases/archives/population/001720.html.* (See Chapter 1 resource list.)

U.S. Census Bureau. "Hispanics and Asians Increasing Faster than Overall Population." Press release (2004). *http://www.census.gov/Press-Release/www/releases/archives/race/001839.html* (See Chapter 1 resource list.)

Visconti, Luke. *http://www.diversityinc.com/public/main.cfm.* Visconti, a former Fortune magazine sales representative, co-founded Diversity Inc. to track diversity in corporations, including news developments, lawsuits and benchmark measures. Diversity Inc. publishes a web site and magazine. (See Chapter 1 resource list.)

Wallace, Linda. "Reaching Cultural Competency." Columbia Journalism Review (July-August 2003). *http://archives.cjr.org/year/03/4/wallace.asp.* The author of this piece on newsroom diversity is a cultural coach and consultant; she spoke on "Cultural Competency" at the 2004 "Let's Do it Better!" Workshop at Columbia University.

Weaver, David, Randal Beam, Bonnie Brownlee, Paul Voakes and G. Cleveland Wilhoit. "Journalists of Color Are Slowly Increasing." The American Journalist Survey, Indiana University (2003). *http://www.poynter.org/content/content_view.asp?id=28787.* The percentage of journalists of color remains well below that of the general U.S. population. Among news operations, television employs the most; weekly newspapers the least. See Chapter 1 section of this list.

Westin, Av. "You've Got to Be Carefully Taught: Racist Encoding in Television Newsrooms." Nieman Reports 1:55 (Spring 2001), 63. (See Chapter 2 resource list.)

CHAPTER 3 CLOSE-UP

Dayton Daily News.
http://www.daytondailynews.com/.

Poynter Institute for Media Studies.
http://www.poynter.org. The Poynter Institute is a school for journalists, future journalists and journalism teachers. Poynter offers seminars in multiple subjects within broadcast/online, education, ethics and diversity, leadership and management, reporting, writing and editing, and visual journalism. The web site features articles and essays to help journalists do a better job.

Society of Professional Journalists.
http://www.spj.org.
(See Chapter 1 resource list.)

Tulsa World. *http://www.tulsaworld.com/.*

Vinita (Okla.) Public Library.
http://www.vinitapl.okpls.org/. The library has information and links to resources such as the Cherokee Nation web site, the Will Rogers Memorial Rodeo, the library genealogy department and the Eastern Trails museum.

CHAPTER 4: REFRAMING DIVERSITY

ABC News and The Washington Post. "Beneath Broad Support for War Are Sharp Divisions in Intensity." Press release for War Update IV – April 7, 2003, ABC News Poll Vault. *http://abcnews.go.com/sections/us/PollVault/PollVault.html.* This telephone poll of more than 1,000 adults found that general support for the war remained high, at 77 percent. Fifty-seven percent said they supported the war "strongly."

ABC News and The Washington Post. "Both Confidence and Concerns Greet the Sudden Fall of Baghdad." Press release for *The Fall of Baghdad – April 9, 2003. http://abcnews.go.com/sections/us/PollVault/PollVault.html.* Nearly two-thirds of the 509 adults polled by telephone said they thought the war would produce a more stable Middle East. Public support for the war was 80 percent.

Associated Press. "New Scholarship Created for Whites Only." (April 18, 2004) *http://www.cnn.com/2004/EDUCATION/02/15/whites.only.ap/.* The College Republicans at Roger Williams University in Rhode Island created this $250 scholarship to protest affirmative action. Applicants had to write an essay about their pride in their white heritage and enclose a recent picture.

Bendixen & Associates, New California Media and the University of Southern California.
"First Multilingual Poll of Immigrant Opinions on War in Iraq. New California Media and University of Southern California Survey." (2003). *http://news.newamericamedia.org/news/view_article.html?article_id=e2fe7ad5d135b75aa6835f3ebf6f7020.* This survey of 1,000 immigrants included U.S. residents who were born in Asia (China, Vietnam, Korea, the Philippines and India), the Middle East and Latin America. Sponsors included NCM, a national association of ethnic news organizations, USC Annenberg School for Communication's Institute for Justice and Journalism and the Chinese American Voter Education Committee. Each community was found to have distinct opinions about the war and its effects. "Immigrants living in the United States worry that the war in Iraq will heighten the threat of terrorism and lead to increased economic instability and government harassment," the multilingual poll concludes.

Bendixen & Associates, New California Media and the University of Southern California. "First-Ever Quantitative Study on the Reach, Impact and Potential of Ethnic Media."
http://news.newamericamedia.org/news/view_article.html?article_id=796. This survey of 2,000 Asian, Hispanic and African Americans, conducted in 12 languages over five months ending in March 2002, tried to quantify the reach, impact and potential of media targeted to the three largest ethnic minority groups in California.

Bendixen & Associates and New California Media. "Ethnic Media in America: The Giant Hidden in Plain Sight." (2005). *http://news.newamericamedia.org/news/view_article.html?article_id=0443821787ac0210cbecebe8b1f576a3.* This poll surveyed 1,895 African American, Hispanic, Asian American, Arab American and Native American adults in the United States on their news media habits. Interviews took place in 10 languages. The researchers concluded, "the ethnic media reach 51 million ethnic Americans – almost a quarter of all (or one in four) American adults. Of these media consumers, 29 million ethnic American adults, or 13 percent of all adult Americans, not only use ethnic media regularly but prefer ethnic media to its mainstream media counterparts." Survey sponsors included The Center for American Progress and the Leadership Conference on Civil Rights Education Fund.

Browning, Rufus, and Holley Shafer, John Rogers and Renatta DeFever. "News Ghettos, Threats to Democracy and Other Myths about the Ethnic Media: Lessons from the Bay Area News Media Survey," San Francisco State University Public Research Institute (June 2003),118-119. *http://pri.sfsu.edu/ethnicmedia.html.* This report is based on a phone survey of 1,600 adults of Chinese, Hispanic, African and European origin in Cantonese, Mandarin, Spanish and English. The authors estimate the audience and assess the role of ethnic media, including its political and social impact. Funded by the Ford Foundation.

Chuang, Angie. Columbia Workshop on Journalism, Race, and Ethnicity. Columbia University (June 10-12, 2004). *http://www.oregonian.com/.* Chuang, a reporter at The Oregonian, outlined tips for successful beat reporting on minority communities.

Close, Sandy. New America Media. *http://www.newamericamedia.org.* Close directs New America Media (formerly New California Media) and Pacific News Service in San Francisco. For an overview of her contributions to journalism and her philosophy, see a profile by the National Association of Minority Media Executives, which awarded her the Lawrence Young Breakthrough Award. *http://www.namme.org/programs/awards/award-winners/2004_close/.*

Columbia Workshop on Race, Journalism and Ethnicity. *http://www.jrn.columbia.edu/events/race/mission.asp.* These workshops, directed by Arlene Notoro Morgan, associate dean of prizes and programs, highlight excellent and courageous coverage of race and ethnicity and provide a forum for journalists to discuss and learn from each other. The web site includes excellent resources on "growing your own," "growing your (newsroom) culture," and "growing your content." Poynter Institute Dean of Faculty Keith Woods, who is highly regarded for his training and analysis on coverage of race, contributed the in-depth "Status Report on Race and Ethnicity."

Dedman, Bill, and Stephen K. Doig. "Does Your Newspaper Reflect its Community?" John S. and James L. Knight Foundation (2003). *http://www.powerreporting.com/knight/2003/.*

This annual report on newsroom minority employment compares editor assessments of the percentage of minorities in their primary circulation area to U.S. Census Bureau data for those ZIP code areas.

Dingle, Derek. "Essence of the Deal." Black Enterprise (March 2005), 69. *http://www.blackenterprise.com/.* Dingle analyzes the takeover by Time Inc. of an enduring black institution and one of the nation's largest black-owned businesses.

Do, Anh, and Teri Sforza, with photography by Cindy Yamanaka. "The Boy Monk." The Orange County Register (2003). *http://www.ocregister.com/features/monk/index.shtml.* "There was something very different about Donald Pham," said the introduction to this four-part, multimedia series. "Even as a child, he seemed strangely wise. His parents came to believe that he was a monk in his previous life and should study in India. We follow his arduous path as a Tibetan Buddhist monk."

Domke, David. *http://www.com.washington.edu/Program/Faculty/Faculty/domke.html.* Domke is an associate professor at the University of Washington, Seattle. He specializes in political elites and the news media, individual values and cognition, and social change.

Fine, Lauren Rich. "State of the Industry: An Investment Year." Journalism & Business Values section, Poynter Online (2004). *http://www.poynter.org/content/content_view.asp?id=61400.* In an excerpt of her annual industry forecast, Fine reviews the loss of ad share and circulation by newspapers and notes the launch of targeted publications to Hispanic and youth markets as one popular response. These niche outlets may not be as profitable as mass market newspapers, but they could attract new readers into the fold, she says. Fine is an advertising/publishing industry analyst at Merrill Lynch. *http://askmerrill.ml.com/res_profile/0,,3704,00.html.*

Gay and Lesbian Alliance Against Defamation. *http://www.glaad.org.* Most reporters know GLAAD from the organization's activist missives or media awards. But true to its tagline, "Fair, Accurate and Inclusive Representation," GLAAD also offers an extensive array of media tools to help journalists understand and cover gay, lesbian, bisexual and transgender issues more accurately. Its Media Reference Guide provides a glossary of terms, including those the organization recommends and the ones it views as offensive or defamatory. The site features tip sheets on topics such as sports, crime, and "conversion therapy," and resource kits on LGBT communities of color, inclusive holidays and hot news topics.

Glasser, Theodore. (2004). "Make the Call: Should Two Gay Journalists Who Marry Be Allowed To Cover The Same-Sex Marriage Story?" Grade the News (2004). *http://www.gradethenews.org/feat/ makethecall/gaymarriage.htm.* San Francisco Chronicle Public Editor Dick Rogers says reporters lose credibility when they are participants in a developing story. But Stanford University journalism professor Ted Glasser argues that objectivity is a pretense. He says the photographers' interest in gay and lesbian rights didn't materialize with their wedding. In fact, Glasser says, the diversity movement is important precisely because it brings journalists with a variety of backgrounds and interests into the newsroom. The argue their case on Grade the News, a media research project and web site that aims to be a Consumer Reports for San Francisco Bay Area news.

Heider, Don. *White News: Why Local News Programs Don't Cover People of Color.* New Jersey: Lawrence Erlbaum Associates, 2000. Former television newsman Heider was floored when he visited Hawaii and saw only "pink" people on the local television news, in contrast to the diverse population on the streets. His shock led to studies of local coverage by two newsrooms in Honolulu and Albuquerque. This book discusses the news production practices and decisions that Heider concluded lead to a systematic exclusion of certain groups of people.

Independent Press Association.
The Independent Press Association offers support to independent publications, including the ethnic media. IPA-NY (*http://indypressny.org*) provides assistance to the ethnic and community press in the New York region, while IPA-Chicago (*http://indypress.org/site/chicago/index.html*) does the same in its area, also offering a guide to more than 200 publications in Chicago. For a compilation of news by member publications translated into English, see Voices That Must Be Heard at the IPA web site.

Indian Country Today. *http://indiancountry.com/.* This 22-year-old newspaper, the largest of its kind, covers American Indians from a national perspective,

with attention to local issues and events as well.

Johnson, Troy. American Indian Studies. *http://e.experience.uces.csulb.edu/AmericanIndian Studies/index.html.* This web reference page compiled by California State University Long Beach professor Troy Johnson features a wealth of web sites with news, history and background information by and about American Indians. Includes tribal and nation homepages, as well as other online, print, video, visual and audio references. Go to "Troy Johnson" under "Activities" to find the reference list.

Kaplan, Martin (Norman Lear Center), Ken Goldstein (University of Madison-Wisconsin) Matthew Hale (Seton Hall University) and Roberto Suro (Pew Hispanic Center). "Spanish Language TV Coverage of the 2004 Campaigns." *http://pewhispanic.org/reports/report.php?ReportID =38.* This study monitored and analyzed 29 days of nightly half-hour network news on Telemundo, Univision, ABC, CBS and NBC leading up to the Nov. 2, 2004, election. It also documented and compared local evening news from 5 to 11:30 p.m. on affiliates of ABC, CBS, FOX, NBC, Telemundo and Univision in three markets. The Spanish-language networks carried nearly as much campaign news as their English-language counterparts and more world news, but focused less coverage on the Iraq War.

Kerner Commission. "Report of the National Advisory Commission on Civil Disorders" (Washington: U.S. Government Printing Office, 1968). President Lyndon Johnson created the National Advisory Commission on Civil Disorders to study the reasons behind the uprisings that had upset major U.S. cities each summer since 1964. In its report, the commission chastised the media for its failure to report on the lives of African Americans and for helping to deepen the racial divide. (See Chapter 1 resource list.)

Kilgannon, Corey. "Thousands Bid Farewell to Ossie Davis." The New York Times (Feb. 13, 2005), 44. *http://www.nytimes.com.* The Times ran a 1,700-word obituary on Feb. 5 and covered the Harlem public viewing with about 800 words on Saturday, Feb. 12. The funeral itself, with eulogies by Harry Belafonte, Maya Angelou, Alan Alda and Bill Clinton, among others, received 414 words on p. 44.

Leonardo, Zeus. "The Color of Supremacy: Beyond the discourse of 'white privilege.'" Educational Philosophy and Theory, 36:2 (2004), 137-151. This article, written for educators, introduces ideas about white privilege, then goes beyond to show how the active participation of white people in accumulating unearned advantages amounts to white supremacy. Leonardo challenges the ways in which discussions about race often tiptoe around the matter of white responsibility.

Loewen, James W. *Lies My Teacher Told Me: Everything Your American History Textbook Got Wrong*. New York: The New Press (distributed by W.W. Norton), 1995. This critique of high school textbooks details the omissions and distortions taught in school that may have led to journalists' own misunderstandings about Native Americans – and at the same time, provides a helpful retelling of a more accurate American history.

Malveaux, Suzanne. "Bush to Declare End of Combat in Iraq: President Will Address Nation Thursday." CNN.com (May 1, 2003). *http://www.cnn.com/2003/ALLPOLITICS/04/30/sprj.irq.bush.combat/*. News report on the end of major combat in Iraq.

Mangan, Katherine S. "Horse Sense or Nonsense?" Chronicle of Higher Education 48:43 (2002), A8. *http://chronicle.com/*. Mangan focuses on the movement to teach medical students' communication skills so they can interact more skillfully with patients, including those from a different cultural background. Describes various curriculum initiatives under way.

Maynard, Dori J. *http://www.maynardije.org/columns/dorimaynard/*. Maynard, president and chief executive of the Robert C. Maynard Institute for Journalism Education, heads the Fault Lines Project and is a well-known advocate for diversity.

Robert C. Maynard Institute for Journalism Education. *http://www.maynardije.org*. Founded in 1977, the institute is dedicated to training journalists of color and to increasing diversity in news staffing, content and business operations. Its web site has a wealth of diversity news, analysis and resources, including Richard Prince's "Journal-isms" column.

Meier, Barry. "A Primary Source Outside Mainstream." New York Newsday (April 13, 1988), 26. *http://www.newsday.com*.

Mencher, Melvin. *News Writing and Reporting*. New York: McGraw-Hill Higher Education, 2002. *http://highered.mcgraw-hill.com/sites/0072564970* A popular text for basic journalism courses.

Morgan, Arlene Notoro, Alice Pifer and Keith Woods. *The Authentic Voice: The Best Reporting on Race and Ethnicity*. New York: Columbia University Press, 2005. The first of its kind, this multimedia textbook of case studies offers a practical teaching tool on covering race and ethnicity for both print and broadcast. The book, developed by three outstanding trainers in inclusive coverage, includes examples of excellent work, essays by the reporters involved, a DVD with interviews of the writers, correspondents and producers, discussion questions, links to related material and a web site offering additional work and a teacher's guide.

Moss, Mitchell. "The Structure of Media in New York City," *Dual City: Restructuring New York*. John Hull Mollenkopf and Manuel Castells, eds. New York: Russell Sage Foundation, 1991. *http://www.mitchellmoss.com/books/nycmedia.html*. Describes the complex print, radio and television media infrastructure that has arisen to serve New York City's ethnically and culturally diverse population. Reviews the differing images of New York conveyed by various media and the populations they serve.

New America Media. A nationwide consortium of over 700 ethnic media. For regular news summaries from member publications, see the NAM Editorial Exchange: *http://news.newamericamedia.org/news/*.

Patterson, Gregory. "Heart and Soul." Minneapolis Star-Tribune (Feb. 6, 2003). An essay on the culinary legacy of soul food from a personal and historical perspective, with recipes.

Peabody Awards Archives. *http://www.peabody.uga.edu/archives/*. For summaries of "POV Flag Wars" and "POV Two Towns of Jasper," search by year for 2003.

Poynter Institute for Media Studies. *http://www.poynter.org/subject.asp?id=5*. The Poynter Institute is a school for journalists, future journalists and journalism teachers. Poynter offers excellent tip sheets, discussions, resources and diversity reports on its web site, along with information about its diversity seminars.

Program on International Policy Attitudes.
"Public Impatient with Iraq Reconstruction: 7 in
10 Now Say UN Should Take Lead." Press release
for a PIPA/Knowledge Networks poll of 712 people
(Dec. 3, 2003). *http://www.pipa.org/online_
reports.html*. Respondents said the processes of
creating a government and developing a police
force to maintain security were going too slowly.
Only 43 percent said that the U.S. presence in Iraq
would improve the prospects for democracy
throughout the Middle East.

Project for Excellence in Journalism.
http://www.stateofthemedia.org/2005/index.asp.
An in-depth annual report on eight forms of news
media and their content, audience, business
outlook, ownership and other essential factors.
Also includes a survey of journalists.

**Radio and Television News Directors
Association.** *http://rtnda.org/asfi/awards/
murrowshow2004.asp* (June 24, 2004). Univision
won a national award in the news series category
for *Mis padres, mis verdugos (My Parents, My
Tormentors)* and in videography for *En busca de un
milagro (In Search of a Miracle)*. A full list of the
awards is on web site.

Shah, H., and M. Thornton. *Newspaper Coverage of
Interethnic Conflict: Competing Visions of America*.
Thousand Oaks, Calif.: Sage Publications, 2003.
http://www.sagepub.com/book.aspx?pid=9723. A
study on general circulation and ethnic minority
media coverage of interethnic conflict in Miami,
Washington and Los Angeles. The authors investi-
gate the roles of these media in defining, construct-
ing and challenging racial ideology and race relations.

Sing Tao Daily. "Patriot Act devastates Chinatown
banking," translated from Chinese by Xiaoqing
Rong (Sept. 26, 2003). *Voices that Must be Heard:
The Best of New York's Immigrant and Ethnic Press*.
*http://www.indypressny.org/article.php3?ArticleID=
1073*. Most of Abacus Federal Savings Bank's
60,000 clients are undocumented Chinese immigrants, who now must provide official U.S. photo
identification to open an account. Sing Tao USA:
http://www.singtaousa.com/.

Smith, Geri. "Can Televisa Conquer the U.S.?"
Business Week 3902 (Oct. 4, 2004), 70. An overview
of the ambitions of the world's largest media empire,
Grupo Televisa. The Mexican company supplies most

of Univision Communications Inc.'s programming.
Televisa's web site is *http://www.esmas.com/
televisahome/* and Univision's is *http://www.univision.
net/corp/intro.jsp*.

Srivastava, S. "Outsourcing God: Mass in Kerala."
Siliconeer (July 20, 2004).
http://www.siliconeer.com/. Roman Catholic
parishes in India receive instructions by e-mail
and payment from dioceses in the United States
to offer Masses or prayers in someone's or something's honor.

Tapaoan, Emelyn. "Strict new guidelines affect
undocumented Filipinos." Filipino Express (Nov. 24,
2002). *http://www.filipinoexpress.com/*
Coverage on the new bank regulations from the
perspective of Filipinos in New York.

Turner, Beauty, Mary C. Johns and Brian J. Rogal.
"Deadly Moves: A Special Report on Chicago's
Murder Rate by Residents' Journal and The Chicago
Reporter." (2004). *http://chicagoreporter.com/
2004/8-2004/8-2004toc.htm* and
*http://www.wethepeoplemedia.org/Backgrounder/
Special.htm*. As the mainbar of the story summarizes:
"In a joint investigation, Residents' Journal and
The Chicago Reporter found ... that the murder
rate in (Chicago Housing Authority) developments
has nearly doubled since 1999, the year before the
city launched its Plan for Transformation, a 10-
year, $1.5 billion redevelopment effort, in which
the CHA moves nearly 25,000 families." For the
Residents' Journal story on the award, see
http://www.wethepeoplemedia.org/Index.html
and for the SPJ press release, *http://www.spj.org/
news.asp?ref=459*.

Wagner, Venise. *http://www.journalism.sfsu.edu/
departmentinfo/wagner.htm*. Wagner is an assistant
professor at San Francisco State University and a
former reporter at several newspapers. She
specializes in civic journalism and coverage of a
diverse community.

WTNH.com. *http://www.wtnh.com/Global/
story.asp?S=3011372* (2005). News Channel 8 in
New Haven, Conn., goes to a New England prep
school to talk with students and their math teacher
about Harvard president Lawrence Summers'
remarks about women and their capabilities for
math and science.

CHAPTER 4 CLOSE-UP

Accrediting Council on Education in Journalism and Mass Communication. *Diversity: Best Practices.* Lawrence, Kansas: Accrediting Council on Education in Journalism and Mass Communications, 2003. *http://www.ku.edu/~acejmc/index.html.* Provides an explanation of the diversity standard, the reasons for it and compliance history. Tabulates the best practices in creating a faculty, student population and campus environment supportive of diversity.

Becker, Lee, with Aswin Punathambekar and Jisu Huh. "Evaluating the Outcomes of Diversification Initiatives: Stability and Change in Journalism & Mass Communication Faculties, 1989-1998." James M. Cox Jr. Center for International Mass Communication Training and Research, Grady College of Journalism and Mass Communication, University of Georgia (2001). *http://www.grady.uga.edu/annualsurveys/.* A report on and analysis of data from the Cox Center's Annual Survey of Journalism & Mass Communication Enrollments. The authors conclude that if journalism programs do not change their practices, the faculty will not be as diverse as *today's* student population until the year 2035. The situation is likely to become far worse, however, because the student body is likely to grow more diverse.

De Uriarte, Mercedes Lynn, with Cristina Bodinger-de Uriarte and José Luis Benavide. *Diversity Disconnects: From Class Room to News Room.* New York: Ford Foundation, 2003. *http://journalism.utexas.edu/faculty/deuriarte/diversity.html.* A study of diversity in both classrooms and newsrooms, including analysis on the historical and institutional reasons for resistance and failure to meet goals.

Hines, Barbara Bealor. "Into the 21st Century: The Challenges of Journalism and Mass Communication Education." *Journalism and Mass Communication Education: 2001 and Beyond*, (March 2001), 29-50. *http://www.aejmc.org/pubs/2001.html.* This report from the Subcommittee on Inclusivity, Association for Education in Journalism and Mass Communication, provides an analysis of the status of diversity on the faculty and in the curriculum, followed by an extensive list of resources.

Mass Communicating: The Forum on Media Diversity. *http://www.masscommunicating.lsu.edu/about* (2005). Offers resources and programming to enhance media diversity education at the college level. The web site aims to be a principal source of information about scholarship on diversity in higher education, journalism and mass communication.

Medsger, B. *Winds of Change: Challenges Confronting Journalism Education.* Arlington, Va.: The Freedom Forum, 1996. A study of journalism education and how well it prepares journalists to meet newsroom challenges and cover a multicultural society. Includes informative surveys of educators, newsroom recruiters and supervisors, and new journalists.

Reznet. *www.reznetnews.org.* An online newspaper for Native American students to share their views and report news about tribal communities and colleges.

Student Press Law Center. *http://www.splc.org.* The Tartan at Carnegie Mellon University shut down voluntarily after complaints about a racially charged cartoon and poems about rape and mutilation, while administrators at the University of Scranton closed The Aquinas for a parody of the movie, *The Passion of the Christ*. The Student Press Law Center advocates free speech for student publications and provides free advice, information and legal support.

Wickham, K. "An examination of diversity issues at Southeast Journalism Conference Newspapers." Newspaper Research Journal 25:3 (2004), 103-109. A study on attention to staffing demographics and guidelines that call for a commitment to diversity. Wickham found that student newspapers are overwhelmingly white and female, and that there are few stated guidelines about the need for diversity. Presented at Association for Education in Journalism and Mass Communication convention in Kansas City, Mo., in 2003. *http://www.aejmc.org.*